Pelican Books
The Emerging Japanese Superstate

Herman Kahn was born in New Jersey in 1922; he took
his B.A. at the University of California and his M.S. at
the California Institute of Technology. From 1945 he
was a laboratory analyst with the Rand Corporation and
went on to teach at the University of Los Angeles. He
later established the Hudson Institute and has been
closely involved with many of the studies produced by
the Institute. His other books include *On Thermonuclear
War*, *Thinking About the Unthinkable*, *The Year 2000*
and *Can We Win in Vietnam?* (with members of the
Hudson Institute). He is also Director of the Staff
Technical Advisory Group of the Atomic Energy
Commission. Herman Kahn is married, with two
children.

Herman Kahn

The Emerging
Japanese Superstate

Challenge and Response

Penguin Books

Penguin Books Ltd, Harmondsworth,
Middlesex, England
Penguin Books Australia Ltd, Ringwood,
Victoria, Australia

First published in U.S.A. 1970
Published in Great Britain by André Deutsch 1971
Published in Pelican Books 1973

Copyright © Hudson Institute, 1970

Made and printed in Great Britain by
Richard Clay (The Chaucer Press) Ltd,
Bungay, Suffolk
Set in Monotype Times

*To the Japanese Superstate
and its successful and peaceful integration into
the international system.*

Contents

Acknowledgements

Grateful acknowledgement is made to those authors and publishers who granted permission to quote from their works.

Additional credits appear in the Chapter Notes and in the Appendix.

Changing Japan by Edward Norbeck, Copyright © 1965 by Holt, Rinehart and Winston, Inc. Reprinted by permission of Holt, Rinehart and Winston, Inc.

John Whitney Hall and Richard K. Beardsley, ed., *Twelve Doors to Japan*, McGraw-Hill Book Company, 1965, copyright 1961.

'Japan-Australian Partnership', *The Oriental Economist*, July, 1969.

Edwin O. Reischauer, *The United States and Japan*. Cambridge, Mass.: Harvard University Press, Copyright 1950, 1957, 1965, by the President and Fellows of Harvard College.

Edward Norbeck and George de Vos, 'Japan', in Francis L. K. Hsu (ed.) *Psychological Anthropology: Approaches to Culture and Personality*, The Dorsey Press, Inc., Homewood, Ill., 1961.

Prefatory Note on the Title

The title *The Emerging Japanese Superstate: Challenge and Response* has been chosen with some care to describe as precisely as possible the subject matter of this book. By using the term 'superstate' I have tried to preclude a prejudgement about whether Japan will become only an economic, technological, and financial giant and retain its current 'low posture' in international affairs, or whether it will also become at least a financial superpower and seek – or develop – 'super' political and/or military power or influence. Indeed it is possible that the Japan of the future may find a role that compromises these factors of power or that exerts them in new ways and in different areas of the world.

I do believe, and argue in this book, that in the next decade or two Japan almost inevitably will achieve giant economic, technological, and financial stature, that very likely it will become financially and politically powerful in international affairs, and that eventually it is likely to strive to become a military superpower as well. In addition, I take account of some – but only a few – of the possible aesthetic, artistic, and cultural aspects of Japan's future – issues of the 'quality of life' and of what is now often called 'meaning and purpose,' particularly as these are affected by the onset of 'post-industrial culture.' (However, I am engaged now in writing a book dealing with all these issues of the 70s and the 80s.[1])

The phrase 'challenge and response' in the title implies not only a challenge to the United States, but even more important, a challenge to the Japanese themselves (who, despite their pride and confidence in current achievements and their desire for national prestige, are often more anxious about the new challenges than anyone else). It also implies a challenge to non-Communist Pacific Asia, to various parts of the Communist bloc, and even to Europe, Latin America, and Canada; all of these areas are affected by some of the characteristics, prerequisites, or consequences of Japan's enormous economic growth. The challenge, and therefore the response to it, will be different in each area, so it might have been better to talk about 'challenges and responses' – but that would have been somewhat pedantic.

Foreword

Many of us believe the 1970s and the 1980s will see a transition in the role of Japan in world affairs not unlike the change brought about in European and world affairs in the 1870s by the rise of Prussia. In addition, it seems likely that the 70s and 80s will be an important period of transition from the industrial to the post-industrial society – at least for the 20 per cent or so of the world population that lives in developed societies. In some respects these processes compete with each other, in others they reinforce one another. The things that might happen will be influenced by the rate at which these two processes, and a few others, go. It therefore seems reasonable, given the growing importance Japan will have in world affairs over the next decade or two, to conduct some studies in sequence – i.e., to study Japan, in much the same way we have studied the Soviet Union, China, and the United States, and then to incorporate it in our general over-all study of the world environment.

We should very soon complete Hudson Institute's second study of the 70s and 80s – that is, a study of the general environment and its interactions with individual nations and special issues, all with an emphasis on this transition to a post-industrial culture.[1] We hope then in our 70–71 study programme to do new 'country studies,' and 'issue studies' – to re-examine a number of separate countries and issues, but now in the over-all context set by the new study of the 70s and 80s. Thus, the study of Japan reported in this book is a kind of prototype of an initial study of a country and a step to a later study. I wish to emphasize, therefore, that the main purpose of this book is to open up discussion, rather than to settle it. For this purpose, a book that sets a context, formulates a number of interesting issues and conjectures, and speculates about the alternatives can be most effective in stimulating other people to make their own contributions to the discussion. Thus, the reader should think of this as a beginning, rather than as an end, and as a portion of a continuing programme. That was true, of course, of several other books I have written, and in those cases, they worked splendidly for the purpose. I can only hope that this book will do as well.

The Emerging Japanese Superstate might be said to owe its existence to the accident of my friendship with Thomas Lipscomb. About a year ago Mr Lipscomb discussed with me the possibility of writing a book based upon some Hudson Institute area studies of the fascinating long-range prospects of Japan. Since I was obliged to do another book on the 70s and 80s, as well as to participate heavily in the Institute's research programme and administration, another project did not seem possible. But Mr Lipscomb returned about a month later with a draft of the book's general contents, which he had put together from various of my briefings and reports. The draft was sound, and I found it impossible to argue that I could not find the time to strengthen and polish it.

In addition to Mr Lipscomb, who continued to work with me on this book even after accepting a position elsewhere, I would like to thank a number of members of the Hudson Institute Staff who have contributed to the book. In particular, I would like to thank Cary Aminoff, Andrew Caranfil, Marylin Chou, John Karlik, Richard Melson, Robert Panero, and Mark Wehle for their help and their many suggestions, and William Pfaff for making editorial comments on the entire manuscript. Without their contributions this book would have been even less complete than it is.

There are other American and Japanese friends, too numerous to list, whom I would like to thank. However, I must at least mention Mr Kei Wakaizumi, who has been good friend and critic for a period of almost a decade. I would like to acknowledge here my many debts to him. I would also like to thank Kyoto Sangyo University, the President, Mr Toschima Araki, and the Chairman of the Board, Mr Ryosuke Ono, for their many, many courtesies

– in particular for their twice inviting me to Japan and thus enabling me conveniently to deepen my knowledge of that extraordinary country. Indeed, the first chapter of this book contains a revised version of a talk I gave at Kyoto Sangyo University on the occasion of the Meiji Centennial in 1968.

In analysing basic economic projections as well as their implications in the 1966–7 Hudson study of Long-Term Japanese Prospects, I drew heavily on such American experts on Japanese affairs as Herbert Passin, James Abegglen, Martin Bronfenbrenner, James Crowley, Paul Langer, James Morley, Hugh Patrick, Robert Scalapino, and various US and Japanese government officials and innumerable Japanese friends and consultants. None of them, however, is in any way directly responsible for the views I now hold; in fact, many of these people would disagree quite sharply with some of my points. But I do wish to give them credit for the help they provided me and the group at Hudson that worked with me. Of the many American experts on Japan who have contributed to my understanding of Japanese issues, Herbert Passin, Robert Scalapino, and James Abegglen have had an especially great influence on me.

I should also note that at Hudson Institute we have no serious experts on Japan as members of the staff – no one at the moment, for example, except for various consultants, who even reads Japanese. But we have continued to think about these issues and to check our ideas with many American and European experts, and even more important, with many Japanese.

One final remark. In preparing this book, I have tried to speculate as honestly and as objectively as I could, and some of these speculations may prove offensive to some of my friends in Japan. I hope not. In any case, I assume that all of these know me well enough to understand that nothing is said in malice or as unfriendly criticism. I have enormous respect and liking for Japan and most things Japanese. Nevertheless, the spectacular rise of Japan does raise many issues that must be considered seriously by those of us who are in the business of thinking through the range of possible futures for various countries and for the world as a whole.

Herman Kahn

Chapter One

An Overview of the Rising Sun

In 1968 Japan officially celebrated the end of the Meiji century, and thus many Japanese have recently been preoccupied both with assessing the last hundred years and with trying to achieve some orientation on the next hundred. This is a particularly characteristic Japanese activity. In some ways the Japanese are among the most forward-looking and future-oriented people in the world – if not the most so. In other ways they cling tenaciously to traditional patterns and ways. Indeed, one can say that the Japanese have roots in both the past and the future, and it is perfectly natural that on an occasion like the Meiji Centennial they should look both ways with about equal intensity.

It was in the Meiji century – the century beginning with the accession of Emperor Mutshuhito in 1867 and the corresponding destruction of the old Tokugawa shogunate – that Japan rapidly accelerated its movement from a closed feudal society into its present position as an advanced industrial power at home and on the international scene. By the time of the Meiji Centennial celebration in 1968, it was becoming increasingly clear that the 'economic miracle' had not yet concluded. The rising sun – the *asahi* – had not yet reached its zenith. It seemed possible that the Japan yet to come would be a superpower in every sense of the word and likely that soon it would possess the most productive economy the world has ever known.

It is not surprising, then, that at least over the last century the Japanese have been very interested in the opinions of them and of their national prospects that various foreigners have had. In addition, I am, in a manner of speaking, a professional futurologist, in that I have spent a good deal of time during the last ten years considering issues of the future and how one goes about speculating, extrapolating, predicting, and forecasting the future, and avoiding or hedging against the problems foreseen. This experience is probably as important a reason for my interest in Japan in the next century, as any special knowledge I have of Japan and of things Japanese.

Very early in this period of studying, among other things, future possibilities in international relations – including issues of economic development and world security – I concluded that one of the most interesting countries to focus on was Japan. My original interest was based on considerations of national character (as discussed in the next chapter), some relatively simple extrapolations of current economic and political trends, and some guesses about how these might interact with each other and with other aspects of Japan's international relations. Despite the fact that at Hudson Institute we have subsequently done a certain amount of detailed work to refine our original conjectures, our underlying assumptions and techniques have not changed significantly – though my faith and confidence in our original 1962 study has been greatly increased.

One result of that 1962 study was a remark that was frequently misquoted in Japan at the time. As I originally made it, the remark went something like this: 'It would not be surprising if the twenty-first century were the Japanese century.' However, I also said in the same context, 'It would also not be surprising if it were the American century; it would be a little surprising if it were the Soviet century; and it would be even more surprising if it were the Chinese century. And then, of course, it might not be anybody's century.'

Since then eight years have passed and I now would be willing to make the remark in a form somewhat closer, though not identical, to the version then quoted in Japan: 'American scientist predicts that the twenty-first century will be the Japanese century.' In the last eight years I have come very close to a belief that the Japanese have, in effect, discovered or developed an ability to grow, economically, with a rapidity that is unlikely to be surpassed in the period at issue – and that might well result, late in the twentieth century or early in the twenty-first, in Japan's possessing the largest gross national product in the world. Whether or not this would result in Japan's becoming the major influence on the politics and society of the twenty-first century remains an open issue. One need not be a simplistic advocate of increasing GNP as a universal panacea to recognize its importance in supporting and generating a large range of national purposes. So it would not be surprising if the dynamism of Japanese growth were accompanied or followed by an equal dynamism in other areas – e.g. scientific, technological, cultural, and religious. Therefore if, as is not unlikely, the Japanese want to exert worldwide influence, they may well succeed in doing so.

Thus the overriding reason for my interest in Japan is its spectacular past and expected future economic growth – better than 10 per cent a year in the last two decades, and likely to be maintained at around that rate for at least the next two or three decades. The time has come to ask what this likely economic – as well as corresponding technological and financial – development means for Japan and the world.

The future, of course, is dependent both upon choices by various groups and upon events, and these can be affected and effected both by controllable and uncontrollable decisions and influences. When I look at Japan I tend to feel that the early and mid-70s will see many occasions for some of the more important of these relatively controllable decisions to arise either for Japan or for the external world, or for both. I have believed this since Hudson's original study, but the case can now be made much more persuasive. Indeed, a number of transitions and turning points may occur during the 1970s that will be almost as sharp and dramatic as any in Japanese history – as occurred, for example, in the early seventeenth century, in the decade or so following 1868, and during the early years of the American occupation.

It is sometimes said that in 1945 Japan went – in a very few days – from being the most militaristic nation in the world to being the most pacifistic. I do not predict a sharp change in the reverse direction. For many reasons such a rapid and deep change would be almost impossible. But I predict that in a short period of time during the early and mid-70s we may find a number of crucial changes occurring in Japanese attitudes towards defence (including nuclear weapons), foreign policy, self-image, as well as national and international expectations.

Let us try to move ourselves to a salient point in this 1970–80 decade – say mid-1975 – and see if we can simulate the thoughts and attitudes of various Japanese at that time. Yet because of the spectacular performance of the Japanese economy in the last three years (growth rates in real GNP in 1967 of 12·9 per cent, in fiscal 1969–70 of 13 per cent, and an estimated rise in fiscal 1970–71 of 12 per cent); because foreign reserves and gold have grown from the usual $1 billion,* or less, to $4 billion (and are still growing); because of the psychological impact of the Osaka Expo-70 exhibition; and because of many other things, the mood of confidence and exhilaration that I attribute to 1975 Japanese may well emerge years earlier.

In 1975, after twenty-five years of high growth rates, Japan will have attained a gross national product in the neighbourhood of a third of a trillion dollars (current estimate by the Japanese Economic Planning Agency). And the now commonly held belief that these growth rates must take a sharp drop in the near or moderate-term future probably will have been shaken; let us at least assume so. In other words, it seems to me at least as likely as not that by 1975 the Japanese – and most of the outside world – will be expecting Japan to enjoy another twenty-five years of much the same growth rates. Or even if by 1975 the Japanese – or others – no longer expect Japan to match the greater than 10 per cent per annum growth rates of the 1950–75 time period, they almost certainly will expect close to 10 per cent and substantially more than the 'usual' 5 per cent or so (a number that will probably represent a reasonably rapid and successful growth rate for almost any other developed nation). In any case, in 1975 Japan will have had the world's third largest gross national product for about six years, and it also will probably have been a major net source of capital for international investment (say $1 to 3 billion per year) for about five years.

Of course, the Japanese often point out that they are approximately twentieth in the world in per capita income. In 1975 it will

* American use of the terms billion and trillion.

not be possible for them to make even this kind of denial of their wealth. Even as a naïve calculation such a comparison in terms of GNP per capita is misleading, because in many ways the Japanese people live better than other nations ranking higher on the formal per capita scale (and also invest a great deal more in future growth). Furthermore, it somehow is neither serious nor informative for Japan to compare itself with Australia, Belgium, Canada, Denmark, Finland, Holland, Kuwait, Luxembourg, New Zealand, Norway, Sweden, and Switzerland. In any case, the Japanese will probably pass the Soviets in per capita product sometime in the mid-70s, and every succeeding year is likely to see a growing Japanese–Soviet gap in the standard of living.

By the mid-1970s there will be every reason for believing that the Japanese will do well in the more distant future. After all, it is very likely that in 1975 they will still be characterized, even as they are today, by:

1. High saving and investment rates (about twice those of the US);
2. Superior education and training (i.e., American scale and European quality through high school);
3. 'Adequate capitalization';
4. Readily available 'risk capital';
5. Technological capabilities competitive with those of the West;
6. Economically and patriotically advancement-oriented, achievement-oriented, work-oriented, deferred-gratification, loyal, enthusiastic employees (probably increasingly so);
7. High morale and commitment to economic growth and to surpassing the West – by government, by management, by labour, and by the general public;
8. Willingness to make necessary adjustments and/or sacrifices;
9. Excellent management of the economy – by government, by business, and, to some degree, by labour; this results in a controlled and, to some degree, collectivist ('Japan, Inc.') but still competitive and market-oriented (but not market-dominated) capitalism;
10. Adequate access – on good and perhaps improving terms – to most world resources and markets;

11. Almost all future technological and economic and most cultural and political developments seem favourable to continuation of the above;
12. Relatively few and/or weak pressures to divert major resources to 'low economic productivity' uses;
13. Many by-products of a high momentum of economic growth.*

I, myself, find that simply looking at and analysing qualitatively the widespread effects of this list is more persuasive than are detailed, input–output type numerical analyses of Japanese GNP growth rates – even when such analyses are done by or for our own staff at Hudson Institute. I am willing to argue that almost any item in the list is worth a major fraction (i.e., more than half) of a per cent of higher Japanese growth rates than those of most Western countries, including the United States. Thus I believe not only that adequate capital and foreign trade opportunities will continue to be available to finance and support this growth rate, but that there will also be sufficient ingenuity and innovativeness to avoid, surmount, or alleviate bottlenecks and to create new opportunities for expansion. Given these assumptions, it is easy to believe that the Japanese growth rates will maintain their current margin over those of the West for most or all of the rest of the century. This is particularly likely to be true if, as I suspect will happen, the Japanese dedicate themselves to accomplishing precisely that goal. In fact, I would conjecture that, given all the attention now being paid to the year 2000, the Japanese will specifically pick that year as their target date for surpassing the most advanced Western countries in economic development. If it turns out to be easy to meet this schedule, then they will undoubtedly meet it; if it turns out to be hard, then they will be perfectly willing to make sacrifices and other efforts.

Of course, I do not wish to imply that Japan's ambitions will be completely materialistic during this period. The Japanese are certain to be interested in participating fully, perhaps even leading, in such areas as sports, scientific achievement, literature, art, architecture, and the like, as well as in participating in other activities for their own sake. They will also be interested in

*All of these issues are discussed further in Chapter 4.

various kinds of aesthetic, recreational, educational, and consumption activities. Doubtless they will want to play an important or central role in Asian development, in various world peace movements, in bringing China into discourse with the rest of the world, in furthering the rapprochement of the United States and the Soviet Union, and so on. Finally, they are clearly going to make major efforts to improve their standard of living – including the social and physical environment.

I also believe there will be an emergence of many new desires, as well as a re-emergence of some old desires that we at the Hudson Institute sometimes call 'youth' and 'third generation' effects. The 'youth effect' is typically an upper middle-class and upper-class phenomenon, and it is in part a revolt against many current ideas simply because it is fashionable and exciting to revolt and because the current ideas are dull and constraining. The American 'third generation effect' may have many points in common with what seems to be happening among young people in Japan.

It is often believed in America that many immigrant families go through the following sequence: The first generation clings desperately to many of its traditional values even while it is attempting an amalgamation with US values. The second generation often violently rejects traditional values; often it is ashamed of them. The third generation, secure in its Americanism and interested in being different and in some degree even chauvinistic, makes at least a partial return to traditional values. This process, which takes three generations in the United States, often takes only one generation in Japan. We will discuss this when we talk about the so-called '*tenkō* transformation' in Chapter 2, and we will also discuss the third generation version as it is currently being manifested by Japanese high school students.

One reason to expect 'youth effects' is that by 1975 World War II will have been over for thirty years. There has already been published in Japan an extensive revisionist literature on the origins and course of World War II, and by the mid-1970s there will have been more such publications. Not only will there be little or no guilt felt about Japanese participation in World War II, there may even be some animosity against and a desire to eliminate obtrusive legacies of World War II and of the subsequent defeat and occupation. It is also possible that the few years between now and the mid-1970s may see even more internal conflict and chaotic conditions – particularly at the universities – than has the last decade. I would conjecture here that this turmoil both on and off campuses will settle down in the relatively immediate future, having given rise to – or been reformed or replaced by – a pervasive drive for and a more satisfying sense of national purpose and cultural identity.

Let me discuss some of these possible 'national purposes'. On the one hand, there will be some desire for Japan to become an integral part of a Western Pacific grouping or of the developed world generally. On the other, there will be inevitable pressure towards an 'Asia for the Asians'. In either case there will be pressure for attaining full status and acceptance of Japan as a superpower. There may be a deliberate search for new political ideas, possibly because the past ones are 'boring' or passé. Many historians, both Japanese and non-Japanese, have detected in Japanese history a kind of oscillation between xenophobia and xenophilia, between chauvinism and internationalism, between over-respect and resentment, between adoration and contempt of the foreigner. Such cycles may occur again to one degree or another.

What might be some of the effects of all the above? One possibility of course would be something like the following:

1. Growing realization of the need for 'Japanese solutions';
2. Pressures against and criticisms of naïve xenophilism and internationalism of any kind, toleration (or even encouragement of) xenophobia and chauvinism;
3. Some degree of political disengagement – even isolationism;
4. Excessive reactions against foreign influence;
5. Some reaction against 'American' political styles and processes or even parliamentary democracy – possibly against the 'American-drafted' constitution;
6. Pressure for at least 'temporary' nuclear armament.

Such developments would in a sense constitute a neo-isolationist and nationalistic trend: nothing so deep, pervasive and critical as a return to the almost total isolationism of Tokugawa Japan or the almost manic nationalism of the 30s, but a small move in both of those directions. Perhaps equally likely is almost the exact opposite: a trend toward cosmopolitanism and a desire to thrust Japan very centrally into world affairs. This desire would no doubt be moderated by a perfectly understandable wish to trade with – and to avoid antagonizing – all possible customers. But that was much the attitude of the British in the nineteenth century when in some ways they were also the world's policemen. I do not suggest that Japan in the year 2000 will aspire to the role of world policeman, at least not by itself. But the Japanese may well wish – indeed, feel obliged because of their pervasive worldwide interests and capabilities – to take part in such a role – and, depending on events, this may be a surprisingly large part.

In discussing these possibilities I do not wish to imply that there will necessarily be clarity or real unity and consensus on any or all of these issues. However, neither would I like to preclude that possibility. The Japanese have shown in the past a surprising and perhaps unsurpassed capacity for purposive, dedicated, communal action and for choosing explicit national goals.

Thus, despite the fact that many other changes are going to occur and that inevitably – at least for a time – there will be confusion about how old concepts and constraints apply and which new concepts and constraints are applicable, there may still emerge an effective consensus on what Japan can and should strive for, and on what it cannot or should not attempt. Incidentally, if such a consensus does not emerge, then this very confusion about ultimate goals makes even more likely a heavy concentration in the immediate future on the simple – and intrinsically attractive – goal of catching up with or surpassing the West economically and technologically. Almost all Japanese probably agree on this last as being at least 'a good thing' in which success is not only worthwhile in itself but likely to facilitate whatever other societal objectives are finally agreed upon – provided, of course, that this catching up is not done at too great cost to the basic culture and environment.

One obvious short-term prediction for Japan, therefore, is simply more of the same. It is easy to believe, then, that in this period of the early and mid-1970s there still will be no really strong centre party, no charismatic leader, and that the current politics of compromise and factionalism will continue, even if some intensity goes out of some of the old issues. The Old Left might still be what I would regard as nationalist, racist, xenophobic, Marxist, dogmatic, and the like. But no doubt there will be a New Left, and it will certainly partake of some of the characteristics of the New Left in the United States, in Western Europe, and in Eastern Europe, as well as have some original characteristics of its own.

On the other hand, Japan in many ways may be much more united and decisive than it has been in the past. For one thing, it is likely to be all too clear that the 'low posture' of the 1950s and 60s may no longer be suitable or even feasible. In the recent past Japan has been able to get along reasonably well with both Koreas, both Chinas, both Germanys, and even both Vietnams. It has also been able to get along with the United States and the Soviet Union, Burma and India, Indonesia and Malaysia, and so on. This kind of juggling act will become relatively difficult – and perhaps seem less desirable – when Japan has clearly become an Asian superpower: at first only an economic and technological superpower it is true, but economic and technological power tends to create or facilitate other kinds of power. Furthermore, the Japanese themselves may feel a need (or desire) for such things as greatly increased international status – politically, culturally, and perhaps even militarily.

There will almost certainly be at least a partial return to prewar values – in part because of what we have already called 'the third generation effect,' in part because of the current and future prevalence of revisionist theories about World War II, but mainly because these prewar values will simply be regarded as both more comfortable and more suitable for the new Japan. Indeed, there may be specific attempts to inculcate and strengthen prewar values – perhaps as an antidote to some of the excess of the post-war reaction against them, and/or as a corrective to some of the less attractive characteristics of the influence on Japan of Western affluent (and nearly post-industrial) societies. Indeed, it is my understanding that one of the major objectives behind the founding of Kyoto Sangyo University was to provide an example and an opportunity for encouraging the best of traditional Japanese values and the adoption of new but 'responsible values' when they seem called for. In any case, it is almost certain that most Japanese, on both the Left and Right, will be interested in asserting various kinds of national independence. Whether this will entail an attempt to be independent of US military or nuclear guarantees is hard to guess. It is possible to imagine it going as far as to include a deliberate attempt to reduce trade with the United States in order to reduce excessive dependence on a single customer, or the independence may instead be relatively limited. For example, the Japanese could still depend on the United States for the nuclear defence of their homeland, or there might possibly be some new arrangements that do not involve Japanese acquisition of national nuclear weapons but do give the Japanese more responsibility and authority in various issues that could arise.

There could be a good many reasons, however, for the Japanese to acquire at least defensive nuclear weapons; just as de Gaulle refused to rely on the United States, they too may refuse to rely wholly on United States protection. They could also argue that they would not be violating Article IX of the Japanese Constitution, which was drafted by Americans during the occupation and forbids the Japanese to possess any warmaking power. At least they would not be violating Article IX more than the existence of the current self-defence forces does, since the nuclear weapons would also be clearly designated defensive. Japan could point out that the Americans and the Russians possess such defensive systems, and since these two nations do not rely completely on deterrence why should the Japanese? In fact, Japan could probably make a better technical and political argument for ballistic missile defence against China than either the Russians or the Americans can make for defending themselves against one another by means of ABM.

It is likely that I have offended some Japanese by raising this delicate issue of nuclear armament. Yet I would have been less than honest if I had not done so. I do not want to be in the position of advising – or even seeming to advise – Japanese on what to do. In many ways I may have more faith in the Japanese than they have in themselves, and I suspect they will come up with perfectly reasonable and satisfactory answers to these problems. I have published two articles[1] discussing how a nation such as Japan might forego acquiring national nuclear weapons in favour of some kind of international or multilateral or similar force whose only purpose would be to deter the use of nuclear weapons and, if deterrence failed, to see to it that the nuclear aggression was punished by some kind of 'talionic' (tit-for-tat) or other response. I believe it is possible to organize such forces on a multinational basis and to design them so that militarily they would be truly defensive and politically they would encourage non-proliferation.

One reason I discuss these possibilities, even relatively prematurely, and with Japanese, is that I believe the Japanese should formulate, study, and work out their own 'solutions' or alternatives to their present position on the defence question. It would be desirable, however, to have some of this work carried out along lines that are not usually considered, rather than by the obvious process of following the paths of France and China.

The reader may also feel that given the current political attitudes of Japan, my concerns about nuclear weapons are absurdly unrealistic. I would be delighted if that were so. I am much more concerned, however, by the opposite charge often made against such a discussion: that the anti-nuclear sentiment in Japan is so precarious that the influence of a foreign commentator may upset the balance and touch off an avalanche of pent-up nuclear ambitions which otherwise would have remained in check. When I examine the reactions I have already had from Japanese, the second charge seems in some ways more realistic than the first, though I think neither is really justified. In any case, I long ago adopted the personal policy that, with very few exceptions, I either do not speak on a subject at all or I speak quite frankly; indeed it is my responsibility to speak frankly. Since I am in the business of worrying about long-term tendencies in trying to study how a more secure world can be achieved – not only in the next five to ten years but in the next ten, twenty, and thirty years and longer – Japanese nuclear aspirations must play a central part in my considerations.

Let me add, however, that even in the short run these concerns are not frivolous ones. By the mid-70s, Japan should have a nuclear-based civilian electric power industry capable, without much difficulty, of being modified to produce some hundreds, perhaps a thousand, small nuclear bombs a year – and doing this without necessarily reducing power production significantly (though the cost of the power might go up slightly). Japanese missile research (currently for peace purposes) will also have created a base for a strategic capability – at least in terms of being able to produce adequate propulsion, guidance, and re-entry vehicles for a strategic weapons system. Japan will also have had a lot of experience in producing and operating large integrated weapons systems. It will certainly have the financial capacity for a defence budget of, say, $6 billion a year (or more than any European nation today), since this sum will only be about 2·0 per cent of the gross national product – about twice the percentage being spent today on defence, but much less than the 5 per cent or so which is typical of England, France, and West Germany, or the 10–15 per cent which has recently been characteristic of US and Soviet defence budgets.

In particular I would point out that it has been more than a dozen years since any nation has explicitly and publicly launched a programme to acquire nuclear weapons. By 1975 it will have been almost twenty years since the last of the current nuclear powers began its programme, and it seems improbable that India, West Germany, or Israel – the three nations usually singled out as most likely to be nuclear power number 6 – actually will have made any such decision. There is, therefore, a very good chance that the Japanese will face, as a practical possibility, the question of whether or not they themselves wish to become nuclear nation number 6. If they decide affirmatively, it will probably lead to tremendous political pressures on the Germans, the Indians, the Italians, and eventually many others to acquire nuclear weapons. This could then be one of the biggest turning points in the twentieth century.

Now it is widely believed both in the world at large and within Japan that the above issue is an academic one – that, on the contrary, the Japanese have an intense, deep-seated, and almost total animosity towards nuclear weapons, even a 'nuclear allergy' because of their experience in World War II as the only nation which had – or yet has had – such weapons used against it. In addition there is often thought to be an overwhelming Japanese desire to contribute to world peace, arms control, and disarmament by 'leading the world' in being non-nuclear and anti-nuclear. I myself tend to think that the 'allergy' and the desire were and are more complex and subtle than is usually understood, even by most Japanese. Although genuine nuclear pacifism and international idealism are unquestionably involved, much of the emotion and activity usually accepted as demonstrating anti-nuclear sentiment are often concerned too with such matters as anti-militarism (in particular, nobody in Japan wants to return to the prewar conditions of the Japanese officer corps and 'government by assassination'), some degree of anti-American-ism, a certain amount of political partisanship directed against the liberal democratic party, an almost inevitable by-product of the 'low posture' foreign policy and internal economic expansion, etc. I would add that one of the most important reasons the Japanese 'nuclear allergy' persists is simply a basic and widespread belief that there is no pressing need, in terms of Japanese security or other current and imperative national interests, for obtaining nuclear weapons at the moment.

Now I would like to note that all these factors seem to be eroding, even today. For example, by 1963 most of the animosity against the 'illegal' Self Defence Forces had dissipated; in 1964 there was a certain revival of war songs and of revisionist theories of the war, and, in general, romantic attitudes about the war began (and continue) to replace the previously total rejection of war or militarism. By 1965 it was possible for visitors to discuss most issues of national security with most Japanese in a relatively unemotional way. By 1966 Japanese were willing to discuss nuclear issues in the same unemotional and objective way. By 1967 there was a somewhat surprising depth of animosity generated in Japan against the non-proliferation treaty negotiations. Not only was the depth and pervasiveness of the emotional reaction surprising to many in the West, but I suspect it was surprising to many Japanese. Since then there has been an increasing tendency for the formation of serious study groups on nuclear issues – even study groups combining participants from both the Right and the Left. This last point is an important one; both the Left and the Right may wish to have 'temporary' nuclear rearmament. The Left may wish to be independent of the United States, and the Right may strive for national prestige and power as well as independence.

I should also mention that in informal polls of Japanese graduate students, even in university departments that were very anti-militaristic and Leftist, the overwhelming majority felt that Japan would acquire nuclear weapons within five, ten, or at most fifteen years. Most felt that such nuclear armament, if it were to take place at all, would occur after West Germany or India had created a precedent. That would make Japan nuclear power number 7 or 8 – which somehow does not seem an act that would 'rock the nuclear boat' excessively. As I have already indicated, however, the pressures, sanctions, and restraints on Germany and India are probably much greater than those on Japan, and if there is a nuclear power number 6 in the 70s it will most likely be Japan.

It should be realized that if Japan does get nuclear weapons, and in particular if it procures them in a relatively 'irresponsible manner' so that further nuclear proliferation is touched off, enormous animosity will be created in much of the rest of the world and especially in Asia. For one thing, there will be a general accusation of trickery and hypocrisy. The Japanese have advertised their peacefulness – and their nuclear allergy – so extensively and so intensely that most people simply cannot now believe that the issue is really either as complex or as subtle as I have indicated or that, despite superficial appearance, a rapid change in Japan's nuclear policy is indeed possible. Having overestimated the depth, pervasiveness, intensity, and permanence of the nuclear 'allergy,' people will overestimate the seeming trickery and hypocrisy involved in policy reversal. South-east Asia, in particular, will then find itself reverting to some degree to the pre- and post-1945 hatreds, fears, and animosities – at least temporarily.

From many points of view, therefore, it may well make sense for the Japanese not to fulfill the 'prediction' I have made but rather to go on through the 70s without nuclear weapons – thus sparing themselves a certain amount of expense and a great deal of trouble. This would in many ways be a more momentous decision for the Japanese than the world realizes; still, they may judge it the least costly policy – in terms of an over-all assessment of the various risks, national security issues, prestige and economic considerations, and other matters. This may even be true if the Japanese intend to attain full great power status in the 80s – including nuclear armament. Premature moves in that direction may retard the attainment of that goal and raise grave risks and other costs.

Let me add a comment on past and recent United States policy and its effect on Japan. American officials often urge the Japanese to take a larger, more active, more aggressive role in Asian and world affairs. It seems to me that what they are really saying is that the United States does not wish to continue shouldering various aid and defence burdens by itself and would like Japan to assume part of them. There is nothing illegitimate in such a request; nevertheless, it is quite unlikely that the Japanese will be willing to allocate very large resources to, in effect, the slavish or un-thinking support of US Asian policy. It seems quite clear that Japan will want to follow its own policies – indeed will consider , other things being equal, that a certain amount of credible and visible independence will be a virtue. Nevertheless, probably these policies will largely agree with ours; at least, when I try to examine what I believe to be Japan's national interest, I do not see in the likely scenarios much occasion for serious quarrels between our two countries, though no doubt there will be many frictions and strains. On the other hand, if the Japanese, in the interest of either national objectives or world peace, decide to forego the acquisition of nuclear weapons, whether national or multi-national, the US probably would be – and should be – more than willing to make whatever financial and other sacrifices are necessary to see that the Japanese do not suffer from their restraint.

In other words, I believe the United States would – and should – be more than willing to continue providing an adequate nuclear umbrella for Japan for some decades to come if the Japanese are satisfied with such an umbrella in lieu of independent nuclear forces. It seems reasonable that if the Japanese were to think it in their national interest, or in the world interest, to forego the ownership of nuclear weapons but feel they need certain kinds of guarantees, then these should in fact be made available.

I once knew quite well a great physicist, Leo Szilard, who was the source of much wisdom about physics and other matters. He once commented to me that a major difference between physics and political science is that in physics we almost always ask, 'What did the man say?' and 'Is it true?' while in political science we tend to ask, 'Who said it?' 'Why did he say it?' 'Why now?' 'Why here?' Clearly both sets of questions are interesting. But I tend to feel that the first set is more interesting than the second. Therefore, as far as I am concerned the main reason for raising these nuclear issues at this time is simply that I feel they are important issues to raise at almost any time and in any place.

Let me make a final and rather personal comment on the second set of questions. About six years ago we started a number of studies at Hudson Institute in an attempt to examine the long-range prospects of the world. We have tried, as much as possible, to incorporate in these studies not only the viewpoint of a president of the United States, but that of a secretary-general of the United Nations, as well as that of a world citizen. We have also tried to incorporate various Asian, Latin American, African, and even Australian and Middle Eastern perspectives, From almost all of these points of view, we have increasingly found ourselves interested in and even focusing on Japan as in many ways a key nation in terms of choices, decisions, and potentialities for these long-range prospects. Further, as I have studied and visited Japan, I have found myself not only knowing more about the Japanese but admiring and respecting them, and even liking them more and more. During this same period of time the Japanese have tended to do exactly the opposite with regard to the Americans. This is not surprising since, as I mentioned earlier, there seems in Japanese history a tendency towards cycles of xenophilia and xenophobia, over-respect and over-resentment, and so on. Many Japanese, particularly intellectuals, currently seem to be going through such an anti-American phase. I rather suspect that this tendency has reached its peak, though I may be wrong. I hope I am not. But whether right or wrong, I believe that despite such movements, and almost irrespective of any of the choices I have been discussing, the future is going to find the United States and Japan with many things to say to each other; they are further going to be closely related in a number of different projects, policies, and areas, and they are going to be deeply concerned with each other's intentions and prospects. I suspect that most of this will occur in a natural and desirable manner, being mutually beneficial and accepted as such, but inevitably also with many frictions and irritations, some of which may be avoidable – and all of which should be containable. I offer the Hudson study as one attempt to anticipate and mitigate many of these frictions and irritations.

Chapter Two

Some Comments on the Japanese Mind

In outlining some of the major issues with which this particular discussion of Japan's future is concerned, I have also tried to explain why I have taken such intense interest in long-term Japanese prospects, even, if necessary, at the cost of diverting attention from many other important issues and nations. One reason for doing this is the newness of this issue. Another is the widespread unfamiliarity and even ignorance about Japan and the Japanese. It would now seem appropriate, therefore, to give more background and context to our study by considering some of the traditional characteristics of the Japanese that seem relevant to this discussion of current conditions and prospects.

In doing so I risk running into a certain degree of psychological opposition, particularly among American readers. It has long been an intellectual article of faith among most Americans that peoples everywhere 'are very much alike'. At some level of abstraction or analysis that of course is correct. However, in observing typical existential behaviour patterns in specific situations, typical values, typical ways of dealing with problems, it is at least as possible to be impressed with the differences among peoples as with their likenesses.

Of course, for a long time in the United States being different often meant being judged inferior; or at least there was a fear that such an implication existed. As a result differences were often emotionally denied. There were great pressures to facilitate the 'melting pot' characteristic of American society by deliberately underestimating the difficulty of 'perfect assimilation' and over-estimating the degrees of success actually achieved. These attitudes were greatly reinforced by intense reactions against the racist theories and practices of the Nazis and the Fascists.

Furthermore, even if none of these factors had existed, the belief that 'everybody is very much alike' would probably have proved more fundamentally in tune with American democratic assumptions than would any theory of national differences. For example, Tocqueville once said:

> He who inhabits a democratic country sees around him on every hand men differing but little from one another; he cannot turn his mind to any one portion of mankind without expanding and dilating his thought till it embraces the whole. All the truths that are applicable to himself appear to him equally and similarly applicable to each of his fellow citizens and fellow men ... men who live in ages of equality have a great deal of curiosity and little leisure; their life is so practical, so confused, so excited, so active, that but little time remains to them for thought. Such men are prone to general ideas ...[1]

It is the basic thesis of this book that the Japanese differ from Americans and Europeans in many important ways, and that it is important for Americans and Europeans to understand these differences. To do so will give us better estimates of what the Japanese may do, and it will help to avoid certain kinds of misunderstanding and other difficulties. For the general reader wishing to pursue this matter of the similarities and differences between Japanese and American national characters perhaps the best book is *The Chrysanthemum and the Sword* by Ruth Benedict.[2] While the Benedict book is now almost a quarter of a century old, most of the points it makes still carry a high degree of validity, though with some caveats due to the passage of time and the significant impact of the wartime and postwar experience, especially on young Japanese but on the whole country as well. I should also note that the Benedict book is extraordinarily readable.* I will use it freely in this chapter – in part because I myself

---

* I should point out that many American Japanese experts think of the Benedict book as superficial, although as far as I know they do not think of it as in any way seriously misleading (except in respect to the effects of the wartime and postwar experience). I hope I will be forgiven by my American friends who happen to be Japanese experts holding this opinion if I impute their judgement in part to the classic problem of the professional dealing with a skilled amateur. When Miss Benedict wrote her book she

found it a most useful introduction whose clarity I see little point in paraphrasing, and in part because it is widely available.

Miss Benedict starts her discussion of the Japanese with some caveats of her own.

... the Japanese have been described in the most fantastic series of 'but also's' ever used for any nation of the world. When a serious observer is writing about peoples other than the Japanese and says they are unprecedentedly polite, he is not likely to add, 'But also insolent and overbearing.' When he says people of some nation are incomparably rigid in their behavior, he does not add, 'But also they adapt themselves readily to extreme innovations.' When he says a people are submissive, he does not explain too that they are not easily amenable to control from above. When he says they are loyal and generous, he does not declare, 'But also treacherous and spiteful.' When he says they are genuinely brave, he does not expatiate on their timidity. When he says they act out of concern for others' opinions, he does not then go on to tell that they have a truly terrifying conscience. When he describes robot-like discipline in their Army, he does not continue by describing the way the sodiers in that Army take the bit in their own teeth even to the point of insubordination. When he describes a people who devote themselves with passion to Western learning, he does not also enlarge on their fervid conservatism. When he writes a book on a nation with a popular cult of aestheticism which gives high honor to actors and to artists and lavishes art upon the cultivation of chrysanthemums, that book does not ordinarily have to be supplemented by another which is devoted to the cult of the sword and the top prestige of the warrior.

All these contradictions, however, are the warp and woof of books on Japan. They are true. Both the sword and the chrysanthemum are a part of the picture. The Japanese are, to the highest degree, both aggressive and unaggressive, both militaristic and aesthetic, both insolent and polite, rigid and adaptable, submissive and resentful of being pushed around, loyal and treacherous, brave and timid, conservative and hospitable to new ways. They are terribly concerned about what

knew no Japanese and had never visited Japan. She based it almost completely on materials available in the United States, mostly upon interviews with various kinds of US experts and with a large number of first, second, and third generation Japanese who lived in this country and were available for such interviews. I have talked to many dozens of Japanese about the book and, to a man, they have thought of it as perceptive, accurate, and – as always, with the important caveat I have noted – accurate and reliable.

other people will think of their behavior, and they are also overcome by guilt when other people know nothing of their misstep. Their soldiers are disciplined to the hilt but are also insubordinate.[3]

I think it should be clear from the above that there are going to be some difficulties in generalizing about so complex a people. In addition to the inherent complexity of the Japanese culture and psychology, we have the complexity of any modern industrial society – in this case a rapidly changing modern society. Then, of course, there is also the inherent complexity and uncertainty in making generalizations about any large population, because, even if it were relatively homogeneous, it would still display a great deal of diversity in the very variables we are generalizing about. This last is in principle a purely technical problem of understanding the kind and degree of internal variation and then using language or quantitative descriptions carefully enough so as not to be too misleading. But in practice it becomes quite diffi- cult – in part because of data problems, in part because it is pedantic to keep adding qualifications and caveats. This is a less serious problem with the Japanese than with other peoples, because to a remarkable degree they are a unified and homo- geneous people with one culture – including of course, many class, regional, age, sex, and occupational differences, but often less significant ones than one finds in other cultures. In any case, the first two difficulties are both intrinsic and difficult enough to deserve more attention than I will be able to give them here. I will therefore try to be as careful as possible, and to be more 'leading' (i.e., orienting) than 'misleading,' but the reader should take almost all the generalizations of this chapter with more than one grain of salt.

Let me begin our discussion of why and how the Japanese are different with a quotation from another very good book on Japan:

For the past two millennia Japan's national development has taken place in a special setting that has conditioned and shaped both events and institutions – culturally, socially, politically, and economically. Insularity and the absence of large-scale migration into the archipelago in historical times have been responsible for the achievement of cultural homogeneity at an early date. The heterogeneous ethnic origins of the Japanese have been largely obliterated by thorough assimilation, although some distinctive physical characteristics still remain. So highly developed is the sense of national solidarity that the people have at times acted like one huge family with the Emperor as its head.

Traditonal Japanese values are not derived from or even influenced to any significant degree by Judeo-Christian traditions. Many things that are taken for granted in the West are therefore completely alien to their culture and are outside their traditional system. There is no public ceremony marking the Emperor's assumption of his position. His ascension to the throne is celebrated in a private ceremony. There is no coronation. Opening sessions of the Diet are not preceded by prayer for there is no chaplain. Instead, the Emperor adds solemnity to the session by delivering a brief message in person. No oath of office is administered to officials.[4]

Following below is a capsulated and synoptic (and therefore superficial but still useful) description of some important aspects of the traditional Japanese culture, society, national character, and political system that are of special interest to this study. Actually at Hudson Institute we have tried for many years to limn the traditional Japanese national character in a few lines and/or pages. Drawing upon some work of Edmund Stillman and mine, I offer the following description with the warning that while it is reasonably acceptable to many experts on Japan, it also is a very 'by and large' and 'largely' type of generalization and contains few if any of the subtleties and tensions that Ruth Benedict indicates are necessary in a careful description of the Japanese and their culture.

1. *Politically Pluralist.* For more than a thousand years national power and authority have nearly always been divided – sometimes between factions and groups (as today) in an almost feudal manner, sometimes between shogun or bakufu and an emperor, sometimes in an even more complex and subtle fashion. Almost never has there been a Caesar-Pope uniting both secular and religious authority in one figure or a totalitarian all-powerful and self-legitimating dictator.

2. *Authoritarian.* Even in today's 'democratic Japan', despite much public rhetoric, there is very little genuine and deeply held feeling that the mass of people have an inalienable right to choose

their leaders or their system of government, although such feeling is increasing. Throughout Japan's history, however, various groups and classes – even those at the bottom – have always had important and traditionally inalienable rights. If these were violated, appeals to the proper governmental authorities for validation of these rights, correction of the damage, and/or punishment of the offender or erring authorities, while dangerous to make, were almost always taken seriously if made appropriately. The system was, in other words, authoritarian rather than totalitarian, dictatorial, or democratic.

3. *Communal.* In nearly all activities and issues the Japanese traditionally think of themselves as members of a group, and their satisfactions are largely expected to come through group fulfillment of group objectives. In traditional Japanese culture, and to an amazing degree today (despite a nominal emphasis on democratic individuality and other erosions of traditional patterns and ties), one of the worst of all sins is to display an egoistic disregard of, disinterest in, or resistance to group mores, attitudes, taboos, totems, traditions, or objectives – or often just to display any individualism at all.

4. *Nationally Egoistic and Assimilative.* The Japanese people have almost always had a very clear conception of themselves as being special, as being Japanese and therefore unique. However, this did not prevent them from deliberately adopting all kinds of ideas, practices, techniques, technologies, concepts, and so on from Chinese and later from various European and American examples. But from the very beginning they were consciously selective, as indicated by the ninth-century slogan 'Chinese knowledge, Japanese spirit.'

5. *Hierarchical.* The Japanese have very little concept of equality. In fact it would be difficult to find a Japanese word by which one could express the concept, 'all men are created equal'. The various Japanese words we would use as synonyms for 'equal' simply do not have an apposite meaning in that phrase.

Traditionally every Japanese is part of a hierarchical structure. There are people who rank above every individual, except the

Emperor and the shogun, and, except for the youngest daughter of a member of the outcast Burakus, there are people beneath. To say in Japan that certain people are equal generally implies they are an equal distance from some common superior – i.e., they are equal in the way two privates or two generals are equal. Both have common rank in a pyramidal hierarchical structure.

The concept starts in the family, where, for example, there is a rigid ordering of rank exhibited in the sequence in which people take their turn using the tub – a sequence from which there is normally no deviation and which faithfully reflects the rank ordering in the family. By learning this sequence each person in the family knows exactly where he stands in the official family hierarchy – and notes that this hierarchical ordering is not only characteristic of his family but is universal: there is nothing idiosyncratic about his family. When he grows older he learns that such an order exists in almost all other spheres as well, and with much the same manner and rigidity of distinction.

This hierarchical system is so strong that it can often operate against what many would consider a 'natural order'. For example, in Tokugawa Japan (the 'classical' period roughly from the end of the sixteenth to the middle of the nineteenth century) the upper class were the Samurai, but many, perhaps most of the Samurai tended after a while (and some inflation) to be among the poorest people in Japan. The next lower social level was assigned to the farmers, who tended on the average to be somewhat better off financially than the Samurai but not as well off as those at the next lower social level, the artisans; the artisans in turn were usually not as well off as the merchants – who were assigned the lowest social rank. Thus the group that was socially at the bottom, the merchant class, also tended to be among the wealthiest in Japan, while those close to the top often suffered from extreme poverty. It was of course difficult to maintain such a state of affairs. Thus merchants often paid Samurai families to adopt their children, or through various other techniques and artifices used their money to raise their social status. Although this reversal of wealth and status has obtained at least for a time and in certain places in other societies, it was relatively widespread and long-lasting in Japan.

6. *Romantic Attitude towards War.* Until their defeat in World War II, the Japanese preserved much of the feudal spirit and feudal attitude towards war, holding it to be an exciting and noble activity of the most exalted kind (and thus, in Tokugawa Japan, restricted to the best classes), in which the finest qualities of human beings were nurtured and brought forth. Further, in Bushido and state Shintoism 'patriotic war' was given a religious and nationalistic coloration, connotation, and fervour (coupled with the new concept of universal participation), which had almost completely disappeared from the European West by the end of World War I (although it reappeared in a different form in the European Fascist movements). We will discuss later the current peace-orientation of the Japanese people and argue that their attitude towards war, while greatly changed from the prewar tradition, has many elements of continuity with the past.

7. *Pervasive and Important Aesthetic (and Aesthetically Emotional) Attitudes and Values (particularly in upper classes and Samurai).* For at least ten centuries Japanese culture has been characterized by such concepts, issues, and activities as personal style, poetry, artistic skill, sensitive and refined ability to appreciate artistic experiences and objects and to feel in harmony with nature – and indeed an almost 'precious' aesthetic attitude toward many relatively ordinary events, special aspects of the environment, and special situations and contexts. To take just one important facet, according to Michiko Inukai:

Again the Japanese, who are endowed by birth with a highly developed aesthetic sense, tend to be better at feeling things than at analyzing them. As a result they have produced less of note in the academic and intellectual fields than in literature relying less for its effect on rhetoric and logic than on intuition and emotion. Thus it was the Japanese who created the *haiku*, that extreme case of the condensed in literature which captures and compresses into artistic form the fleeting intuition and the emotion of the moment. Even today, there are said to be several tens of millions of *haiku* poets in Japan – a fact which I find extremely interesting and striking. Although the 17 syllables which make up the *haiku* have, of course, meaning simply as words, almost the whole of its effect derives, not from the words which are arranged visibly into the 17-syllable form, but in the emotional overtones which hover invisibly about them. This remarkable literary form is of extra-ordinary beauty and refinement, but it lacks entirely the Western-style rhetoric which presents things for all to see, analyzes them, then makes doubly sure that its meaning is quite clear. *Haiku* is not a literature of speaking one's mind. In the same way, it seems to me that the Japanese manner of arguing has *haiku*-like qualities, and that their ways of thought in general betray the same traits.[5]

8. *Competent Perfective Technology*. Throughout their history the Japanese have admired good craftsmanship and have been able to master almost any technology available to them. In addition they not only were able to copy another nation's technology but usually were able to change and perfect it in such a way that it became either typically Japanese or at least better for their purposes than the original model. It is thus clear that they can be reasonably creative with technology – or at least it is clear that they have been so in the twentieth century. It is still an open issue whether their creativity will rank with that of the English, French, Germans, and, to a lesser degree, Americans and Soviets, and in what areas.

9. *Assertive Attitude towards Environment*. Here we would argue the Japanese are something between the West, with its general Faustian attitudes and concept of 'dominion over land and animal,' and China, India, and many primitive cultures, which usually try to fit man into the environment in a natural, non-coercive, and non-disturbing manner. The Japanese are somewhat willing to make changes in the environment and to assert their will and fulfill their objectives, but they tend to do so less grossly, less starkly, and with greater moderation, care, and even love for the environment than is characteristic of the root-and-branch restructuring common in Western tradition. Oddly enough, when it comes to such things as gardens everything must be disciplined and planned – the natural and spontaneous have no place unless they are carefully planned for and designed into the system.

10. *Approving Attitude towards Private Property*. While the Japanese have tended to be very communal in the psychological, social,

and political senses, and have fulfilled many of their basic internalized pressures and drives by satisfying communal objectives and requirements, property has always been, in one way or another, lodged in the individual or his family. Even when the government claimed to own everything, it assigned relatively permanent rights of property use to various people. The Japanese, of course, have had the institution of the extended family, where every member of the family had some kind of claim on the resources of every other member of the family, to be exercised in certain circumstances and under certain conditions. But this did not contradict the essential institution of private property. Yet there was no concept in Japan of laissez-faire – of a basic right to unrestricted use of one's property. Although the property was the individual's (or his family's), he had to use it for traditional objectives and in accord with traditional social obligations.

11. *Purposive Attitude towards History* (*a working out of the national destiny*). Partly as a result of their great consciousness of being Japanese and therefore belonging to a special group; partly because of their isolation, which allowed them to carry through plans of their own, ordinarily without suffering great interference from the outside world (before World War II, in a period of almost 2,000 years, there had been only two serious attempts at an invasion of Japan, both by Mongols in the thirteenth century); and partly because of the nature of the challenges they have been faced with, the Japanese have grown to conceive of history as something to be consciously determined by the national will. This often has been a mystic concept associated in turn with other mystic concepts such as *kokutai* (national essence or national polity), attaining one's rightful or proper status in the international hierarchy, etc.

12. *Faithful Samurai Warrior* (*and/or Faithful Servitor*) *and Responsible Paternalistic Confucian Master as Ideal Types*. Ideal types of character are an important indication of a nation's culture. Probably to a degree unmatched in any other culture, the Japanese have exalted such qualities as loyalty, faithfulness, devotion, dedication, etc., as associated with the faithful culti-

vated warrior (and/or other 'committed' servitor) and the corresponding qualities of loyalty, protection, meticulous regard for ritual, codes, obligations, rules, other proper behaviour, etc., appropriate to the responsible, paternalistic Confucian master. This is presumably one of the reasons the Japanese factory works so well; it is also, of course, another source of the unsurpassed ability of the Japanese at purposive, communal action. Japanese literature in particular has emphasized the requirements for and desirability of these two types of human being.

Let me conclude this part of my discussion of Japanese national character by noting that individual male Japanese often describe themselves with such terms as egoistic, emotional, introspective, illogical, hypochondriac, stoical, persevering, disciplined, conformist, diligent, respectful, loyal, honest, polite, and unbelievably rigid about the requirements of various kinds of duty, but as less interested in the letter of a written agreement than in its emotional connotation and context, very anxious to avoid stark confrontations and uncertainty in almost all situations (social, business, governmental), tending to dislike and look down upon Koreans, and finally as having a realistic ability to learn, indeed almost always to be interested in self- or national-improvement.

Many readers will be affronted by the many seemingly simplistic and sweeping generalizations I have just made. Other readers will yearn for a somewhat simpler description. While I can be somewhat sympathetic with the first group if the issue is rigorous accuracy and objectivity, I can have only empathy, not sympathy, for the second. The purpose here is to give a useful picture, and thus a certain complexity is essential. Indeed, the rest of this chapter elaborates and embellishes the above by discussing certain aspects and issues in more detail, though it still falls far short of being a rigorously accurate description of the complex and changing Japanese reality.

We shall turn now to some twenty or so specific Japanese characteristics, concepts, and institutions that are of special relevance to our purposes. These characteristics as formulated may appear to many readers a fairly miscellaneous congery. The principle of selection will become clearer as the reader notes the role these concepts play in later discussions. Using this 'congery format' seems the best way to cover a large range of issues and yet not take up too much space on equally interesting but – from the narrow point of view of this study – less central issues.

The Surprising and Perhaps Unsurpassed Japanese Capacity for Purposive, Dedicated, and Communal Action

The remarkable feat of the Japanese in carrying out a conscious and deliberate modernization process in the late nineteenth and early twentieth century (the Meiji era) not only was the first really successful example of modernization by a non-European nation, but it was accomplished with an efficiency, skill, intensity, continuity, and perseverance that is still the wonder of the world. In part this success was due to an increasing flexibility and willingness to experiment – to try almost anything once.

John Whitney Hall has argued that 'One of the outstanding features of the "Japanese mind" throughout history has been its persistent inquisitiveness and flexibility in the face of new demonstrably superior intellectual systems . . . [While] other societies have resisted or even rejected intellectual intrusions uncongenial to their traditional values, . . . the Japanese somehow have managed to accept [or at least acknowledge] quite readily the entire range of thought currents emanating from the West. In doing this, they have remained persistently eclectic, despite cycles of feverish imitation or resurgent xenophobia, so that the result has often been a distinctly Japanese adaptation of Western ideas or methods, an adaptation in which the Japanese have somehow been able to prove a modicum of their individuality.'[6] However, there are costs to this kind of a process, but even here the Japanese seem to have ways of limiting them. Thus according to Robert Jay Lifton:

Ever since the time just before Meiji Restoration, . . . educated Japanese have looked to the West with a uniquely intense ambivalence. They have felt impelled to immerse themselves in Western ideas and styles of life in order to be able to feel themselves the equals of Westerners, and at the same time they have waged a constant struggle against being psychologically inundated by these same Western influences. In the process they have experimented with a greater variety of ideas, of belief-systems, of political, religious, social and scientific ways of thinking and feeling than perhaps any other people in the world. And they have as individuals learned to move quickly and relatively easily from one of these patterns to another, to compartmentalize their beliefs and identifications and thereby maintain effective psychological function.[7]

Before reviewing these and other aspects and incidents of the modernization process, it is worth mentioning that the nineteenth century was not the first time in history that the Japanese accomplished something like this. In the sixth to eighth centuries they, in effect, 'sinicized' their culture – at least superficially – by copying aspects of the Sui and Tang cultures. As in the nineteenth century, the copying was not only deliberate and conscious but very selective and with much modification, so that what resulted was a very Japanese system. In fact, the Japanese cut off relations with China and went into a period of final and creative synthesis – fully living up to the slogan of the day, 'Chinese knowledge, Japanese spirit.'

They repeated part of this process with Sung China and then stopped, among other reasons because of the conquest of China by the Mongols, which again resulted in the typical Japanese reaction of a period of withdrawal and isolationism. Another round of much the same process was begun in the late fifteenth and sixteenth centuries with Ming China when, mainly as a result of the initial impact of the West, the Japanese changed their mind in the middle of the process and began almost 250 years of relative – indeed, at first almost total – isolation. This retreat into isolation was carried out with the same intelligent and communal purposiveness that had characterized previous periods of relative acculturation. Indeed, in its own way the outcome – Tokugawa Japan – was another wonder of planned social engineering: some 250 years of more or less designed stability (and an unintended evolution towards a commercial society).

The destruction of this system and the emergence of Tokugawa Japan onto the world scene has generally been credited to actions by the Americans in the two Perry expeditions in 1853 and 1854, with an assist by the Russians, British, and French. It can be argued, however, that in many ways Tokugawa Japan was ripe for such emergence. A lot of things were occurring at the end of the Tokugawa period, including some years of clandestine education by many Japanese in so-called 'Dutch knowledge' at Nagasaki (the Dutch were the only Europeans allowed into Japan), and the culmination of almost two centuries of limited but very significant commercial, technological, educational, and bureaucratic development. These activities during the period of Tokugawa isolation helped lay the basis for subsequent modernization in the Meiji period. Japan is not an example of an overnight modernization of a primitive culture or even of an advanced but non-commercial society such as Indian or Chinese culture.

Finally, one can argue that perhaps since 1948 – and almost certainly since the signing of the Japanese Peace Treaty in San Francisco in 1952 – the Japanese have re-engaged themselves in the same kind of common purposive enterprise, in this case 'catching up with the West' (except that the slogan has recently been quietly changed to 'surpassing the West').

But let us briefly examine the Meiji Restoration to gain some orientation towards what was involved in this process of consciously synthesizing selected aspects of an external culture with their own.

The Meiji Restoration

When in the mid-nineteenth century the West began pressing on the isolation of Japan, the Japanese began to see that they probably would not have the material or military strength to resist Western penetration or other Western demands. Accordingly the shogun circulated a questionnaire among the various *daimyo* (the feudal lords among whom all of the country, except the lands of the shogun himself, were divided). The outer lords, particularly the clans of Satsuma, Choshu, Tosa, and Hizen, who were among those *daimyo* historically less loyal to the shogun, took this as a sign of his weakness. After the shogun made some concessions to the West, a movement began among these clans under the slogan, 'expel the foreigner and honour the emperor'. It should be noted that this is exactly the slogan used by the Boxer Rebellion some four decades later.

The big difference between the Japanese and Chinese responses to Western exploitation is that when the Japanese rebels became influential they immediately realized the impracticality of expelling the foreigner and concluded that the sacred land of Japan was, in fact, in danger of being successfully invaded. They also carefully noted what had happened to other countries that had not had the ability to withstand Western power.

After some preliminary confusion the younger Samurai in particular managed to effect a number of changes. First, they got the great *daimyo* to voluntarily resign their feudal privileges – in effect they convinced the upper class to carry through a voluntary social revolution.

There is a lot of controversy about exactly what did happen at this point in Japanese history, and there is a certain tendency, especially among Japanese intellectuals, to downgrade this feat – particularly since it left the composition of the middle and upper classes more or less the same. But several historical examples have shown that most revolutions, including the Russian and the French, did not change the class structure anywhere near as much as most people think. The important thing was that this Japanese revolution was initiated by the upper classes and carried through by and with their co-operation. Although there was some resistance and some bloodshed, the entire programme was accomplished from the top downward, and not, as is usually regarded as normal today, with the active revolutionary presence – or even revolutionary cooperation – of the lower classes, or in any other way from the bottom up.

A number of interesting incidents occurred during this process. At one point, for example, some Satsuma forts got into a fight with a British and the French naval force and found their shore installations reduced to rubble by the superior guns of the Western nations. Rather than holding a grudge, the Satsuma immediately made friendly overtures to these Westerners to find out just how those marvellous guns were made.

During this period the Japanese interest in both wealth and technology was as a means rather than as an end. It is interesting to note that the great families thought of their wealth as a trust. For example, they often built two houses: one a large, elaborate Western-style house filled with luxuries for use in entertaining foreigners, and the other a classic, austere, ascetic, aesthetic Japanese house where they could live a disciplined and very simple life in their day-to-day existence.

There were many manic and even ludicrous aspects and inefficiencies during this process of acculturation, but as a whole it was worked through with a purposiveness, care, and thought that diminished such inefficiencies to probably as low a point as was consistent with rapidity and thoroughness.

Of course, it is now a matter of history that the Japanese carried out all the programmes indicated by the slogans, and did so with remarkable success. Unfortunately their role in World War II on the side of Germany and against the United States was, to put it mildly, a premature assertion of power. They had no real theory of victory, only some kind of faith either in their ability to rise to the occasion or that their early victories would discourage the US from undertaking to pay the cost in blood and treasure that would be necessary to reconquer the Pacific. They learned that America had not only the material resources but also the spiritual resources to carry through the programme. But we will turn to this again when we discuss the issue of spiritual versus material resources.

The war was in any case a great miscalculation on the part of the Japanese and one they firmly intend not to repeat. It should be understood, however, that at the time they clearly saw their sin as the miscalculation rather than the attempt itself. There have since been important changes in Japanese culture, and it is difficult, given both their historical record and recent events – as well, of course, as the effects of the specific and perhaps atypical context of the existential moment of choice – to get any reliable sense of how the Japanese now would act under many circumstances. But we will try to do so in subsequent chapters.

Let me return to the story of the pre-World War I modernization of Japan. As is well known, the Japanese sent out emissaries to study the West and take the best from everybody. They started by copying the French military system (which possessed all the glamour of the revolutionary and Napoleonic Wars), the British navy, the form of the English parliamentary system but without its real content, parts of the American educational system (it would seem that even the Japanese can make mistakes), and so on. When Germany beat France in 1870 the success-oriented Japanese switched their working military model from the French to the Prussian, but it should be emphasized that they already had assimilated many basic French ideas. Actually, the nation that made the greatest impression on them during this period probably was Germany, and there are thousands of words in the Japanese language that come from German roots and entered the language during this and subsequent periods. (It might also be noted that there are now probably twenty thousand or so words of English origin in the Japanese language.) It is interesting to see that while in polls today the average Japanese seems strongly to prefer Americans to all other nationalities, that is not true of Japanese intellectuals, who still tend to admire Germany.

There were a number of incidents during this new period that are worth noting. First, in the Boxer Rebellion the Japanese joined with the Western expeditionary force, and their troops behaved extremely well, both on the field of battle and in terms of the code of military honour. They found to their shock, however, that the Western troops in no sense lived up to their pretensions about the code of honour. This discovery did not affect the Japanese behaviour against the Russian Army in the War of 1904, but it seems to have had a noticeable long-term effect.

As successful as the Meiji modernization programme was, the internal strains were very great, so that eventually the whole character of leadership changed and gave way to what came to be described as 'government by assassination', followed by an equally manic assertion of the sense of uniqueness and of having a special mission. Thus, the Japanese experience, competent and successful as it was, would seem to validate a prevalent belief that rapid modernization can be very disruptive of a culture and, in effect, breed neuroses and social pathology. But this does not necessarily slow down dramatically the rate of modernization.

There were two more important turning points, at least in terms of the psychology of the Japanese vis-à-vis the West. These were the refusal of President Wilson during the Versailles Treaty negotiations to add a racial equality clause to the League of Nations Treaty and the Oriental Exclusion Act passed by Congress in 1924. Both of these were more or less accidental, and probably could have been avoided by better diplomacy on the part of either the Japanese or those they dealt with. When the Oriental Exclusion Act was being considered, for example, there was already a tacit agreement in Washington not to insult the Japanese in this deadly way. But the Japanese Ambassador did not fully understand that and sent a note to the Congressional Committee concerned, pointing out how seriously passage of this act would affect US–Japanese relationships. In reading his message today one can only agree that it was simply an attempt to give the committee information it ought to have and was in no sense a threat. Unfortunately the committee took it as a threat, promptly broke the previous agreement, and passed the legislation.

One can argue that another event of the same general period bears a lesson for the Japanese – and perhaps for the US. Rather soon after the Franco-Prussian war it became clear to most British leaders that the new Germany would eventually surpass England in industrial capability. The British, nonetheless, felt friendly to the new Germany. There had been several centuries of good relations between Englishmen and Germans and their two countries were very close, so most of the British were willing to live with the new situation. But in 1890 the German Emperor fired Bismarck and began to formulate German policies by himself or with the help of less cautious and less wise advisers. In particular, he began to build a German navy to rival that of the British, though he understood that his navy would never be more than half the size of the British navy.

Kaiser Frederick Wilhelm had a pet theory (devised by Tirpitz) that the British would be deterred by this navy, because they could not risk any action with it that might result in their suffering so much damage that they would be unable to fight the French navy, the French being the 500-year-old enemy of the British. The British reaction was quite unexpected. They made up with their 500-year-old enemy France. They simply refused to live with a Germany that was both a great industrial power and a naval rival. One can argue that the German decision to build a navy diverted important resources from the main German efforts – their land army and their general industrialization programme – to a second priority programme and one that irrevocably antagonized their major friend and ally. It seems reasonable to suppose that if the Germans had not done that, their Berlin to Baghdad Railway would have been built and they would have become the hegemonial power in Central Europe, having under their control most of what is now Eastern Europe and Austria, as well as a good deal of the Middle East, presumably stopping short of the Suez Canal, where British-controlled territory would start.

The analogy to Japan is reasonably clear. There are many 'unnecessary' types of military expansion or political aggression the Japanese could initiate that might have the unhappy effect for Japan of forcing the United States and other developed – and underdeveloped – countries to reconsider their current indulgence of the general Japanese trade offensive in the international marketplace. This, indeed, is one of the reasons for a recent re-emphasis in Japan of the 'low posture' foreign policy – of avoiding premature 'great powerism'.

Hierarchy, Prestige, Shame, Guilt, and Pride

According to Ruth Benedict, the Japanese character

was in large measure the product of explicit training in the need for self-sacrificing pursuit of duty – of duty towards the Emperor, the nation, the family, status, superiors and personal benefactors, and of the duty to maintain one's good name in order to retain the esteem of one's group – a preoccupation which made shame rather than guilt the major moral sanction. Since the duties were particular duties relating to particular spheres of conduct and particular social relations, large areas of life were left free for innocent sensual enjoyment, untroubled,

if there was no conflict with duty, by any sense of guilt. And this dichotomy was exemplified and reinforced by the discontinuity of childhood
training – the indulgence of early childhood contrasting with the sudden
requirement of conformist responsible behavior later on. The Japanese
had, in short, . . . a 'situational ethic,' which made them a well-dis-
ciplined moral people in familiar situations but lacking in guide-lines
for behavior when – as in wartime – they were faced with new ones.[8]

One of the important things that has happened in postwar Japan
is the movement of almost a third of the population from rural
areas to urban areas – a movement that has tended to break down
a good many of the traditional 'situations' in which the situational
ethic described by Miss Benedict prevailed. According to Edward
Norbeck, there is as a result a widespread feeling of a breakdown
of moral standards, but this feeling may be exaggerated. Thus he
says:

A putative general decline in moral standards is a matter of national
concern, at least to the extent that it is frequently the subject of public
expressions of alarm. Everywhere civic leaders plead for improved
standards of morality, and they often refer to sexual morality. Almost
any urban citizen of mature years will state that the family system has
collapsed, that old values have disappeared, and that confusion reigns.
But he generally makes these statements with composure, and it is
evident that he has found a way to live with peace of mind.[9]

With regard to both of the above quotations, consider the remarkable fact that many Japanese who were captured during World
War II were unconscious. When they recovered they often asked
to be killed, but 'if [American] customs do not allow this' they
tended to be model prisoners and for all practical purposes
changed sides. They often voluntarily flew in our observation
planes and pointed out Japanese military installations or otherwise provided information about their former comrades. They not
only felt they were as good as dead, but they also suffered an
almost complete conversion. This is of course very similar to the
conversion in the 1950s of the Kikuyus in Kenya who became
Mau Maus after first violating the most sacred taboos of their
tribe, or to the practice in some radical movements of forcing
young people (for example, the Chinese, in repudiation of the
Confucian ethic) to turn in their parents to the authorities. In some

ways the final surrender was a similar shock to the Japanese and perhaps temporarily provoked this kind of conversion. How deep it went, how long it seems likely to persist, are all matters we will discuss later.

However, at least initially, surrender convinced the Japanese that 'their proper place' was far beneath that of the Western powers. This concept of 'taking a proper place' has dominated much of recent Japanese history. For example, the preamble to the Tripartite Treaty with Germany and Italy reads: 'the governments of Japan, Germany, and Italy considered it as a condition precedent to any lasting peace that all nations of the world be given each its proper station. . .' The Imperial Rescript accompanying the signing of the pact repeated the objective in the following terms: 'The task of enabling each nation to find its proper place and all individuals to live in peace and security is of the greatest magnitude. It is unparalleled in history. The goal is still far distant. . .' Finally, on the very day of the attack on Pearl Harbor the Japanese envoys handed a declaration of war to Secretary of State Cordell Hull that again repeated the point: 'It is the inimitable policy of the Japanese government to enable each nation to find its proper place in the world. The Japanese government cannot tolerate the perpetuation of the present situation since it runs directly counter to Japan's fundamental policies to enable each nation to enjoy its proper station in the world.'

This moral issue among the Japanese is going to come up again when, if current conjectures on the Japanese growth rate are proven correct, the Japanese attain 'super' status as an economic, technological, and financial power and have the capability of becoming a superpolitical and supermilitary power. In fact, the essence of the 'challenge' specified in the title of this book refers less to the Japanese challenge as an economic, technological, and financial superstate than to the political and military consequences of that challenge. Japan's decisions on this issue will be a challenge to the Japanese themselves, to the Americans, the Europeans, the Soviets, the Chinese, and especially to those nations that we will discuss later as occupying 'non-communist Pacific Asia' (or as we shall designate it, 'NOCPA').

It is often said that the sense of hierarchy has been diluted in postwar Japan. Certainly the part of the Japanese language that is 'respect language' – having the characteristic that the user cannot communicate without choosing words and modes of expression that define (for himself, the person he is addressing, and all hearers) the precise relationship between him and the person he is talking to – is to some degree beginning to erode. In particular, this respect language has been somewhat modified by the younger people of Japan. And it is conceivable that respect language eventually will fall almost completely into disuse in Japan, just as it did in the United States. It should be noted, however, that in many areas of Europe the distinction between 'thou' and 'you' has been maintained to the present day (although the frequency and degree of the distinction have been greatly eroded in the last ten years or so); one would tend to feel that the much more complex and graduated respect language of the Japanese may become more attenuated in many ways but still play a dominating role in displaying, reinforcing, and even forcing certain modes of thought and behaviour on the Japanese.

The sense of hierarchy is so great that many men in the street have no sense at all of participating in the government, because to them such participation would have no real meaning. Thus, if one polls the average Japanese as to whether he is concerned with national prestige and personal happiness, he generally answers that personal happiness is his major concern.

On the other hand, if you ask him, 'Could you be happy if foreigners were making fun of Japan or even if Japan did not count in the world?' he would probably answer with a rather violent or emotional 'No.' He does not normally get concerned with national prestige issues, because they are the government's concern. It is particularly the conservatives and the elderly businessmen running the country who are very much involved with questions of national prestige; therefore the 'common man' does not have to worry about such issues. But if the national leaders did not, he would very much tend to reject them as being unworthy of their trust.

The Japanese Sense of Being on Display and of Being Judged and Evaluated

One purpose of the last section was to provide some context for discussing one of the most important characteristics of the Japanese people – at least as far as our interests in this study are concerned. That is the tremendous interest displayed by Japanese, both as individuals and as members of groups, in foreign opinion about Japan and the Japanese. The practical importance of all of the characteristics just described is greatly reinforced by the associated feeling that other people judge them in much the same way they judge each other, and that these judgements are important. Thus, even today the Japanese have an intense feeling of being 'on-stage' – a feeling that is as easily associated with feelings of inferiority as of superiority. Herbert Passin and other well-known observers of the Japanese scene have remarked that Japanese are constantly aware of rank order, and they are constantly asking themselves: How high do we rank? How high should we rank? What can we do to improve our rank? And since ranking is not only a matter of self-estimation, but also of the estimation of others, the Japanese are extremely attentive to what others think of them. If Americans appear always to want to be loved and are anxious about their popularity rating, then this is all the more true for the Japanese when they are abroad – in fact, they show a constant preoccupation with the problem.

During the war the Japanese newspapers and military commanders continually reminded Japanese soldiers that 'the eyes of the world were upon them' and that it therefore behooved every member of the armed forces to be conscious of himself as a representative of Japan. Japanese seamen were warned that in the event an order was given to abandon ship they should man the lifeboats with the utmost decorum or 'the world will laugh at you'. Indeed, 'The Americans will take movies of you and show them in New York.'

To give some mundane examples of how powerful an agent of change this characteristic can be, consider the following vignettes: Japanese men used to strip down to their undershorts on public conveyances in order to be comfortable. The government notified them that it embarrassed European travellers and made these Europeans judge the country to be uncivilized. Almost overnight the Japanese adopted the European standards – at least in accommodations normally used by Europeans. The same thing occurred when Haneda Airport was first opened near Tokyo. People who came to watch airplanes come in and take off would gather on a special balcony. In hot weather the men often stripped to their shorts to cool off. No Japanese seemed to mind, but it struck visiting Europeans and Americans as odd. So it was stopped.

Similarly, at one point when I was in Tokyo the Police Department issued a statement that the taxi drivers' excessive use of car horns was bothering foreign visitors, particularly the Americans. I was later told that this resulted in a sharp decrease in that particular source of noise.

Or consider the extraordinary institution of 'weeding' (infanticide of defective children up to the age of two), which was common at least in rural Japan at the time of the Meiji Restoration. As the reader may know, the Japanese in some ways tend to treat young children with even greater permissiveness than Americans do. For example, it is almost unthinkable for an adult to slap or physically punish a five-year-old child. (It is true, however, that if the child misbehaves too continuously, they will often burn *mogusa*, a cauterizing substance, on his wrist, producing a very painful burn. But the purpose of this measure is to drive out the evil spirits and not to punish the child, though it may work both ways.) Thus we see in Japan a culture that formerly practised infanticide when the child was as old as two years. That is, if a child developed traits that indicated he was seriously defective, the custom of the country permitted exposing or otherwise disposing of the child. In this, Japanese culture may have been unique. Though many other cultures have practised infanticide, or have more or less callously exposed young children to great risks in the expectation that the fittest or best would survive (e.g., Mongolians on their annual movements following pasturage), these societies did not 'commit' so emotionally to the unborn or very young child, but as far as I know none of them ever practised delayed infanticide. Japanese culture, with its greater sense of discipline and its greater concern for fitness and wholeness, was able to combine infanticide with commitment. The whole institution disappeared because of the horror Europeans expressed when they learned of it.

Or, even more extraordinary, consider the following observation by Michiko Inukai:

The excessive preoccupation with the self makes the Japanese, both as a nation and as individuals, almost morbidly worried about what others are thinking of them. At the same time, one should not neglect the fact that, since every weakness has its directly corresponding virtue, this same preoccupation with the self has also helped bring Japan very great advantages. It was the desire not to appear inferior in the eyes of foreigners which, giving an added spur to the innate vitality of the Japanese people, enabled them to carry through an astonishing modernization of their country in such a short time. In the same way, they build new roads not so much for themselves but so that they shall not be ashamed for foreigners (for example, at the time of the Olympics) to see them – in other words, in order to present their nation in a better light to foreigners.[10]

In summarizing this particular issue, it is important to distinguish the Japanese sense of being onstage from a similar but very different – and much weaker – traditional American concept. From the beginning of the Republic, Americans have had a sense that the American form of society represents the wave of the future and that an American exists to convert the rest of the world to that future (but – at least in the early days of the Republic – by example and precept, not by intervention). They were, therefore, very conscious of the impression they made on the rest of the world. To a remarkable degree Europeans and others were willing to concede to America this role. Thus the still famous epigram of Goethe's: 'Amerika, du hast es besser.' And of course to a remarkable degree various Latin American constitutions are modelled on that of the US, rather than on the British or French. America played a similar role as the example to be emulated in the Soviet revolution. To a degree that would startle many pro- as well as many anti-Communists, American practice and usage was used as an example to inspire and guide many Soviet efforts.

It is probably very important for most Americans that we have some such message for the rest of the world. It would not be satisfactory for this country to find that while our system worked very well as far as we Americans were concerned, it was a system unique to this country and could not be exported. Indeed, when we do run into a special situation in which 'the American experience' is to a greater or lesser degree irrelevant, we often simply refuse to recognize the fact, or we go through one or another kind of traumatic experience, sometimes finally even doubting the validity of our system for ourselves – or all others – if it cannot be made to work in a particular foreign context.

The Japanese have no such problem. They could not care less whether or not it is possible for other countries to adopt their institutions and their techniques. After all, they think of themselves as a unique race. It would not surprise them if their techniques were so special that they could not be exported. But what is important to them is that the unique Japanese be admired and respected – that they be acknowledged as counting in the world – and the more unique and special the techniques used to attain status, the better.

Social and Group Unity and Harmony

Japan is probably the only large country in the world in which almost everybody concerned – management, labour, consumers, family, the general public – tends to identify the success of a business firm with the success of the nation and with his own individual success. The firm's triumph is the nation's triumph and also his own triumph. Not only is this true of those closely associated with a firm, but it also somewhat resembles the situation in a homogeneous and closely knit community where one may root for one's own relative to win a race, but if the boy next door wins one still has a sense of sharing in his triumph – and is even willing to contribute to making it feasible.

This kind of unity shows up in Japan's foreign trade. The Japanese often cooperate with each other to a remarkable degree even while they are competing. That is, they try as hard as possible to further the interest of their own firm, but they take almost as much pleasure in any Japanese success, since to some degree it is Japan against the world – and cooperation, of course, can be very helpful. One effect of this cooperative attitude is a kind of 'open society' in which competitors discuss relatively freely services and information that in the West would be regarded as proprietary and therefore private and secret. This interchange is most helpful in creating an informal and flexible society. All of these kinds of cooperation are furthered by the government ministries, but it would occur even without formal arrangements. A recent *Newsweek* article (9 March 1970)* suggests:

How did Japan achieve its economic miracle? A good part of the answer lies in the intricacies of the Japanese character – disciplined, group-minded and capable of extraordinary efforts in pursuit of the common good. 'The company is like the father,' explains a Japanese executive in London. 'It looks after you for your whole life. And you give it devotion.' Indeed, the Japanese see themselves not as a society of individuals, but a national family in which all the people and all the companies cooperate to make the nation stronger. The country, says *Newsweek*'s Tokyo bureau chief, Bernard Krisher, is not merely Japan – it is Japan, Inc. The very word for individualistic – *kojin-teki* – has an unpleasant connotation of pride and arrogance. . .

In a nation where watching the gross national product is a gross national pastime, trade representatives come close to being culture heroes. Departing from Tokyo's Haneda Airport for their three- to six-year assignments in the field, they are usually seen off by delegations of colleagues waving banners and shouting '*banzai!*' Their exploits are publicized like battlefield heroics, and a truly dedicated *shosha-in* can get national recognition.

It should be noted, however, that, heroic as the assignment is and heroic as the individual is treated, there is, as is almost inevitable with the Japanese, another side. Thus *Asahi* comments that,

there is no more pitiful sight than a Japanese on an airplane leaving Tokyo airport for his first flight abroad. . . He will be so preoccupied with behaving correctly that the last thing he is capable of is being helpful and considerate. He is as tense as a soldier who has landed in enemy

* 'Japan – Salesman to the World'. Copyright Newsweek, Inc., 9 March, 1970.

territory. I know of no more telling or depressing evidence of the lack of self-confidence of Japanese men, or at least of a large number of them. And these are the same people who, once safely returned to Japan, will blossom forth with loud confident statements about Japan's great national strength.[11]

The younger generation, while ostensibly revolting against group unity and stressing individualist values, more often than not also craves some form of group life. As Robert Jay Lifton notes:

In Japanese youth, cultural and historical influences have brought about diffusion and dislocation of unusual magnitude. One of the ways in which young people attempt to deal with this predicament is by stressing a developing awareness of their own being, by delineating the self... They speak much of individual freedom in relation to family and society, and strongly criticize the negation of the individual person in traditional and contemporary Japanese practice. They respond strongly to those elements of Marxist thought which refer to self-realization, and they frequently combine their Marxism with existentialism...

But underneath this ideal of selfhood, however strongly maintained, one can frequently detect an even more profound craving for renewed group life, for solidarity, even for the chance to 'melt' completely into a small group, a professional organization, or a mass movement...

One feels this tension between the ideal of individualism and the need for the group in the concern of young people with that... elusive, sometimes near-mystical but always highly desirable entity known as *shutaisei*. [It] literally means 'subjecthood' and is a modern Japanese word derived from German philosophy, coined by Japanese philosophers to introduce into Japanese thought the German philosophical ideal of man as subject rather than object... [Currently] young people use *shutaisei* to mean two things: first, holding and living by personal convictions—here *shutaisei* comes close to meaning selfhood; and second having the capacity to act in a way that is effective in furthering historical goals and... joining forces with like-minded people in order to do so – here the word means something like social commitment.[12]

It is significant that young Japanese undergo psychoanalysis in order to adjust themselves to social and group unity concepts. Bruno Bettelheim says:

How the problem of generations can differ in different cultures may be illustrated by a controversy between American and Japanese psychoanalysts: in Japan the psychoanalyst's task was seen to consist in helping the young individual to give up his search for self-identity; his self-realization was to be sought not in individuation but in accepting his place within the family in the traditional subservient position of the son toward his father. Thus a Japanese patient 'as he approached the successful conclusion of his treatment said, "During my vacation my mother told me on one occasion that I was now pleasing my father better." The psychoanalyst, in reviewing the changes in the patient's personality, says, "His psychic state is now as harmonious a one as can ever be reached by human beings" i.e., in accordance with the national mores and aspirations of Japan.'[13]

And Robert Huntington comments that 'The Japanese personality has weak, indistinct, permeable boundaries between the self and other; is dependent as opposed to independent, group-cooperative rather than self-reliant; conforming rather than innovative, and accepting of personal rather than rational-legal authority.'[14]

The Politics and Techniques of Group-Centred Decision-Making, Japanese Style – The Institution of Ringi

According to James Abegglen of the Boston Consulting Group, the Japanese employ 'a diffuse, group-centred decision-making apparatus'. He argues that the usual use of the word 'consensus' to describe this Japanese process of decision-making probably raises inappropriate images and connotations. In this Japanese process of 'group-centred decision-making' the views of all parties who have an interest in the decision are canvassed, and an attempt is made to accommodate each of these views. Direct confrontations are avoided whenever possible, and many institutional mechanisms, including the use of middlemen, are employed to prevent them. A dissident party may also be placated by granting him a concession on some issue totally unrelated to the decision at hand – or by conceding an obligation to make up, whenever the opportunity occurs, any losses suffered by a generous concession on the matter at issue.

An example of this aspect of Japan could be obtained by

analogy with the American democratic family. Imagine a husband and wife and, let's say, five girls. Six out of seven members of the family want to go to the mountains for their vacations. But one of the girls has a boyfriend at the beach and she is desperately anxious to go there. It is judged unreasonable to allow the one to outweigh the six. As a result the family goes to the mountains. However, everybody remembers that this girl's quite legitimate desire to go to the beach has been neglected. The next time an issue like this comes up her vote will be given extra weight; in fact she may get an overriding vote, simply because the family does not wish to frustrate her so severely twice in a row. She will almost certainly get the overriding vote if such an issue is raised a third time.

The Japanese system is a bit like that. Everybody who has been generous in concession or who has done something out of the ordinary to facilitate consensus is remembered, and to a remarkable degree – partly because of the *giri* and *on* systems of duty and obligation, which I shall discuss later in this chapter – he is eventually repaid. This is true if it is a matter of a favour a corporation has done for the government or a favour an individual has done for a corporation.

In most cases the process is less simple than I have indicated. Being so diffuse, it is difficult to isolate the source of the initiative behind an idea; an initiative can come from almost anyone and often originates quite low in organizations. A similar difficulty exists in determining who is the effective decision-maker, since the decision is in a sense made by all the interested parties, each of whom has veto power. Frequently the man with the senior position in an organization is not necessarily the one who wields effective power or possesses the ability to satisfy dissidents. And though the government has a voice in almost all major business decisions and may itself assemble the views of various interested parties, it by no means exercises final decision-making power. Even when the government is involved and has nominal authority, an effort must be made to accommodate each viewpoint – including those of interested private parties.

A virtue of the Japanese system is that the effort to keep all parties satisfied practically eliminates the demoralizing squeaky-wheel phenomenon. But if some party or group remains – despite all discussions and compromise – opposed to a given initiative, the result is usually a non-decision – i.e., a decision to stall and keep the question circulating indefinitely until the matter is either dropped or a change in conditions permits unanimous agreement.

In some cases one group may ram through a decision against the wishes of a weaker opposition group; Japanese characterize the resulting state as a 'tyranny of the majority'. Thus, to the Japanese, action based on a ten to two vote does not represent a group decision; it reflects instead the domination of a tyrannical majority over the firmly held desires of the minority. The proper outcome should be some form of temporizing 'non-decision'.

Therefore, achieving a consensus in a Japanese organization or government bureau is sometimes a little like producing a nomination for Prime Minister in the Conservative Party in England. It would be unthinkable for the decision to come from the top down. Nor could it be done by an open and 'destructive' political campaign – or by a majority vote of the masses. Somebody, usually senior, typically an elder statesman who is not himself competing, will go around and consult people's opinions, trade their views, do a little politicking – but not very much, and almost always of the 'soft sell' sort. Finally, after a great deal of discussion, a consensus emerges. At this point the consensus may not be unanimous, but in the Japanese system, under some circumstances at least, a father figure (or emperor figure) may come forth and announce the decision. All will then agree.

One result of this technique is a thorough discussion of the issues by all who are affected and an equally thorough educational process. All involved parties receive and contribute to this discussion of the options, facts, and philosophy behind a decision before that decision is finally made. Each party carefully prepares arguments backing its position, and this information is circulated. Thus, once an accommodation is reached, the staff work has been completed and each party is aware of its role in executing the decision. Typically the Japanese are prepared to move very quickly once an issue is resolved. On the other hand, if no means can be found to satisfy all interested parties, the understanding among them is that each – within reasonable limits – will do more or less what he wants; but it is also understood that the issue is not resolved and will be raised again and again until an accommodation is reached.

It is interesting to make a comparison with the usual American decision-making process. In this system there are several possibilities. The decision may simply be promulgated from the top down, those on the top having more than ample authority to do so. Or some group, presumably a small one, may study a problem or an issue, usually at the request of those at the top, while other people pretty much tend to their own jobs. One way or another the issue is brought to the top decision-makers who – as the term implies – make a decision which the organization is then supposed to implement. The top decision-makers may or may not explain their decision in detail. If they do, there may be a more or less trivial attempt at a formal discussion and explanation. There may even be a little internal debate and consultation on minor details before the decision is made 'irrevocable', but nothing as thoroughgoing as is required in the Japanese system. As a result , there is often a tendency in the US system for junior people, or for various vested or informed interests, to oppose the decisions, because they feel they have not been fully consulted, because they really do not understand all the implications, or even because they feel the decision really is counter-productive. It may take a great deal of time before this internal opposition, even sometimes internal sabotage, is overcome by persuasion, by threats, or simply by the passage of time.

Let us now compare the two systems. If we make a distinction between innovative and implementational decisions, then in Japan the former requires accommodation among the interested parties, while implementational decisions – even when they involve apparent changes in direction – can usually be done very rapidly, and at about any level, since all those people involved understand the policy, the facts, and the philosophy behind that policy. Almost the opposite is true in the United States. Innovative decisions often come down from the top and, in principle at least, do not require consensus. Implementation decisions usually cannot be carried out unless people know and support what they are doing, and since often in the US the consensus was not achieved ahead of time, it must be subsequently achieved.

Yet it seems that the length of time it takes to make a complete decision – including both the innovative and implementational aspects – and thereby get the system moving in a purposive 'communal' fashion is about the same in American and Japanese business firms. The difference is that in a Japanese firm the debate is carried on in such a way as to increase morale and the general sense of participation, while in the American firm the debate that takes place after the decision has been made is – almost by definition – subversive, or at least against official policy. It therefore is more likely to hurt morale and the sense of participation. In the Japanese system, since the debate is aboveboard and understood as necessary, everybody contributes wholeheartedly to facilitating it and conducting it as efficiently as is reasonably compatible with the objectives and customs. In the case of the American debate, since it is underground and subversive, it is difficult to facilitate or organize efficiently.

It is important to notice that the Japanese system has many elements of what we in the US now call participatory democracy. It also has elements in common with the famous Hawthorne experiments conducted by Western Electric from 1927–32.* While both of these issues are worth examining in more detail, it would take us somewhat afield to do so. I will just note here that the participatory democracy aspect works, in part, because of other aspects of the Japanese character already discussed (e.g., communal spirit, urge to conformity, rigid requirement to repay even the slightest obligation, urge to further group harmony and unity, etc.). I would not expect this kind of participatory democracy to work in any culture that stresses individuality or egoistic motivation. The Hawthorne experiments are relevant when we consider that they indicate Americans might become much more productive under the stimulus of a system not unlike the Japanese system.

---

* In these experiments a variety of changes in working conditions, some contradicting others, all resulted in increased productivity. The conclusion reached was that it was not the actual changes that were decisive but rather the impression conveyed to workers that management was interested in them and in their views, as well as in their circumstances.

One of the most interesting bureaucratic manifestations of the politics of consensus and the way it can be used or applied is through the institution of what is sometimes called *Ringi*. As this is normally applied in large government bureaucracies, and even in large private bureaucracies, junior people in a department achieve a consensus among themselves on an issue on which they think a decision should be made, and then they draft a paper on it. The department head will approve the paper. This paper will then be circulated in other departments, usually at the lower levels, with much discussion and correction ensuing. The paper may go back and forth a number of times as changes are made, and eventually a reasonable consensus is achieved at the lower levels. The paper is then passed on to the department heads and from there to the corporate heads, who now are under rather serious pressure to sign and forward it to the president's office or other centralized decision-making point for final implementation.

Thus *Ringi* is simply a special institutional arrangement for obtaining the kind of consensus we have just described, but one in which most of the initiative comes from the bottom or middle levels. Where it is still used (there is some pressure in Japan to abandon or de-emphasize the system) it really represents a kind of decision-making from below – almost a grass-roots form of participatory democracy – yet placed in a very authoritarian and hierarchical structure.

Another method of achieving agreement is called *matomari* – which can be part of the *Ringi* process or independent of it. As described by Richard Halloran the process is as follows:

. . . A typical decision-making meeting opens with a statement of the problem by the group's senior member. Each member then exposes a slight portion of his thinking, never coming out with a full-blown, thoroughly persuasive presentation. After this, he sits back to listen to the same sort of exposition from the others. The Japanese, who has a tremendously sensitive ego, does not wish to put himself in a position where he is holding a minority or, worse, an isolated view. Nor does he wish to risk offending an associate by coming out bluntly with a proposal that might run contrary to his colleague's thoughts. The discussion goes on at great length, each person slowly and carefully presenting his opinion, gradually sensing out the feelings of other people,

making a pitch subtly, following it without pressing if he finds it acceptable, quietly backing off and adjusting his views to those of the others
if he finds himself not in tune with the evolving consensus. When the
leader of the group believes that all are in basic agreement with a
minimally acceptable decision, he sums up the thinking of the group,
asks whether all are agreed, and looks around to receive their consent-
ing nods. Nothing is crammed down anyone's throat. If, by chance, a
consensus does not emerge and a deadlock seems likely, the group
leader does not press for a decision, does not ask for a vote, does not
rule that no consensus seems possible and thus embarrass people.
Instead, he suggests that perhaps more time is needed to think about
the problem, and sets a date for another meeting. The people involved
can then meet informally to adjust views or, if there are positions that
are wide apart, mediators will go back and forth between the people
holding the opposing positions and attempt to narrow down the differences. By the time the next meeting is called, the differences most
likely will have been straightened out and the process can move forward
to a final decison. In all of this, the most important principle is not to
stand on principle but to reach agreement. All else is subordinate to
this point.[15]

Affecting Japanese Decision-Making from the Outside

It should be clear that this process of 'group-centred decision-
making' is a relatively autonomous one, at least as far as outsiders are concerned, and can more easily be affected negatively
than positively. That is, any pressures to accelerate it or to make it
reach an immediate decision are likely to be regarded with intense
hostility and suspicion. But that is not to say that Americans have
not occasionally been able to get such decisions facilitated. The
author knows of at least one case where an American company
pointed out to the Trade Ministry (MITI) authorities that under
present conditions, Japanese operations were just not worth the
company's time any more, and as far as the chief executive was
concerned, he intended to cut losses unless the Ministry came up
with an immediate decision. The MITI authorities managed to
do so. (But only two junior Japanese officials were on hand to see
him off at the airport when he left the country – in contrast to the
seven or so who greeted him upon his arrival.)

If an outsider can anticipate the eventual form of the consensus to emerge and can articulate it at the appropriate moment, he may perform a valuable service to the Japanese discussion. And sometimes the outsider has an advantageous perspective for attempting to do exactly that. It is, of course, particularly important that such an outside solution be advanced in time to influence the discussion and before the chief negotiator – or an important group – has adopted positions that are more or less contrary to the outsider's proposed consensus.

In any case, it is clear that the outsider could go to some pains to provide the Japanese discussants with relevant information and to explain the reasons for his own preferences. He should not wait until the consensus has been largely achieved before joining the discussion, nor should he expect immediate results. (He cannot possibly convince the individuals he is talking to, as they represent a larger communal constituency, which must be consulted.) Therefore, to the extent the outsider has relevant and important information, ideas, concepts, arguments, etc., he should attempt to get them in as early as possible, subject, of course, to all the other constraints that such outsiders always have.

For many issues on which such decisions are being made, there are out-groups not directly consulted, at least in the particular 'game'. In the political arena these might include newspapers, intellectuals, students, workers, radicals, the opposition political party, and so on. In any particular context there will be some such out-groups of varying degrees of importance. They can sometimes influence both the content and the timing of the decision by threatening to precipitate a confrontation before the accommodation process has had sufficient time to work. In particular, they can exert enormous delaying influence, since it is extremely difficult, if not impossible, for even a pronounced majority to ram through legislative or administrative decisions against the will of a determined minority, for, as indicated earlier, to do so would be thought of by the Japanese as a 'tyranny of the majority'.

As suggested, therefore, an outside business firm, government bureau, or other organization should not normally try to rush the decision process, because to do so will often only result in the erection of barriers and animosity. Instead, one should find out where the staff work on a problem is being done, provide the staff with relevant information, and present opinions – mostly when the Japanese ask for them. Since the Japanese do intensive staff work to educate themselves, any effort to rush or channel this process is likely to raise suspicions of deception. Unsolicited opinions should be presented only as the process goes on. In particular, one normally should not take a rigid position; otherwise the Japanese might become frustrated and give up any hope of accommodation. Also, one may take a lesson from the Japanese and occasionally propose side deals or suggest other means of accommodation to make it easier for the Japanese to move appreciably in the desired direction. And, since decisions are reached only after an extended period of discussion among the large number of interested Japanese parties who often hold widely divergent views, anyone anticipating the eventual agreement and articulating it at the right moment may not only facilitate but sometimes influence the decision. Therefore, if an outsider should succeed in formulating a reasonable accommodation, his leadership value would increase immensely, especially since by the time all the various factions are accommodated, the position of their chief negotiator may be practically frozen.

Duty – On, Giri, *and* Ninjo

Because the issue is so important, I will quote extensively from several writers on this concept:

Perhaps no other emotional force in Japanese society is as powerful and propulsive as that which inheres in the sense of obligation or indebtedness which is known as *on*. From the cradle to the grave, this emotional force, in all its variations and manifestations, propels the individuals in his actions. Life is an endless succession of favors received for which repayment must be made with diligence. The social behavior of the people becomes unintelligible without adequate consideration of this peculiarly Japanese concept and practice. The fabric of society is thus woven with the warp and woof of mutual and reciprocal indebtedness and obligations. Obligations bind the individual to individuals and groups in a tight web of relationships which ignore individual rights and desires. What exists is a hierarchy of obligations beginning at the top with loyalty to the emperor and the state, to society at large, to the family as manifested in filial piety, to one's superiors, teachers, friends, in-laws, and even to subordinates and servants. . .

Traditionally loyalty to the state and the emperor has been at the very top of the hierarchy of obligations. In feudal times, the primary loyalty was to one's lord and only indirectly and secondarily did loyalty reach the emperor if at all. But in the nineteenth century, this obligation was transformed into absolute loyalty to the emperor who became the personification of the state. This was achieved in the Imperial Rescript on Education (1890) and the rescript to the soldiers and sailors (1882). Although the obligations to the family and to the state are unlimited, the latter take precedence over the former. In China, filial piety or family loyalty always took precedence over loyalty to the Emperor but when the Japanese took over from her continental neighbor the political philosophy of Confucianism, they reversed the order while rejecting completely the idea of revolution.

Filial piety is a form of repaying the heavy burden of obligation to one's parents and is one of the very first lessons a child learns in life. On this obligation the authority of the parents is firmly based, especially that of the father who is the head of the family. Filial piety is loyalty to the family and as such is of a primary nature. Aside from the two principal loyalties there exist a myriad of loyalties which determine the behavior of individuals.[16]

Thus says Chitoshi Yanaga.

On *giri*, human obligational relationships, Yanaga writes:

The whole gamut of human obligational relationships is included in the concept of *giri* which is all-embracing in its implications. No facet of life could exist outside it. Everybody must and does move within its orbit. Merely to give all the different connotations the word conveys to a Japanese would be an impossible task. It means duty, justice, honor, face, decency, respectability, courtesy, charity, humanity, love, circumstance, gratitude, claim.

Giri is an all-pervading force in the behavior of all classes of people and in all walks of life: the prime minister, the official, the politician, the businessman, financier, industrialist, intellectual, student, parent, the factory worker, and the farmer. Although the complexities and ambivalences of *giri* must be taken into account, it operates because of the universal need for respecting and expressing 'human feelings' (*ninjo*) in social life that exists in closely knit communities. . . The sanctions of *giri* are to be found in society in the mores, customs, and folkways, and not in the laws.

The obsessive behavior regarding honor or 'face' is inextricably tied in with the demands of *giri*. In a negative sense it operates to prevent shame or disgrace to one's name, while in a positive sense it becomes a desire for fame and prestige. In feudal society, loss of honor either by insult, dereliction of duty, failure, or cowardice called for vendetta or suicide, both of which are forms of redressing a wrong or a disgrace. There was also another way out of such dishonor, namely, renouncing the world by taking the tonsure and leading a cloistered life in a Buddhist monastery. While these methods are no longer employed in their original forms, the spirit of vengeance or retaliation is still very much in evidence especially in the political sphere.

Suicide, the most extreme form of aggressive action that a Japanese can resort to, has been a part of the operational code of *giri*. Not only is it condoned but in the Tokugawa period it was even glorified in literature for those who committed suicide in romantic love pacts. There has never been any stigma of cowardice attached to suicide. On the contrary the act has been regarded as the final demonstration of a man's courage and determination. Properly carried out, it will remove the stigma or disgrace attached to a person's name. It serves as an apology to atone for one's failure, as a protest to induce a change of heart in someone thereby changing a course of action, or as a final desperate method of winning an argument in a controversy. Used as a threat, it has effectively forestalled, prevented, or induced action. To commit suicide to avoid the disgrace of capture by the enemy has been a common practice since feudal times. Suicide has often been an alternative to destroying others.[17]

Beardsley adds,

Giri obligations often are mutual and reciprocal, especially within a collectivity. . . [It] works well in a society of lifelong neighbors and associates. It is measured not from a single incident or transaction but from its coloring of an association that is expected to extend indefinitely through time. . . Since such mutual support often extends to a network of persons, *giri* relations may link not just two but a whole row of participants. . .

Giri inevitably loses its effect in an environment of impersonal transactions among strangers and incidental acquaintances.

On is a beneficence handed down from one's superior. It institutes an obligation (*ongaeshi*) to the superior on the part of the person who receives it or enjoys its benefits. By its very nature, *on* always connotes a hierarchical relation between two specific actors; the obligations that rise from *on* therefore are not part of an abstract code or principle but have at least shades of difference, inasmuch as the specific participants in one relation differ from another.

To some Japanese today, *giri* is the blanket term for obligations between specific persons in concrete, actual situations, as contrasted with a universalist ethic of duty, and *on* or *ongaeshi* are merely special forms of *giri*. Others draw the following distinction: two individual persons are always hierarchically linked through *on*, whereas *giri* relations include obligations towards groups and do not necessarily establish superiority on one side and inferiority on the other. . .[18]

Ninjo refers to what one would like to do as a human being and equally to what one finds distasteful or abhorrent out of personal sentiment. *Giri* pertains to what one must do or avoid doing because of status and group membership.[19]

We can summarize much of the above by reproducing the following table from *The Chrysanthemum and the Sword*.[20]

Schematic Table of Japanese Obligations and Their Reciprocals

I. *On:* obligations passively incurred. One 'receives an *on*'; one 'wears an *on*,' i.e., *on* are obligations from the point of view of the passive recipient.

> *ko on. On* received from the Emperor.
>
> *oya on. On* received from parents.
>
> *nushi no on. On* received from one's lord.
>
> *shi no on. On* received from one's teacher.
>
> *on* received in all contacts in the course of one's life.
>
> NOTE: All these persons from whom one receives *on* become one's *on jun*, '*on* man'.

II. Reciprocals of *on*. One 'pays' these debts, one 'returns these obligations' to the *on* man, i.e., these are obligations regarded from the point of view of active repayment.

A. *Gimu*. The fullest repayment of these obligations is still no more than partial and there is no time limit.

> *chu.* Duty to the Emperor, the law, Japan.

ko. Duty to parents and ancestors (by implication, to descendants).

nimmu. Duty to one's work.

B. *Giri*. These debts are regarded as having to be repaid with mathematical equivalence to the favor received and there are time limits.

1. *Giri*-to-the-world.

   Duties to liege lord.

   Duties to affinal family.

   Duties to non-related persons due to *on* received, e.g., on a gift of money, on a favor, on work contributed (as a 'work party').

   Duties to persons not sufficiently closely related (aunts, uncles, nephews, nieces) due to *on* received not from them but from common ancestors.

2. *Giri*-to-one's-name. This is a Japanese version of *die Ehre*.

   One's duty to 'clear' one's reputation of insult or imputation of failure, i.e., the duty of feuding or vendetta. (N.B. This evening of scores is not reckoned as aggression.)

   One's duty to admit no (professional) failure or ignorance.

   One's duty to fulfill the Japanese proprieties, e.g., observing all respect behavior, not living above one's station in life, curbing all displays of emotion on inappropriate occasions, etc.

Expendability of 'Damaged' or 'Inadequate' People or Things

Let me begin with an anecdote Ruth Benedict tells about Japanese attitudes towards the expendability of their fighting forces. She notes the shocked incredulity with which the Japanese received news of the US Navy's wartime decoration of Admiral John S. McCain Jr, commander of a task force off Formosa, who successfully nursed two damaged ships across the Pacific to San Francisco for repair. According to the Japanese,

... The official reason for the decoration was not that Commander John S. McCain was able to put the Japanese to flight, though we don't see why not since that is what the Nimitz communique claimed . . . Well, the reason given for Admiral McCain's decoration was that he was able successfully to rescue two damaged American warships and escort them safely to their home base. What makes this bit of information important is not that it is a fiction but that it is the truth . . . So we are not questioning the veracity of Admiral McCain's rescuing two ships, but the point we want you to see is the curious fact that the rescuing of damaged ships merits decoration in the United States.[21]

It was perfectly clear to the Japanese that saving those two ships helped the American fighting effort greatly. They could therefore sympathize with an American admiral who, since the Americans needed the ships badly, did try to save them instead of acting in a truly honourable way and letting them go to the bottom of the sea, the fate they deserved for being damaged. It is not always possible in wartime to take the proper and honourable path. What the Japanese could not understand was that having carried through this shameful act, the Americans would advertise what they had done. As Ruth Benedict puts it,

Americans thrill to all rescue, all aid to those pressed to the wall. A valiant deed is all the more a hero's act if it saves the 'damaged.' Japanese valor repudiates such salvaging. Even the safety devices installed in our B-29's and fighter planes raised their cry of 'Cowardice.' The press and the radio returned to the theme over and over again. There was virtue only in accepting life and death risks; precautions were unworthy. This attitude found expression also in the case of the wounded and of malarial patients. Such soldiers were damaged goods and the medical services provided were utterly inadequate even for reasonable effectiveness of the fighting force. As time went on, supply difficulties of all kinds aggravated this lack of medical care, but that was not the whole story. Japanese scorn of materialism played a part in it; her soldiers were taught that death itself was a victory of the spirit and our kind of care of the sick was an interference with heroism – like safety devices in bombing planes. Nor are the Japanese used to such reliance on physicians and surgeons in civilian life as Americans are. Preoccupation with mercy toward the damaged rather than with other welfare measures is especially high in the United States, and is often commented on even by visitors from some European countries in peacetime. It is certainly alien to the Japanese. At all events, during the war the Japanese army had no trained rescue teams to remove the wounded under fire and to give first aid; it had no medical system of front line, behind-the-lines and distant recuperative hospitals. Its attention to medical supplies was lamentable. In certain emergencies the hospitalized were simply killed. Especially in New Guinea and the Philippines, the Japanese often had to retreat from a position where there was a hospital. There was no routine of evacuating the sick and wounded while there was still opportunity; only when the 'planned withdrawal' of the battalion was actually taking place or the enemy was occupying was anything done. Then, the medical officer in charge often shot the inmates of the hospital before he left or they killed themselves with hand grenades.[22]

Japanese Patriotism – Kokutai *– Mystic Sense of Being Special and Distinct*

Kokutai is usually translated as 'national polity' or 'national essence,' but it also conveys the sense of 'body' or 'substance,' and its nature is impossible to define precisely. Included in *kokutai* are the concepts of 'national structure,' particularly the emperor system; 'national basis,' the myth of the divine origin of Japan and of its imperial dynasty; and 'national character,' those special Japanese moral virtues, stemming from both native and Confucian influences, that are considered indispensable for individual behavior and social cohesion. . . Although *kokutai* is a relatively modern concept – manipulated for political purposes during the Meiji era and again in association with pre-World War II militarism – it had profound roots in Japanese cultural experience and embraced something in the cultural identity of all Japanese.

[World War II defeat undermined the mystical-ideological concept of *kokutai*.] Most young people . . . today no longer take *kokutai* seriously; they dismiss it as the propanganda of militarists. . . Nevertheless the dishonoring of *kokutai* has created in many Japanese youth a sense of their own past as dishonored. . . The sudden collapse of *kokutai* revealed its tenuousness as an ideological system. But it also created an ideological void and thus encouraged the polarizing tendencies that still haunt Japanese thought – the urge to recover *kokutai* and make things just as they were, and the opposite urge to break away entirely from every remnant of *kokutai* and make all things new.[23]

The distortion of *kokutai* by the prewar militarists contributed to the rise of Japanese totalitarianism. The book *Fundamentals of Our National Essence*, published by the Ministry of Education, expressed the official doctrine of *Kokutai No Hongi*. Used as a school guide in national ideology, it attempted to reformulate Japan's unique *Kokutai*, to warn against Western influence, and to stress the importance of the nation over the individual. The book emphasized the values of loyalty, harmony, filial piety, selflessness, the martial spirit of *bushido*, and devotion to the Emperor. The people were exhorted to create 'a new Japanese culture by adopting and sublimating Western cultures with our national essence as the basis.'

It will not be at all surprising if, as many are beginning to expect, the immediate future brings a sharp turn towards the 'right' and towards patriotism, as well as a revival of some aspects of *kokutai*. While no one, including this author, expects the manic intensity of interwar Japan, some of the traditional and not necessarily unhealthy spirit, as characterized for example by Meiji Japan, may be restored.

The Tenkō *Transformation*

One of the strongest 'institutions' the Japanese culture has produced, the so-called *tenkō* transformation, is most important to an understanding of the likely future course of many current Japanese protest groups. The word *tenkō* means *conversion*, with implications of accommodation to a greater power. Thus it has been used to describe the accommodation to militarism made in the prewar years by some formerly Marxist or liberal intellectuals. *Tenkō* is currently said to apply to students who are quite radical while in school but 'sell out' their radical views when they leave school and begin their careers. Yet the overtones of the word are not wholly negative. The *tenkō* process has an air of appropriateness and inevitability about it, as if it represents the individual's necessary (and desirable) subordination of himself to the community and its authority.

Thus *tenkō* is basic to Japanese psychology: it reflects patterns of aesthetic romanticism, obscurantism, and often shallow experimentation with ideals prior to *tenkō* itself; and it also reflects the ultimate need felt by most Japanese to submit and become part of existing authority, to gain a safe place in the human matrix, rather than risk standing alone. Young Japanese go back on their ideals because their society virtually forces them to; but their own emotional inclinations contribute to this 'self-betrayal.'[24]

In the past, *tenkō* has also been used to denote the following:

1. passionate embrace of some Western ideology;
2. a resulting alienation from and rebellion against Japanese society and mores;
3. a searching investigation into the new faith;
4. eventual disillusionment with the practices of this Western ideology (or even just its theories);
5. excessive reaction (apostasy);
6. restoration of (or return to) original Japanese values but now often with a chauvinistic and xenophobic intensity.

It should be noted that 'eventual disillusionment' is inevitable. That is, the investigation is made so searching that it finally and inevitably finds some central hypocrisy, significant internal contradictions, or other skeleton in the closet (either in practice or theory). Since no system is perfect, an intense but basically destructive investigation, even if conducted under the aegis of an effort to fully understand, must eventually result in disillusionment.

There is no implication intended in the above that this process is consciously deliberate, but it seems to me that, if only unconsciously, it has played an important role in the life of many Japanese – at least part of the time and particularly in the life history of many Japanese intellectuals before World War II. It also should be noticed that the ability to carry through this process is useful in ways other than just enabling intellectuals to submit voluntarily to authority. If one wishes to pick up some aspects of a foreign ideology, culture, technology, or technique, and if one follows the above scenario, one will end up knowing everything that one's own country would wish one to know about the foreign mode. Yet one will remain irrevocably Japanese and even be able to apply the new knowledge to Japanese conditions in a creative fashion while abandoning the excess baggage of the foreign system.

The *tenkō* process involving student radicalism and its later replacement by vocational conservatism is common in the West too – although it is nowhere nearly as pervasive, intense, and dramatic as in Japan; this *tenkō* transformation should be contrasted to the common Western scenario in which the first step is as likely to create more or less permanent expatriates, alienated individuals, or foreign enthusiasts as it is an eventual return to the original American pattern.

The Kanji (*Language*) *Barrier*

Let us start by quoting John Whitney Hall:

The process . . . of education and style of mind [was deeply influenced] by the Japanese language itself. Despite the remarkable success which the Japanese had in modernizing the language, the retention of the ideographs (*kanji*) perpetuated a host of educational problems. Many observers have concluded that the complexity of the Japanese language has been a formidable barrier to early elementary education and has restricted the rapid and exact communication of ideas either within the culture or from outside it.

The habits of rote learning required in mastering the characters, it is also claimed, have been carried over into other fields of learning and have tended to encourage uncritical acceptance of officially approved ideas and dogmas. . .[25]

Another illuminating description of the barrier created by the Japanese language is given by Inatomi Eijiro:

. . . Japanese [are] devoid of 'self-consciousness' . . . as [evidenced by] the lack of clear distinction between the parts of speech in Japanese as contrasted with the European languages. [In the latter, all sentences are composed of individual words, each] independent of one another. . . . In Japanese, on the contrary, there are some characters that can be clearly distinguished as forming independent 'parts of speech' and there are also not a few that cannot be strictly separated from other words. . . A Japanese sentence is a composite whole, and not an aggregate of individual words or phrases. This corresponds with the fact that in actual life a Japanese has no clear consciousness of his individual self, but recognizes his own existence only in the composite life of the world. . .

[The Japanese language] is a perfect symbol of the . . . people in its peculiarity of lacking a definite sense of the individual self. . . This 'perfectly corresponds with the lack of the individual. The blank of the self, that is to be seen in the clothing, food and shelter of the Japanese in their daily life.'[26]

From our point of view, perhaps the two most important aspects of the Japanese language are that it is a respect language and that it tends towards what might be called 'an emotionally rich ambiguity'. This last is a bit like the distinction Marshall McLuhan has made between radio, which he calls 'a visual medium', and television, which he thinks of as an 'auditory medium'. In television everything is within a precise box with all the images specified; therefore, little or nothing is left to the imagination of the viewer, who therefore concentrates on the auditory message. In radio, on the other hand, almost nothing visual is specified. The viewer hears only the voices, suggestive sounds, and some descriptions; he is free to make up his own images, which are often very vivid and attractive to him. If the reader will refer to the first quotation from Michiko Inukai he will notice that the *haiku* has much the same character. It is intended to be interpreted by the reader, and both the author and the language allow a good deal of freedom in such interpretation. In general, the Japanese language tends to have exactly this kind of vagueness about it (somewhat like a radio programme), while English tends to be relatively precise and limiting (somewhat like the television screen) and to the Japanese quite constraining. Many Japanese have recognized this, and the Japanese Nobel Prize winning physicist Yukawa has stated several times that he personally finds it difficult to think scientifically and precisely in Japanese and much easier to do so in English.

In addition, it is rather difficult for the Japanese to prepare original material in written form. It is therefore much easier to emphasize the spoken word and face-to-face exchanges in business and professional communication, leaving the written word more for artistic, literary, and emotional purposes. There is little activity in Japan that corresponds to the enormous interchange of correspondence in most American governmental or private offices – indeed, many Japanese secretaries do not take dictation.

The Japanese Emphasis of the Spiritual (and the Apparent) over the Material and the Real.

This takes a number of different forms. In looking at the duality of the politics of Japan, for example, one notices that historically there have generally been people whom an American would call 'front men'; their behaviour is honourable and exemplary, and it is almost always in accord with valued principles and traditions; it is to them that loyalty and respect are due. Then there are others behind the scenes who manipulate the system and are often very practical and pragmatic; but they are considered unworthy even of discussion. Indeed, in many cases the Japanese seem to wish to take the apparent as more important than the real. I remember one discussion with a Japanese scientist who worked on experimental rockets despite his being a pacifist. He was very willing to work on the programme as long as it was done under the Office of Education, but the moment it went to the Office of Science and Technology (OST), he felt it had officially become a military programme and he was no longer willing to work on it. He also realized however, that the major part of his work for the Office of Education was destined to be the basis of the OST programme. But he did not care so long as it was not yet official. At least as far as public discussion of issues is concerned, the Japanese often demonstrate an unwillingness to come to grips with simple facts, preferring instead a discussion of the higher moral issues – sometimes in a way that a Westerner would judge to be an outright denial of reality. Perhaps one of the oddest and clearest examples of this phenomenon is a common Japanese attitude towards sleep. Consider the following remarks by my favourite author on Japan:

Sleeping is another favored indulgence. It is one of the most accomplished arts of the Japanese. They sleep with complete relaxation, in any position, and under circumstances we regard as sheer impossibilities. This has surprised many Western students of the Japanese. Americans make insomnia almost a synonym for psychic tenseness, and according to our standard there are high tensions in the Japanese character. But they make child's play of good sleeping. They go to bed early, too, and it is hard to find another Oriental nation that does that.

The villagers, all asleep shortly after nightfall, are not following our maxim of storing up energy for the morrow for they do not have that kind of calculus. One Westerner, who knew them well, wrote: 'When one goes to Japan one must cease to believe that it is a bounden duty to prepare for work tomorrow by sleep and rest tonight. One is to con- sider sleep apart from questions of recuperation, rest and recreation.' It should stand, just as a proposal to work should, too, 'on its own legs, having no reference to any known fact of life or death.' Americans are used to rating sleeping as something one does to keep up one's strength and the first thought of most of us when we wake up in the morning is to calculate how many hours we slept that night. The length of our slumbers tells us how much energy and efficiency we will have that day. The Japanese sleep for other reasons. They like sleeping and when the coast is clear they gladly go to sleep.

By the same token they are ruthless in sacrificing sleep. A student preparing for examinations works night and day, uncurbed by any notion that sleep would equip him better for the test. In Army training, sleep is simply something to sacrifice to discipline. Colonel Harold Doud, attached to the Japanese Army from 1934 to 1935, tells of his conversation with a Captain Teshima. During peacetime maneuvers the troops 'twice went three days and two nights without sleep except what could be snatched during ten-minute halts and brief lulls in the situa- tion. Sometimes the men slept while walking. Our junior lieutenant caused much amusement by marching squarely into a lumber pile on the side of the road while sound asleep.' When camp was finally struck, still no one got a chance to sleep; they were all assigned to outpost and patrol duty. ' "But why not let some of them sleep?" I asked. "Oh no!" he said. "That is not necessary. They already know how to sleep. They need training in how to stay awake." ' That puts the Japa- nese view in a nutshell.[27]

It should be noted, however, that there now seems to be a decided trend among younger Japanese intellectuals to be prag- matic, matter of fact, detached, and cool – in contrast to the recent pattern, which I can only categorize as dogmatic, moral- istic, ideological (Marxist), and more interested in appearance and intention than in reality and actuality.

Finally, I might note that in the Japanese attack on Pearl Harbor the planners found that on the average their planes could not quite make it from Formosa to Clark Field and back. The official orders said, 'The pilots will rise to the occasion.'

Cliques (Batsu)

One of the remarkable aspects of Western culture is its *relative* freedom from government by – or excessive influence of – secret societies, special cults, or even private political factions. I must of course, emphasize the word 'relative'. Such institutions have caused plenty of problems in almost every Western country at one time or another; a good deal of the history of various Western countries often concerns the role of this or that clique, cult, secret society, or faction and the difficulties the nation had in finally coping with it. But in the West it is almost always thought that the power of cliques is bad for government, and it is rare to have cults, factions, secret societies, and the like possess anything like the influence and permanence they enjoy in many Asian countries. Indeed, in this sense Japan is more like the rest of the world than is the United States, though the clique structure of Japanese government, culture, and society has peculiarly Japanese elements to it. Thus the Japanese term for clique, *batsu*, is pervasive in Japanese life, indicating the importance of these groups.

A famous critique of the *batsu* in politics (*habatsu*) was written in 1918 by Ozaki Yukio – a liberal and progressive member of the Diet who did not like the *habatsu* form of operating.

Here in the Orient we have had the conception of a faction; but none of a public party. A political party is an association of people having for its exclusive object the discussion of public affairs of state and the enforcement of their views thereon. But when political parties are transplanted in the East, they at once partake of the nature of factions, pursuing private and personal interests instead of the interests of the state. . . Besides, the customs and usages of feudal times are so deeply impressed upon the minds of men here that even the idea of political parties, as soon as it enters the brains of our countrymen, germinates and grows according to feudal notions. . . A politician scrupulous enough to join or desert a party for the sake of principle is denounced as a political traitor or renegade. That political faith should be kept not *vis-à-vis* its leader or its officers but *vis-à-vis* its principles and views is not understood. They foolishly think that the proverb 'a faithful servant never serves two masters: a chaste wife never sees two husbands' is equally applicable to the members of a political party. In their erroneous opinion, it is a loyal act on the part of a member of a party to change his principles and views in accordance with orders from headquarters, while in the event of headquarters changing their views it is unlawful to desert them.

While the *habatsu* still dominate Japanese politics – and while polls indicate some degree of approval of 'voting for the man and not the politics' – genuine party organization and party politics in the Western sense have gotten a foothold and might develop, if for no other reason than that the young Japanese seem to prefer it. Or this might be like so many other things in Japan – a façade of Western appearance with a reality of Japanese tradition and practice.

Almost everybody had heard of the *zaibatsu*, which were, if you will, prewar business 'conglomerates', though under much tighter control and unified operation than the typical American or European conglomerate. To the extent that business had an important voice in Japanese government before World War II, this voice was exercised through the *zaibatsu*, though actually the *kambatsu* (bureaucratic cliques) and the military groups (*gumbatsu*) in many cases had more influence. Since World War II the exercise of political power by the business world has been accomplished more through something called the *zaikai* (or the business leader clique) than through the current *zaibatsu* groupings, and the military have practically no clique power at all. The *kambatsu* (the bureaucratic cliques) structure came through World War II more or less unscathed, and for a while achieved a kind of peak of power. Today one thinks of the *zaikai* (business leader clique) as being of greater importance than the bureaucratic or political cliques but in no sense always dominant. Also important, both before and after World War II but much more since the war, have been the *keibatsu* (extended family clique) and the *gakubatsu* (university clique).

Usually the cliques have a structure within themselves that is very dependent on the *oyabun-kobun* relation. This basically resembles the Confucian father-son relationship. Almost any superior who takes an early interest in any particular subordinate may establish an *oyabun-kobun* relationship that lasts even if both are transferred into different departments. Indeed, in Japan this is a characteristic pattern of many superior-subordinate relationships – for example, mentor-protégé, senior-junior, master-apprentice, teacher-student, gangleader-gangster, foreman-labourer relations. The relationship can be very subtle and/or very pervasive, and it almost always exists – to some degree – for life, even if the original reasons for the relationship have long disappeared.

Finally, we should note that though the easiest way to rise in Japanese society is to go to a good university, admittance to a university is largely on the basis of merit. Nevertheless, the *keibatsu* (clique based on marriage or kinship) are still extremely important and not even in a clandestine fashion. Being of good family or being related to good families is considered perfectly reasonable ground for advancement and preferment, and few in Japan would criticize such appointments unless the individual concerned was unlikely or obviously unfit for the appointment.

Japan Incorporated (*or Japan: Conglomerate of Conglomerates*)

I should probably start this section by admitting that the title will be misleading to most readers for whom the terms 'incorporated' or 'conglomerate' will immediately bring to mind the Western models. The model one really needs is that of the Japanese corporation or the Japanese 'conglomerate' (i.e., *zaibatsu*) – a business run as an extended democratic family but in a conforming, communal-minded culture and with an authoritarian hierarchy.

I mentioned in the introduction to this chapter that Japan was both authoritarian and pluralistic. Nothing illustrates this better than the current government of Japan. First and foremost, there is no sense in which the government is a neutral mediator or referee between various factions of the people. We must remember that the entire modernization and industrialization process of Japan occurred under the leadership of what would now be called a 'modernizing élite,' but we can think of it as simply the government of Japan. The opposition between government and business, which is such an important theme in US history (sometimes varied by corruption undermining government's duty to be separate and independent of business and to regulate it), is absent from Japanese history. The current government leaders, decision-makers, administrators, and big business leaders all have the same basic goals determined by a consensus that has developed in some of the complex ways suggested earlier, and, of course, sometimes in even more complex ways. A rather good summary illustrating the pluralist/authoritarian character of government rule in Japan today, despite its democratic forms and formalities, has been given by Chitoshi Yanaga as follows:

There seems to be general agreement among students of Japanese politics that the nation is [now] governed jointly by organized business, the party government, and the administrative bureaucracy.

As to which of the three groups is most powerful, there is no agreement. Any judgement must necessarily be highly subjective and is likely to be biased. Professional politicians believe that the administrators are running the country. Businessmen are quick to assert that the party politicians determine national policies. Administrators are convinced that organized business, working through the party in power, is in control of national policies.

In terms of economic policies, it is easy to conclude that organized business rules supreme. The power of the administrative bureaucracy over organized business is quite apparent when it comes to power to regulate and control business, and to grant or withhold licences, government loans, and subsidies. The party is no match against the power of organized business. Yet there have been instances where the party in power was able to exert a decisive influence over bureaucracy. This three-power relationship is analogous to that of the three-sided 'tossing game' called *janken*, in which paper, stone, and scissors are featured. Paper is stronger than stone, which it can wrap; stone is stronger than scissors, which it can break; and scissors win out over paper, which they can cut.[28]

The sceptical or hostile critic will often think of the three groups as rather unprincipled, buying one another off on one occasion and threatening and coercing each other on another. He will point out that business by its contributions of cash tries to buy the party in power, and the party in power in turn attempts to create an environment in which business can make profits. In the meantime the administrative departments are run by ambitious graduates of

Tokyo University, who have joined them mainly because promotion is rapid and administration is one of the basic preparing
grounds for eventually going into the business or political worlds
– the one to be chosen depending, in a more or less opportunistic
fashion, upon the rewards to be reaped at the time.

There is a fair amount of accuracy in this picture, but because it
leaves out so much that is important it is on the whole misleading.
A much better formulation and a much clearer one would emphasize the basic cooperative, communal, and patriotic nature of
the enterprise. We all know that in any enterprise there is a good
deal of factional politics, and different groups line up against each
other and jockey for advantage. However, if the enterprise is at all
healthy, day-to-day politics, even though for factional advantage,
take place within a basic structure of activity that fulfills the
objectives of the enterprise as a whole; if there is any serious
conflict between factional and over-all objectives, the faction will
find itself either suppressed or doing its own suppressing of
factional advantage. Therefore, I much prefer this description by
Chitoshi Yanaga:

> The spectacle of Japanese politics is in a sense a dramatic production,
> presented jointly by the business community, the ruling party, and the
> administrative bureaucracy. Organized business is the playwright as
> well as the financier. The ruling party, as producer, director, and stage
> manager, adapts the play and makes sure that the production meets
> with the approval of the playwright-financier. It is also responsible for
> picking the leading actor, who must be persona grata to the financier.
> The administrative bureaucracy utilizes its expertise in looking after
> the technical details as well as the business end of the production.[29]

It is in the above sense that we must think of Japan as 'Japan
Incorporated' or as a 'conglomerate of conglomerates'. Currently
the basic objective of this corporate enterprise is to increase the
rate of economic growth and of technological expertise, while, as
a kind of prudential measure, gradually building up the nation's
defensive capability (hedging against various kinds of developments or creating new opportunities). All of this is done in such a
way as to meet the economic, political, and financial demands of
the mass of Japanese people as well as of various special interests.

I will later discuss some of the issues that are likely to arise as this drama plays itself out. We will take note of the fact that there are many other players present who either want to organize their own play or at least are unenthusiastic about the current production and would like to revise or junk it. However, I will argue that despite many cultural changes and social strains, it seems likely that the current production is going to have a very long run, even though other competing patterns are being organized, and even though there is a certain amount of sabotaging of the current production. In part, the very success of the play makes it impossible to organize serious alternatives or to focus criticism. However, the main point is that by and large the Japanese like the current system (i.e., are anxious for the play to succeed as a play).

'The Todai Club'

Todai, or more accurately Tokyo University, can be thought of as the most exclusive club in Japan, and if any 'establishment' or clique runs Japan, it is this group. If one can attain membership in the club, it establishes one's eligibility for the highest positions in the realm in much the same manner (but more so) as graduation from Cambridge and Oxford did (and does) for the British or the Grandes Écoles does for the French, and far more than a Harvard degree does for Americans. Of the ten postwar Prime Ministers since 1945, seven have been members of this Todai Club. Government ministries are traditional strongholds of Todai graduates, as can be seen by the following list (which gives the percentage of Todai graduates among section chiefs and higher officials but not including vice-ministers and parliamentary vice-ministers as of 1963):[30]

Finance Ministry	62 per cent
Ministry of Internatonal Trade and Industry	63
Transportation Ministry	53
Construction Ministry	58
Education Ministry	66
Local Government Ministry	73

It is important to realize, too, that particularly since the war the University of Tokyo has been almost equally influential in business circles. Consider for example the following two tables:[31]

Todai Corporation Executives Compared with Graduates of Other Universities

University	Number	Percentage
Tokyo	630	21·0
Kyoto	210	7·0
Keio	196	6·6
Hitotsubashi	175	5·8
Waseda	116	3·8
Others	1,673	55·8
	3,000	100·0

Prominent Business Leaders According to the Universities They Attended

University	Number	Percentage
Tokyo	54	40·6
Hitotsubashi	13	9·8
Keio	8	6·0
Kyoto	7	5·3
Kobe	6	4·5
Waseda	4	3·0
Kyushu	2	1·5
Others	39	29·3
	133	100·0

It is commonly argued in Japan that Keio University has also been prominent in producing business leaders, and particularly that it is the most prominent of the private universities in doing so. The above table would not seem to bear out this contention – except perhaps as far as competition with other private universities goes (Tokyo, Kyoto, and Hitotsubashi are government schools). In any case, the effect does not seem to be very dramatic. (This last impression might be changed somewhat if we looked at the actual names of the individuals.) It is also common lore in Japan that Waseda University used to produce a disproportionately large number of the political leaders and journalists, and to some degree still does, but that now it too is heavily engaged in producing business leaders. The chart certainly indicates that it is not unimportant in business, but again the effect does not seem to be dramatic in comparison with the overwhelming predominance of Tokyo and other universities. However, I am told that if one cannot get into Tokyo University, it is a good idea to go to Waseda or Keio.

The main point about these tables is that they illustrate how the *gakubatsu* (i.e., university cliques) preserve their authority simply by dominating the positions of power and by preserving a close degree of cooperation with each other both within and between the other *batsu*. It is also interesting to note that there has been an increase in the prestige of business, or at least in the good jobs given by business. Consider the following table on the distribution of Tokyo University graduates between business and government:[32]

	Sept. 1900	*Sept. 1926*	*March 1958*
Government service	383	2,046	5,500
Banks and corporations	187	3,580	10,681

This table reflects only initial entry into government or business and does not reflect the 'raiding' of government by business – a practice that was unheard of before World War II. It is now common to find business men selecting topnotch government bureaucrats and inducing them to enter their businesses. There is little resentment of the practice – rather the opposite. As a result, many Tokyo graduates now enter government administration fully expecting to later go into business. As a result of their detour they increase their flexibility and evade some of the time-consuming necessities of the normal 'escalator system'.

The new respectability of the business and industrial community is a direct result of the postwar economic revival. From the beginning of the postwar period, the business community gradually earned the admiration of the entire nation by rebuilding the Japanese economy and, in the process, restoring the nation's self-respect. At the same time, the business community acquired a much stronger voice, often a decisive one, in the nation's affairs.

Inevitably the Japanese realized that the economic power controlled by these men could easily operate, too, as formidable political power. In the early 1950s, therefore, the press began to pay much greater attention to the views and opinions of the nation's business leaders. And as the economic revival of the country progressed, this emphasis in the press increased.

Dramatic evidence of the new status of the business community was provided by the selection of a crown princess. Despite the large number of candidates of royal or noble blood, the imperial family chose the daughter of a successful corporation president. Many Japanese took this as the highest recognition of the new power of the business community in shaping the nation's affairs.

The importance of this will become clearer when we discuss the probable national goals of the Japanese nation in the next decade or two and the likelihood that social strains or cultural changes may start to decrease the momentum of the Japanese economic miracle.

The current status of the business community, of course, is in startling contrast with the attitudes held in Tokugawa Japan where, as we have already remarked, the business or merchant class was at the bottom of the social ladder, beneath artisans and farmers, and often was looked down upon as parasites of society. That attitude has eroded during the last hundred years until today there is almost nothing left of it.

Thus one can argue that business – and business-oriented people – are now more or less in charge. This 'establishment,' however, is not monolithic and, in addition to the limitations imposed by economic conditions, military realities, and the opinion of intellectuals, its power is occasionally blocked by popular sentiment, itself a growing power. Further, the 'business establishment' is divided into subgroups, with the subgroup that possesses authority varying with the content of the decision at hand. At times one group in the establishment may impose its will on another, as when the government overrules the objections of industrialists and follows economic policies that some businessmen find objectionable but that the government regards as in the best interests of Japanese business as a whole.

Japanese Politics

By now the reader will not be surprised to learn that the most crucial point about Japanese politics is that it is so very Japanese, despite the fact that it has taken on the veneer of Western democratic forms and practices. The situation is rather similar to that in the seventh to ninth centuries, when the Japanese adopted a Confucian model but never really adopted the Chinese Mandarin system of promotion by examination and merit. (Once again, 'Chinese knowledge, Japanese spirit.') Rather, they took this Confucian model and absorbed it into an extremely hierarchical society. The success of the Japanese in managing to fit these two together was similar to their success in borrowing the Chinese written language and using it for their own, although in many ways the two spoken languages are so different that it is miraculous that one can express Japanese words and thoughts in Chinese characters at all.

Let us therefore summarize the situation of political democracy in Japan by contrasting usual American and Japanese attitudes and practices as follows:[33]

	Anglo-American Countries	Japan
Political Sovereignty	Rests with the people and works from the bottom up	Rests with the rulers and trickles from the top down
Citizens	Can be active participants in the processes of government	Normally politically passive, usually consenting to the rule of the establishment
Popular Attitudes towards Government	Inherently distrusts or is sceptical of governmental authority; strives to restrain the exercise of political power	Basically trusts governmental authority and accepts the application of its power

	Anglo-American Countries	Japan
Political Decisions	Ideal is for decisions to be made by the majority for the greatest good of the greatest number, without infringing on the basic rights of the minority or the individual	Made by consensus or compromise for the greatest good of the nation-family
Basic assumptions about human beings and the meaning and purpose of men and communities	1. Western society strives for human fulfillment of the individual	1. Japanese society strives for subordination of the individual to attain harmony within the group
	2. Men are believed to be created equal, even if they are not always treated so	2. Men are inherently unequal and each has his station in a hierarchy
	3. The Western democrat ideally is tolerant and accepts diversity in society	3. The Japanese is intolerant and strives for conformity
	4. The Westerner believes that as a free man he has certain inalienable rights	4. The Japanese believes that as a member of the national family he has certain duties and obligations
Role of the State	The role of the state in a Western democracy is to protect and enhance individual rights	The role of the Japanese state is to preserve a benevolent social order
Rule of Law	Western democracies are founded on the rule of law, to which all men are equally subject	Japanese politics is based on the rule of men, who are supposed to govern for the common good but who do so with different standards for superiors and inferiors

Such a table provides, of course, a very simplistic dichotomy and really describes neither political system accurately, being much too black and white in its contrasts. However, we should not fall victim to the problems of those who have difficulty in detecting these kinds of qualitative differences because of twilight zone or gray zone-type problems. Japan is surely much more of a democracy and more individualistic than this table indicates, and the United States is much more authoritarian, hierarchical, and communal. Their differences, however, are quite important and are likely to be quite persistent, even if they are not quite as simple and dramatic as first indicated.

Contracts and Litigations

Generally speaking, people of different cultures have very different attitudes towards written agreements or contracts. In very few cultures are contracts taken as seriously as in the US where, for example, the written agreement is generally regarded as virtually sacrosanct, overriding all other relationships. Presumably this characteristic can be attributed to the fact that there are comparatively few relationships in the United States based in tradition and culture. In a sense, the contract is all the social cement we have.

In some cases (particularly treaties such as NATO) we tend to think of contracts as being a marriage made for life rather than a liaison made for convenience. Until recently, for example, Americans almost never thought of the NATO Treaty as something that could be easily changed or – from the psychological point of view – lightly picked up or dropped. Europeans, on the other hand, clearly have not taken it so seriously. Similarly, Americans generally regard the US Constitution as a unique, complete, everlasting document: one that created our nation and will endure for its duration. In comparison, the French, who are now in their Fifth Republic, are little concerned with the temporary nature of their written constitutions. For them the nation as the embodiment of the French people is sacred, while the written framework is treated almost as frivolously as we would treat the fashions of an era, as a dress that is discarded when out-worn – or even just out of style.

The Japanese are even more casual about written documents. Where Americans in cases of dispute tend to say, 'Let us return to the document on which the relationship is based and see what it said,' many Japanese would not think the matter of sufficient importance to be mentioned. For most Japanese, the critical issue is the present and past emotional background of a relationship, the personal issues and attributes that led to its creation, and the current power or bargaining situation. The Japanese would want to know: what was the ambience of the situation in which the document was signed; what events have occurred since the signing and what are the current relationships of the concerned parties? – all things that are usually irrelevant to an American involved in a dispute over a 'contractual issue'.

Halloran and George, for example, describe this characteristic Japanese attitude as follows:

Japanese businessmen avoid precedent and deprecate legal, contractual obligations because they believe an agreement valid only so long as the conditions under which it was reached continue to hold true. They view contracts with suspicion and draw them up with an eye to flexibility, in contrast to the American practice of trying to close every conceivable loophole. Few disputes between Japanese businesses ever go to court because this would be an admission that they have not been able to negotiate a compromise. Courts operate on the same theory and endeavor to mediate a compromise if a dispute comes to them in desperation. Courts are deliberately slow, not only because care is required but because the longer a court holds off, the better the chance the two parties will be forced to compromise.[34]

. . . A Westerner entering into a contract with a Japanese individual or firm will find that a contract is often considered an agreement to enter into a general course of conduct rather than something fixing the precise terms of performance. As a result, there may be basic disagreement over whether or not the agreement has been breached. . .[35]

Much the same attitude discussed here with regard to business relationships also holds for treaties and other international agreements and understandings. If there is a change in power or other relationships but new emotional relationships have not been built up, then no treaty is likely to have serious moral binding effect on the Japanese.

The Japanese Press

In most respects the Japanese press seems to be virtually identical to the American press. Japanese newspapers have the usual staff of investigative reporters, editorial writers, and foreign correspondents. They use the same standard layout and printing techniques as the rest of the world. By American standards, however, the circulation of most Japanese newspapers is enormous. The three main national newspapers – the *Mainichi Shimbun*, the *Asahi Shimbun*, and the *Yomiuri Shimbun* – literally blanket the entire country with as many as fourteen editions a day printed in various key cities throughout the Japanese islands. The national circulation of *Mainichi*, for example, is roughly 7·5 million, more than three times the circulation of the largest newspaper in the United States (the New York *Daily News*).

But there is also a much more subtle difference between the Japanese press and the American press, particularly in the conception of their roles in society. Generalizing about the American press has always been a risky proposition, but it should be safe to say that most American journalists see themselves primarily as 'watchdogs' of society in general and of the government in particular. Of course, journalism also has a much broader role in American society, which it performs with varying effectiveness, but it is not one of its recognized functions to consciously promote harmony in the nation – except possibly in times of war. And this is precisely where Japanese journalists and their American counterparts disagree. As Richard Halloran has observed,

The theoretically ideal role of the press is to foster harmony, but it is not always unified in its views and must make adjustments like other segments of Japanese society. The opposition of the press or a particular newspaper to a proposal in its formative stages does not mean that the press opposes the Establishment or the government. It is merely partaking in the endless discussion that is part of the process of reaching consensus. The closer to consensus the Establishment gets, the more the press falls into line.[36]

Throughout this process the press also tends to act as a major force in shaping public opinion. News stories on significant issues or political leaders are written without interpretation, independent judgement, or variation from the official line. In other countries, especially Great Britain or the United States, this would be considered journalistic treason, but in Japan it is the accepted custom. The Japanese press feels that its main responsibility is to publicize the decisions of the nation's leaders once they have been made, and then to persuade the public to support them. Accordingly its general policy and news judgement are not governed by the relative importance of any one story, or by the public's right to know, but by the impact a story will have on the nation and Japanese national interests.

It should be noted that even when editorials criticize a speech that was a trial balloon for a new policy, the new policy is sometimes, in effect, given a kind of backhand support. First, the seemingly on-trial editorials give the ideas exposed in the speech wide publicity and importance, and secondly, they often make the criticism so routinely and in such cliché terms that it has no real sting. In this way Japanese newspapers can, in effect, prepare the general public for a change in policy without looking like they themselves have all of a sudden meekly and uncritically accepted the change.

This is not to imply, however, that the press is completely subservient to the Japanese leadership, although such was the case before World War II. Indeed, there is considerable discussion in the press of major policy issues, but it is important to recognize that such discussion is almost always conducted within the limits imposed by the existing consensus. And once the debate is concluded, the press usually accepts the decision, in much the same manner as any other loyal member of the national leadership or establishment. For the press – and this is the major change in its traditional role in Japanese society – is actually a member of the national establishment rather than a subordinate of it, and it has major responsibility for maintaining the consensus and thereby reinforcing national solidarity and unity.

Japanese Racism and Exclusiveness

The Japanese do not think of themselves as being racist. I once brought sharp surprise to a number of senior Americans and Japanese with whom I was having dinner by suggesting that in some ways Japan is the most racist nation in the world. One of them asked me to explain what I meant. I started, of course, with the obvious point that the Japanese, at least in comparison with other groups, are relatively pure racially. There are, so to speak, no blond Japanese, no red-haired Japanese, no blue-eyed Japanese. And the attitude of the Japanese toward miscegenation is very different from that of, say, the French or the Chinese. If somebody is born of a mixed marriage in France or China but grows up perfectly familiar with and skilled in the indigenous culture, he is largely accepted. That is not true in Japan. The children of mixed marriages are more or less permanently barred from participating fully and comfortably in the society. Those bars also hold against children born in Japan but of Korean or Chinese parentage. One crucial point in the discussion was that the Japanese do not normally notice that they discriminate against these minorities, because the discrimination is so thorough that the issue usually does not arise. I asked the Japanese if they could imagine, for example, having a General of Korean parentage. They could not. I pointed out that it was perfectly possible in China.

An important consequence of this is that the Japanese are not going to be willing to import inexpensive labour into their country. Indeed, most Japanese would very much like to get rid of the current indigenous Koreans and Chinese.

This attitude also implies that when they go to other countries to exploit the skilled inexpensive labour there, they will probably do it with very little intermarriage – and perhaps without easy social intercourse – in contrast to the Portuguese, to whom both come easily. There is a real possibility here for all kinds of issues arising in the future, some of which we will discuss further. The particular characteristics of Japanese society and institutions discussed here are by no means presented as curiosities or minor items of information. As we shall see, in many cases they are important to an understanding of the mechanisms by which a decision will be made or avoided and the conditions under which it will be implemented. A Westerner attempting to shortcut an understanding of or a sensitivity to these special characteristics is likely to be in for a rude shock in his dealings with the Japanese. Attempts at salesmanship with the finest and most persuasive of Western presentations are quite likely to fail. Negotiations in almost any area can become impossible. Yet generally the Westerner will have done his best, will have received a warm reception, and will have no idea why his plans have made no progress.

Finally, it is important to remember that the Japanese have no intention of imposing their culture upon the world in the way Americans are often accused of doing. As far as I can tell, they could not care less if it is desirable or possible for other countries to adopt their specialized and idiosyncratic institutions or techniques.

Let me close this chapter with a most important reminder. I have left out of my discussion of 'The Japanese Mind' almost all those characteristics that make the Japanese so charming, agreeable, and pleasant – and, equally important, many of the things about Japanese society that make it of such great interest from the wider aesthetic and cultural point of view. I have bypassed these aspects of Japanese society not through any lack of appreciation – even though I have much to learn about them – but only because they are not relevant to the main theme of this book. Therefore, no reader should take the material in this chapter as being intended to provide a balanced portrait of Japan and of things Japanese. And, of course, it is very likely that given the biases and perspectives I have picked up in my studies of those Japanese issues presented, I may easily have been even less balanced than I intended. To the extent that any of this results in a somewhat distorted view of the Japanese mind, let me indicate my regret and apologies.

Chapter Three

The Post-World War II Japanese Economic Miracle

For the Japanese economy, World War II was unquestionably a disaster of the first magnitude. Japan had tried a basically nineteenth-century Western policy of imperialistic expansion in an attempt to set up a 'co-prosperity sphere' – complete with overtones of a 'yellow man's burden' attitude towards the under-developed regions of the Pacific Basin. The attempt was in many ways a natural conclusion to the process of Westernization that had characterized the Meiji century. But the empire created by that process was reduced to rubble, and the cities of the homeland were largely destroyed. As far as I can tell, no one – Japanese or American – thought the Japanese economy would ever really recover from this catastrophe. Certainly not in the sense of once more becoming a modern, dynamic, highly technological economy of the first rank. And certainly no one thought it would surpass all its old records, much less imagined the rate at which this has been accomplished. There was a general belief that the Japanese would have to be very austere and abstemious in the future, and while undoubtedly living above traditional Asian standards, doing so by no large factor. Calculations were even made of how the Japanese could live at a relatively low but self-supporting level, without much foreign trade.

There was a period of two or three years when there was a kind of apathy in Japan and then, in 1947–8, the recovery started. And there were many reasons for the recovery and subsequent growth going as rapidly as they did in the 1950s and the early 1960s. Some arose directly out of the Japanese national character as described in the previous chapter and included such things as:

1. A great deal of available energy and dedication and the general Japanese capacity for purposive, communal action;

2. Stringent population limitation;
3. Appropriate and available organizational skills, judgement, and motivation – both governmental and private;
4. Relatively high technological and educational levels;
5. High savings and investment rate;
6. Japanese version of free enterprise;
7. Skilful government direction and intervention (and a reasonably cooperative and sensible policy on the part of the United States);
8. All kinds of pressures to attain 'higher market shares' and to go into advanced technology and industries of the future;
9. Ruthless refusal to support – or even actively 'sabotage' – 'obsolete' or 'not for Japanese' business; equally ruthless support and protection of modern growth industries and advantageous export industries;
10. Willingness to switch to 'economic growth' as major tactic in 'catching up with the West';
11. Desirable and inexpensive work force readily available;
12. Some of the qualities as in the list in Chapter 4.

There were also a number of favourable international political and economic conditions that contributed to rapid Japanese growth rates. Among these were:

1. Less than 1 per cent of the GNP allotted to defence;
2. Stimulus of Korean War (and later Vietnam War);
3. Influx of American capital;
4. US a prosperous and avid customer;
5. Technology available at bargain rates – first from the Americans and later from the Europeans;
6. General atmosphere of free trade and rising levels of world trade;
7. Discovery in Australia and elsewhere of large new mineral deposits;
8. Developments in ocean transport.

These two lists are by no means exhaustive – nor shall we discuss in detail all the items on them.

The first and foremost cause of Japanese economic growth was the general energy and dedication of the Japanese and their capacity for purposive communal action which, when it was finally reactivated and focused on the problem of recovery, performed with its usual skill and dynamism. Secondly (and, in its own way, another expression of purposive and communal action), after a surge in the birth rate as the soldiers returned from the war, the Japanese government established abortion clinics all over the islands – and in an unbelievable display of social solidarity and community responsibility, the birth rate was forced down in a few years from a high of 34 per 1,000 in 1947 to the current rate of around or below 20 per 1,000. It was reduced by a factor of almost two in about five years. Of course, by Western standards the method used was a relatively inconvenient and heroic one – but it was also quite reliable.

This reduction in birth rate produced a double bonus for Japan. As the demographic age profile below indicates, in the postwar years the Japanese were in the ideal position of having relatively few young people to train and support, as well as relatively few old people to support. In the future this transition advantage will disappear.

The Japanese also had high-level organizational skills (as, to a lesser extent, did Tokugawa Japan), which enabled them to put a complex and advanced 'society' together again despite enormous wartime disruption. And they were able to do so quite rapidly and with enough flexibility to make up for the changes caused by the war, the Occupation, and the various constraints, conditions, and necessities of the new environment – including changed access to resources and markets.

But they were not starting from scratch or with inappropriate human resources for industrialization, as so many Afro-Asian countries need to do. Compared to other Asian nations, of course, the Japanese enjoyed very high technological and educational levels, which, despite the pressure of other demands on their resources, they promptly raised even farther. They also had many advantages in being able – once Occupation controls were lifted – to combine a mixture of planning and free enterprise. Thus, unless a Japanese entrepreneur ran into conflict with other

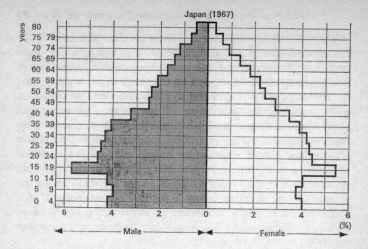

Japan (1967)

Male ◄─────────► ◄─────── Female

Japanese objectives (either of the government or of other parts of the Japanese community), he was able to use his own energy, entrepreneurship, wisdom, and financial resources to the limit. And not only did he take his own risks, but he was often backed by the government or big banks. All the while he was being spurred on to heroic efforts by a combination of personal, familial, communal, and patriotic motives and objectives.

Even in the beginning, government direction and intervention

(8) Population by Age and Sex (1967)
(1000 persons)

Age	Total	Male	Female	Age	Total	Male	Female
All ages	101 408	49 803	51 605	40–44	6 969	3 414	3 555
0–4	8 478	4 346	4 132	45–49	5 321	2 350	2 970
5–9	7 883	4 017	3 866	50–54	4 716	2 159	2 557
10–14	8 061	4 103	3 959	55–59	4 329	2 024	2 306
15–19	10 464	5 303	5 162	60–64	3 486	1 675	1 811
20–24	9 588	4 801	4 788	65–69	2 869	1 357	1 512
25–29	8 838	4 376	4 462	70–74	1 979	896	1 083
30–34	8 389	4 183	4 206	75–79	1 191	495	695
35–39	7 986	4 010	3 976	80–84	578	212	366
				85–	283	84	199

Source: Bureau of Statistics, Office of the Prime Minister.

were very skilful. For example, while the Japanese wisely and correctly accepted the Dodge currency reform of 1951, they also understood from the very beginning that they did not have to accept all the financial shibboleths of Western bankers and economists. They began operating what to Western eyes was an unbelievably risky economy, but they did it with discipline and skill. (Since the war the Japanese have had several government-instigated depressions, all of which were quite painful but which – in retrospect as well as in prospect – were also of about the right intensity to cool off an overheated economy in a few months. Compare this with American – or British – performance.) Of course, they did not have to put much of their gross national product into defence; and the Korean War, which suddenly made Japan a convenient major source of offshore procurement, provided a very important though not an essential stimulus. There was also great encouragement by the US government and the Occupation authorities for American capital to invest in Japan and to bring in US technology. The US in turn opened up its own markets to Japanese trade and later acted in such a way as to encourage other markets to open for the Japanese.

The fact that the Japanese businessmen, as in the Meiji restoration, put community welfare and other national interests above simple maximization of profits, probably – and rather paradoxically – led on the whole to the kinds of practices that were beneficial in terms of both growth rates and, to a lesser extent, profits. Thus, the fact that the Japanese industrial groupings often compete with each other more for market shares and growth than for profits probably has led to a correction of certain kinds of psychological errors and biases. It clearly compensates for the excessive caution of most businessmen. Indeed, from the viewpoint of Japanese society in the 50s, and 60s, increasing volume may well have been the right economic criterion – almost certainly from the long-term viewpoint of Japanese society (given likely Japanese objectives and desires).

Thus, if one of the *zaibatsu* or other groupings introduced some kind of new industrial product or process, or was otherwise involved in some kind of new and modern activity, the others often felt compelled to follow suit in the new field, if only out of a desire to preserve their self-respect. In practice this meant incredibly rapid movement into new fields and an equally incredible willingness to put capital and management time into these new fields.

During this entire post-World War II period, the Japanese have been very hard bargainers with the West. For example, compared to what might be thought of as the cost Europeans have had to pay for American technology, the Japanese got it at bargain-basement rates and even sub-bargain-basement rates. Further-more, Japanese businessmen have not been particularly grateful for this. I have talked to a number of American businessmen who have negotiated sales of technology to the Japanese, and they almost invariably have the same kind of story to tell. Originally they wanted to buy a plant or buy into the Japanese market with some kind of cooperative enterprise in which American capital dominated or would soon dominate, much as Americans did in Europe. They found that in almost all cases (the number of exceptions is really quite small and will be discussed later) they could not do it. They finally turned to a straight sale arrangement, in which they collected royalties for the new technology. Then they found that the agreement went to MITI (the Ministry of International Trade and Investment) for approval – an approval which did not come. Rather, the agreement was disallowed on the grounds that it was unfair to the Japanese firm concerned, and there was a whole new round of negotiations in which the entire agreement was written downward.

In effect, the Japanese were using government control as a method of getting monopoly gains and other tactical bargaining advantages over American businessmen. There are many reasons – justifiable and not – for their doing this. In any case, it resulted in advanced and proprietary technology being transferred to them under very good terms.

The Japanese were also willing to be astonishingly ruthless in getting rid of inefficient industries or those that were somehow not suitable. Consider the following table, which summarizes one aspect of a study the London *Economist* made of Japanese growth rates.[1] They pointed out that there were certain kinds of industries the Japanese thought of as 'throw-away industries,' because not only was Japan no longer competitive in these industries but she regarded it as a mistake to try to gain a competitive position.

'Throw-away Industries' (Japan Uncompetitive)	'Early-Stage Industrialization' Sector (No Longer Wishes to Compete)
Coal	
Non-ferrous metals	Cotton textiles
Paper pulp	Sewing machines
Agricultural products, etc.	Bicycles
	Pottery, etc.
'Second-Stage Industrialization' Sector (Wartime Stimulus; Postwar Growth)	'Third-Stage Industrialization' Sector (Official Stimulus Today) Automobiles
Iron and steel	Precision tools
Shipbuilding	Large-scale construction equipment
Trucks and buses	Computer electronics, etc.
Television and radio	
Railroad rolling stock	
Optical equipment, etc.	

While the Japanese were not quite as ruthless as the term 'throw-away' indicates, they were very close to it. In fact, as indicated by the second set of items on the above table, the early-stage industrialization sector, there was a strong belief among many Japanese that certain activities – manufacturing simple white cotton textiles, for example, or simple kinds of sewing machines, or simple bicycles or pottery – should be deliberately forced to the wall by governmental financial practices, even though they might be kept in competitive status. Therefore, the companies had to release men, materials, and resources for more efficient enterprises. It is, of course, exactly this transfer from the less efficient to the more efficient sectors that facilitates rapid economic growth. But more than that was involved: there was the matter of 'face' and prestige. Simple cotton textiles, sewing machines, bicycles, or pottery might be suitable for Egyptian or Indian manufacture, but 'they are not for the Japanese.'

The *Economist* also pointed out that for more than a decade the major Japanese growth rates were gained in what they called the

'Second-Stage Industrialization Sector'. These were the industries that had been fostered by the military during the 20s, 30s and early 40s, industries in which the military had to pick up the bill even if Japan was not competitive. Any lack of competitiveness simply showed up either in less efficient equipment on the battlefield or in subsidized operations (in smaller forces, a reduction in peacetime standard of living or growth rates). The *Economist* added that even though the Japanese were very good at this second-stage industrialization, it took them from ten to twenty years after World War II to really attain an internationally competitive status in the third-stage industrialization sector. They are now clearly in this third stage and, in fact, are moving into the forefront with the most advanced nations. But again, it was the ruthlessness with regard to the sectors that were dragging (or from which resources could better be displaced) that accelerated the development. And it was an almost total commitment to the most advanced and most prestigious areas, rather than straight business calculations of profit and loss, that drove the Japanese economy in the very successful directions it took.

As a result of all the factors described above, the Japanese were able to deal with two of their most important problems, the high population 'resources' ratio and their postwar legacy of ill-will. The reason I put the word 'resources' in quotation marks is that I mean here traditional resources such as raw materials and land. Actually, Japan is very rich in the resources that count most – the right kinds of people. They are skilled, competent, dedicated, and possess all kinds of traditions, habits, and cultural traits that make unbelievably rapid growth rates possible.

However, the first postwar impression of many Americans who examined Japanese practices was not an optimistic one. Most knowledgeable Americans believed Japan had severe problems that would retard economic growth, and that unless the Japanese made some big changes in their culture and practices, they would face very serious difficulties. For example, in the operation of their large firms, those that were going to spearhead the recovery, the Japanese had practices that by American estimates seemed extremely inefficient. Some of these were (1) a low to almost non-existent labour mobility in the big firms (the so-called lifetime employment system); (2) promotion mainly – and indeed up to the vice-president level almost completely – by seniority; (3) compulsory retirement at 55 (except for vice-president and director levels); (4) diffused responsibility; (5) non-competitive practices; (6) financial operation at a very high debt/equity ratio (in the 50s often at about a ten to one ratio, as compared with US practice, which usually frowns on one to one – much less two to one).

In the postwar Japanese context, all these supposed 'weaknesses' turned out to be assets – at least during the 1950s and 1960s – and to some degree they may be assets in the 1970s as well. (It is worth noting that Japanese – despite their reputation for mindless imitation – did not make any changes in their practices to conform to US concepts, even though they were very forcibly and emotionally pressed to do so.)

Consider, for example, the employment practices of the large Japanese firms. A person first going to work as a regular employee is making a lifetime contract – or rather, both sides are at least morally committed to such a contract. This is true even at the executive level. Consequently, one of the most agonizing decisions a young college graduate has to make is his choice of a company, as it is in a very real form an act of marriage. Head hunting and job hopping towards advancement in a profession are unheard of in Japan.

In the United States this would be an incredibly risky financial policy. American firms simply could not afford to guarantee lifetime employment to a large portion of their work force irrespective of the economy's level of activity and of changes in operating practices. Further, it would be economically inefficient from the national point of view, since if conditions were to change there would be low and/or inefficient labour utilization for that firm and a great deal of useful labour would be denied to other firms that could use it. Therefore, when American managerial experts examine the practices of other countries, low labour mobility is generally scored as a significant negative. What then makes it so different in the Japanese context?

First of all, Japanese firms are growing very rapidly – by 10, 20, even 30 per cent a year – so there is usually a high demand for labour, and adjustments can be made by selective hiring and normal attrition rather than by firing. Thus even if operating conditions change, the high rate of the firm's expansion makes it easy to find useful work for all those to whom the firm is obligated. Indeed, in this respect the Japanese have a superior mobility. Having mainly company unions, there are little or no intra-firm restrictions on labour mobility – in sharp contrast to usual American practices. Also, once the *zaibatsu* were re-established, they did not have as big a problem of artificial barriers, divisions of labour, and other restrictions on the use of labour within the *zaibatsu* group as we have between different companies. All this allows great mobility both within the firm and between firms of the same 'conglomerate.' And it may be a much more important kind of flexibility, not only for labour but for capital funds, management skills, and the like, than the much lower level of 'hiring and firing' flexibility in the US. Even the various 'departments' or subcompanies of an American conglomerate operate relatively independently, and there is little or no transfer of normal labour (though there may be transfers of management or capital) among these departments or subcompanies. This is also true (but less so) of normal labour in Japan, but in abnormal circumstances some such transfer can be made – or a merger can be arranged or forced. However, labour rigidity within an American firm is high because of labour rules and other reasons, and hiring and firing is such a big step that there is some inter-firm rigidity as well. Thus in many ways our economy is much more rigid with regard to labour mobility than the seemingly rigid Japanese system.

Consider a second aspect of the Japanese firm – the use of strict seniority rules in most promotions. This (along with some other practices) was so surprising to many in the West that when the original study on the Japanese factory was done by James Abegglen, many publishers refused to believe the results and would not publish the book. In the large Japanese firm there is an almost total concentration on strict seniority rules for promotions up to about the vice-presidential level. Indeed, if you know the age of a Japanese individual, his family status, the school he graduated from, and the firm he works for, you can ordinarily name his title and salary.

Once again in the postwar Japanese context, this practice turned out to be quite helpful. First of all, an individual who enters one of these lifetime contracts generally must consider his income over the entire period of the contract. The way the Japanese contract is written he is really underpaid for the first fifteen to twenty years of work but correspondingly overpaid for the last fifteen to twenty years. While the contract may average out over the individual's lifetime, the fact is that since most Japanese employees – particularly those of the large and rapidly expanding firms – are young, the firm gets remarkably dedicated and competent labour at a very low price, and this labour cannot be enticed away from the firm.

Another effect is that the firm can afford to invest a great deal of money and other resources in educating its labour, because the benefits of that education will remain with the firm. Finally, in a rapidly changing situation one finds that the Japanese firm can be incredibly quick and flexible in its adaptation, because the individuals concerned do not feel threatened – at least as far as their title and salary are concerned – even by major changes. I know of several American firms that introduced computers in the late 50s and early 60s, not because they really needed them but because doing so created a convenient occasion for making management changes that would otherwise have been impossible because of the large human cost. I know of other cases, and they are presumably more significant, where companies refused to introduce such upsetting innovations as computers because of the large human costs involved in carrying through the changes.

The Japanese firm neither had to resort to the first kind of fakery nor worry about the second kind of fears. Each individual knew that no matter what happened, as far as title, status, and salary went few would suffer much, if at all, from even the most dramatic changes in the company. This confidence in one's status, along with the peculiar Japanese politics of consensus (which allow a large number of individuals, almost regardless of how low their status, to place their ideas into the system) and the enormous community pressures for the firm to do well competitively and absolutely (pressures felt by the individual at his own level of concern), meant that the organization did not hesitate at innovation or the introduction of new ideas.

I have discussed in a previous chapter how decisions are made and how explicit responsibility for the decisions is so diffused that it is sometimes impossible to assign credit to the originator of innovations or ideas. In speaking to many individual Japanese today, I have noticed that, particularly among very competent people and among those who have travelled outside Japan and seen how things are done in the West, there is a certain bitterness about not getting credit for their ideas and about not being allowed to carry them out but having them given instead to others to carry out. There is something of a general protest today against this whole 'escalator system' of lifetime employment, automatic but initially slow promotion by strict seniority, deferment of reward, anonymity, and lack of individual reward for individual effort and creativity. This frustration is not as un-Japanese as it is usually thought to be. It always has been there – what is new are these first tentative and unsure steps to express it. In fact, it is important to note, as I will discuss later, that this kind of resentment against the system is common in Japan, past and present. Under normal conditions it is sufficiently restrained, suppressed, and sublimated so that it does not actually interfere with the operation of the system. Though presently it clearly interferes with the operation of the universities, this situation is not likely to last – nor is it likely to have much effect on economic growth rates in the short and medium term.

One can also argue that the Japanese institution of compulsory retirement at fifty-five – at least under the conditions that obtained in the postwar years – encouraged rapid economic growth. We in the United States are familiar by now with the 'Peter Principle,' which argues that every man rises to his level of incompetence. There is certainly a sense in which this is true, particularly at the middle and upper middle levels of management. It is particularly likely to be true if there is a rapidly changing situation and promotion is by seniority. In these circumstances much of the experience the individual has gained is only partially relevant. The Japanese have dealt with this situation very well; they simply retire these middle management men early.

Further, the potential economic contribution of the retired men is not completely lost, as they are usually given a lump pension that is not quite sufficient for their needs. In order to supplement their lump retirement benefit they often go to work – at a lesser salary – in an allied business, usually one that is close to or a member of the same *zaibatsu* from which they retired or is otherwise close to the original business (perhaps a subcontractor). In that case they may also contribute some capital to the business. Their contacts with the original business are now very useful, and their special experience, while not needed in the old business, may be of enormous benefit to the new and rising business. As a result, everybody gains in some way: the original business by opening up spaces for advancement; the new business by getting a seasoned man they could not otherwise get; and even the individual himself gains – at least he does not lose too much, because his income does not go down spectacularly, the combination of the lessened salary plus his retirement benefits being quite reasonable.

In short, even Japan's non-competitive practices probably accelerated growth rates in the postwar context. One problem with rapid growth is that often the growth rates of various portions of the economy become unbalanced, and adjustments have to be made before the imbalance gets out of control. The Japanese government by its direct pressures and its indicative planning was often able to prevent these imbalances from growing too large. It was also often able to alleviate them by cooperative actions with and among Japanese businessmen. And, of course, it was also willing to have government-instigated recessions, which caused rapid if very painful adjustments; however, it was possible for the establishment to distribute the pain (i.e., the level of readjustment) in the way they judged most acceptable. And in the end the Japanese people agreed, for as Richard Halloran has said about Japan's foreign trade,

They believe they are dependent on the rest of the world for markets and that it matters less that an export product was made by a given company than that it was made in Japan. In international competition, it is Japan against the world, Japanese steel against American steel, Japanese cameras against German cameras, Japanese textiles against

British textiles. To achieve this regulation, the Japanese have made a way of life of investment, production, and trade targets; of cartels, quotas, and fixed prices; and of combining the influences of the bureaucracy, the political world, and the business community in economic decision making.[2]

With a government and industry firmly resolved to work together to reach the goal of economic leadership, and with a gross national product consistently growing at a rate twice that of the United States, there can be little doubt that what was a possibility – a Japanese economy of super proportions – is rapidly becoming fact. The only question now is how long it will take and the effects upon the world.

Chapter Four

Japan Inc.: The Future of the Economic Miracle

It is now almost inevitable that at some point in the 70s or early 80s the Japanese economy will attain a level entitling it to such descriptions as 'giant' and 'super'. One can quite plausibly make this argument almost solely on the grounds of economic momentum – of Japan's simply carrying through the many projects already begun and doing more of the same. At this point the burden of proof is on the sceptic if he is to argue that Japanese growth rates will turn down so dramatically that Japan is not 'one of the three economic powers' rather than just a leader of the second-ranking economic powers.

Of course, a number of problems could arise and present serious difficulties to the continuation of Japan's current economic growth rate. Therefore, we will ask in this chapter in what ways might the Japanese get into trouble? What are the internal contradictions or external forces that must eventually emerge to slow down this tale of uninterrupted economic growth and technological advancement? What other kinds of things could happen that could stop this second rise of the rising sun?

We will identify later some of the factors that could change one aspect or another of the projections I have set forth. However, I suspect we should start by trying to dispose of one common belief among Western experts on Japan and among many anti-establishment Japanese intellectuals; that because a number of cracks are beginning to emerge in Japan's economy and society, those cracks disclose something that is significant enough to erode the nation's growth rates dramatically. If one looks at the history of the West, one sees that the trick of economic growth was first learned in the eighteenth century and demonstrated to the world by the British in the industrial revolution. Despite a great number of cracks that subsequently appeared in Great Britain's economy and society, its yearly economic growth was sustained with unbelievable persistence at about 2 per cent per capita until today. The same story seems to be true of many other nations.[1] Indeed, economic growth, while not easily achieved, is not a fragile child once it is achieved, despite the disruptive and opposing movements and all the other issues it creates or that can otherwise occur.

It should also be realized that despite all cracks, internal contradictions, and other factors discussed in this chapter, for more than one hundred years now the basic national goal of the Japanese nation has focused on one purpose – to catch up with and surpass the West. In the past this has meant military, political, administrative, scientific, technological, and economic successes. It now seems that this hundred-year goal can be largely accomplished through current economic and technological policies, which, if they continue to be successful, can lay the basis for further advance in any other sector deemed desirable or useful.

The phenomenal postwar recovery and growth of Japan that was necessary to achieve the present position was not simply the result of individual enterprise using individual resources (as we would use these terms in the United States), although such individual effort played a role. The basic driving power was a result of the effective utilization of state power, of state financial organization, of state funding, and of the mobilization of other state-owned or controlled resources. All were used to support private enterprises in whatever ways needed. Even the original privately owned *zaibatsu* in the nineteenth century were begun by the government; the government started the business and then sold them at low prices to certain Samurai families. And, as we have seen, even today the government can influence to a remarkable degree which business shall succeed and which shall not.

There has almost never been any feeling of division or clash between the government and the businessman in this enterprise. In fact, there has been little sense of clash or conflict between the government–businessmen combination and the people as a whole

– certainly not so far as concerns the workers within those enterprises chosen to carry out the national policies.

The situation in Japan is very different from that in the United States. Probably more than 50 per cent of all Japanese government officials devote their time to improving the prospects of business. However, one would conjecture that in the United States more than 50 per cent of all government officials devote their time to almost the opposite task – many of them to sponsoring groups with grudges against the business system and the establishment, or groups that are anti-business, anti-economic growth, anti-capitalist, and even anti-rationalist, at least from the economic point of view.

As a result, from the viewpoint of business the United States government has literally become a strain-creating organization, an expense-raising, expense-creating organization, rather than a facilitating and growth-creating organization.

I should note that in many cases (but not all) I agree with these activities of the American government. For example, the United States is a very rich country and does not need to grow economically at the cost of destroying the environment and polluting our reservoirs of pure air, pure water, desirable recreational land, and the like. I do, however, object to the fact that many of our government's activities are strain-creating for business when they need not be so. They could, in fact, be carried on with relatively little disturbance to business or to our economic growth. But public policies are often formulated with a disregard of creative and ingenious technological possibilities, as well as of economic and business concerns and other 'realities'. This is often caused by official rigidity, lack of imagination and/or a basic indifference or a fanatical hostility towards business's needs. I would rather argue that this kind of thing could simply never happen in present-day Japan.

Indeed, the opposite is occurring. There is beginning to develop among the Japanese an almost manic enthusiasm for completing their self-appointed task of surpassing the West. To a remarkable degree, this enthusiasm is missed by many Western observers who, insisting on wearing Western spectacles, note the absence of effort and of a concentration on Japan's version of the 'ills',

102 The Emerging Japanese Superstate

'aches,' and 'pains' approach to societal issues so characteristic of Western society today.

However, the Japanese are no longer de-emphasizing so many of those issues; they too are beginning to worry about the good society and about those aspects of the standard of living other than GNP. One result is that the Ministry of Finance has put together a twenty-year plan for dealing with these issues. If it is successful it may well make Japan into a kind of ideal community living in a garden, and it will have accomplished all that without interrupting or even significantly slowing down the nation's spectacular economic and technological growth. And it should be noted that the mere promise of such development – focusing attention on it – may go very far to assuage certain immediate difficulties and to retain the basic loyalty and enthusiasm of most Japanese for the task at hand, the task of surpassing the West by every reasonable and desirable criterion and of creating an example for the world in a Japanese way of life that the world may not be able to emulate but that it surely has to admire.

So what is most interesting about Japan is less the development of cracks in the economic situation than something like the opposite. To give an example, the Soka Gakkai, one of the 'new religions,' is – among other things – dedicated to success, hard work, advancement, etc. In other words, even an 'extremist' group shares, in this respect at least, the establishment consensus. Upon examining many of the social trends and cultural changes occurring in Japan, one finds they seem far more likely to reinforce the momentum of economic growth than to hurt it; and that, of course, is to be expected. In some ways nothing succeeds like success – at least for a time.

It should be noted that polls can be misleading in this regard. As we discussed earlier, if one stops an average Japanese on the street and asks him 'What are your main concerns: are they focused on personal happiness or national prestige?' he will almost inevitably answer, 'personal happiness.' However, normally the man on the street is apathetic towards national concerns, not because he is disinterested in them but simply because they are not his business. I would quite confidently conjecture that if you asked him if he could be happy if Japan were an object of scorn or if it didn't count in the world, he would say 'No,' that his happiness is greatly increased if Japan counts in the world and he feels very bad if it does not.

This is also a function of time. Herbert Passin has pointed out to me that the Japanese word *Nippon* not only denotes Japan but carries a connotation of 'big', 'important', 'prestigious', while the word *Nihon* has the same denotation but carries a connotation of 'warm', 'homey', 'nurturant' and 'a little soft'. Passin believes, and I too believe from purely anecdotal evidence, that *Nippon* is increasingly acceptable as the proper name and adjective for Japan. Further, as I have noted (and again I have only anecdotal evidence and the opinion of some knowledgeable Japanese), there seems to be a strong current among Japanese high school seniors to be less (some say much less) apathetic on the issues of national prestige, of nationalism, and of being Japanese than some of their elders. This seems to be an example of 'third-generation effect,' a return to basic values – in this case a reaction against excessive Americanization, a feeling that it is time to bring in some corrections. One can, perhaps misleadingly, think of this as being a kind of 'movement to the right' among the high school students, but that is a rather bad way to describe it. It also should be pointed out that there is a small minority of extremists on the left which, while minute, is very intense indeed and could cause its own kinds of issues to arise and even appear quite prominent.

As modern thinkers, influenced by Marx, we must be conscious of the fact that such internal contradictions always exist, and they may grow even in the current Japanese context. However, it seems reasonable, as I will try to explain below, that almost all of Japan's present-day 'contradictions' are of the sort that normally do not interfere with economic growth – or that usually become important in doing so only if the initial momentum has been halted by other causes or barriers. One rather suspects that this will continue to be true throughout the rest of the century. No matter what internal strains and other changes develop, unless the momentum of economic growth either runs into external barriers or suffers very large decreases in marginal return per unit of marginal effort, it is not likely to be stopped because of 'contradictory' internal developments. I would conjecture that if this slowing down occurs and turns out to be more or less permanent, many other problems are likely to develop as well. In fact, it is not unlikely that if a slowing down were to develop soon, a most severe political, social, and economic crisis would also develop. But from the Japanese point of view, all of this further strengthens the need and motivation to maintain high growth rates.

None of the above, of course, implies there are no arguments that can be made for expecting an economic slowdown or even a turndown. Sceptics can, for example, focus on any of the following propositions:

1. The cream has been skimmed off European and American technology, and gains are now going to be more difficult. Furthermore, such technology may no longer be available on as good terms as it was in the past. In any case, the disparities between Japan and the West that were easy to exploit have already been exploited – now only the hard ones remain.

2. The total size of the Japanese work force is not increasing as rapidly as it did in the past. The work force is also becoming relatively older. Indeed, one of Japan's greatest assets, cheap young Japanese labour with at least an elementary school education, is no longer available. (Indeed, there are more than a million unfilled positions for this category of people.) Finally, a good many of the gains to be achieved by shifting labour from low productivity work to occupations with higher productivity have already been achieved.

3. It is going to be very important for the Japanese to build up their social, economic, and public works infrastructure and to take a more serious interest in welfare. Japan is seriously short on such things as roads, utilities of all kinds, homes, schools, transportation, and so on, and it treats quite badly many sections of the population that have been left behind in general prosperity. All of this is going to take a great deal of money and effort to correct. It will be expensive for the Japanese to procure even the most desperately needed elements for the infrastructure – that is, to put in enough to have a balanced system, proportional to their general productivity and general standard of living; and it will be very expensive

indeed if their new programmes also have to include giving adequate welfare to the less fortunate.

4. There are likely to be greater sums of money in the Japanese budget allocated to defence. Currently the Japanese spend about $1·6 billion, or less than 1 per cent of their gross national product (and less than 8 per cent of the national budget) on defence. It seems reasonable to expect this expenditure to go much higher.

5. There may be serious difficulties with foreign trade. Japan has gone from having about 1·3 per cent of the world export trade in 1950 to about 6·6 per cent in 1970, and it anticipates having about 10 per cent in 1980 – a share that may be necessary to be consistent with the kinds of growth rates discussed later. Yet Japan may have difficulty holding its current percentage, much less increasing it markedly.

6. Many Japanese seem to be less interested than they were in economic growth; others have at least lost some of their enthusiasm for working long hours per day and many days per week. Almost all Japanese are becoming more interested in vacations, in enjoyment, in higher living standards. Indeed, what is called 'my home-ism' is an almost overwhelming movement among the younger people. But such hedonistic attitudes are not confined to the young. They are gradually becoming quite common in all sectors of Japanese society. Eventually this should show up in a general erosion of national effort and dedication.

7. The rebellion against the established system of values and priorities is most important among the young people who resent the so-called escalator system of employment, promotion, and remuneration, as well as other traditional Japanese practices. They object to the anonymity of the Japanese decision-making and innovation-adapting machinery and to the communal system generally, which does not really reward the individual for his personal initiative and success. This general feeling of resentment is increased by the feelings of modern Japanese wives who also resent certain aspects of the system, particularly the evenings systematically devoted by their husbands to 'business meetings' in restaurants and bars.

All this adds to the general social strain and is likely to weaken the drive toward increased productivity.

8. There may be other serious political strains in the system. In 1969 student unrest caused the closing of something like 250 schools; other internal political challenges are coming up.
9. As Japanese firms grow in size and complexity they are becoming managerial monstrosities. Eventually the impersonality, slow-footedness, alienation, lack of firm control, and so on, that afflict so many Western behemoths will afflict the new Japanese behemoth as well.
10. As Japan and the various firms grow bigger, the tight cosiness of Japan, Inc. and the feeling of 'one big family' are beginning to break down. That in itself will result in costly national competition and in uncertain guidance.

One could of course go on and list more items that are possible sources of trouble. But I would argue that while all these points, as well as others I have not listed, have some validity, they seem to be – at least as given above or as usually given:

1. Overstated;
2. Assumed to affect growth rates too rapidly: if they affect growth rates at all it will take time;
3. Assumed to have too great effectiveness;
4. Subject to being negated – or at least limited to acceptable levels – by proper policies and/or likely events;
5. At least uncertain in their effects – or actually an economically or politically useful adaptation to Japan's new status and context rather than a difficulty.

In any case, none of the liabilities I have become aware of appear likely to have a very dramatic impact in the near future. In fact, one can argue that, under virtually any competent administration or in any probable international economic environment, Japan's momentum is unlikely to falter so early and so much that the Japanese economy will fail to achieve a 'giant' or 'super' status in the next decade or two. Indeed, it seems almost certain that Japan's rate of growth will maintain itself throughout the early 70s, which should result – in 1975 or soon after – in a $400 billion GNP (1970 prices). And (as I shall indicate in the next chapter) by the end of the century the GNP will almost inevitably reach something between $1·5 and 4·5 trillion. Even the low figures – or perhaps just the attainment of the $400 billion and the promise of more of the same – will entitle Japan to the coveted adjectives. And I myself will be surprised if by the end of the century they do not become *dai-ichi* (number one).

But let us consider some of the negatives in more detail. One rather common argument – and the first given in the list – is that the cream has been skimmed by Japan from European and American technology, and further progress will be much more difficult. I would argue the opposite case. The Japanese breakthrough to what we have called 'the third stage of industrialization,' as well as the general approach of the developed world (including Japan), to what is often called the 'emerging post-industrial culture', have indeed changed the conditions for further growth – but I think to Japan's advantage. First of all, the Japanese are not bedevilled by two serious difficulties current in the West – a loss of morale (including a loss of nerve) and the continuance from the 20s and 30s of a dramatic erosion (at least among the upper and upper middle classes) of those values that lead to an orientation towards work, achievement, growth, national prestige, etc. Perhaps more important, the Japanese are just now coming into a position to exploit modern technology, the economics of doing things on a super scale, and an emphasis on the 'knowledge industries' (in which their superior education, interest in rational thought, and 'unsurpassed ability for purposeful communal action' are all going to be enormous advantages in increasing productivity).

Therefore, the fact that the United States has more than twice the GNP per capita of the Japanese and about three times the productivity per hour – with relatively few Americans working nearly as hard or as long hours or thinking or planning as hard – indicates a lot of room between where the Japanese are now and where they can expect to get. Without going into any careful analyses, I would conjecture that if the Japanese were to take over and operate the US economy in the way they operate the Japanese economy, there would be some losses in productivity per man hour in some areas, but in many there would be an enormous gain; furthermore, as soon as they learned how to really operate their great US economy they would probably not only equal but perhaps double the current $5,000 GNP per capita, and do so in a very few years. Since presumably their own economy eventually will operate that way, either largely approximating or surpassing the US, one can argue that under current conditions they still have a factor of about five or ten to go from their current $2,000 per capita to their potential $10,000 to $20,000 per capita (figures which they seem likely to achieve by the end of the century). I, at least, certainly expect that the Japanese will maintain much of their competitive edge over the Americans – and I must emphasize again that this will be a relative competitive edge, as both groups are likely to slip somewhat – if for no other reason than that the erosion of economic productivity motivations has been going on in the United States for about fifty years, while in Japan over the twenty-five year postwar experience it has been less sustained and one-sided. I would judge that by the year 2000 the Japanese should certainly be capable of a per capita income well in the $5–20,000 range implicit in the prediction of a GNP between $1·5 and 4 trillion. All this involves some very qualitative and approximate arguments, and therefore is not rigorously valid. But the arguments can be developed to make plausible the position that there is no obvious reason for serious 'topping out' in Japanese growth during the next ten, twenty, and perhaps thirty years because of any intrinsic limitations of Japanese technology, management, and access to raw materials and markets.

The second point from our list, the current slow rise in total size of the Japanese work force, is accurate. According to figures issued by the Economic Planning Agency, the annual increase of productive population was approximately $1\frac{1}{2}$ million during the 1960–1965 period (because of the postwar baby boom), but it declined sharply during the past five years to an annual increase of about 900,000. Between 1970 and 1975 this is expected to become 600,000, and between 1975 and 1985 it may drop by another 20 per cent or so. Thus it is anticipated that the increase in labour force will also decline steadily. In addition, the working population increasingly will become older, which could certainly add to Japanese costs.

When all these factors are combined, however, the effect turns out to be relatively small. The big increases in production now come from increases in the productivity of the existing labour force, not in the size of the recruited labour force (last year the labour force increased by only 1 per cent, but GNP increased by 18 per cent). As a result, the trends in the domestic work force include simply an upgrading of the whole labour force to more skilled work, an upgrading which, as we indicated earlier, clearly can be accomplished.

The slow increase in the size of the work force should lower the economic growth rate by approximately 1 per cent. But it may not even do that. First of all, married Japanese women are increasingly willing to work. More important, the Japanese are beginning, as described in the next chapter, to invest large sums of money in what we call 'Non-Communist Pacific Asia' in order to take advantage of the cheap labour force there.

It should be realized that from the viewpoint of the Japanese economy it may not make a great deal of difference if the cheap labour portion of the work is done in Tokyo or Seoul or Taiwan. The system as a whole will operate, and, as always, the big profits and the gravy will go to the complicated part of the process that takes expensive not inexpensive people. The inexpensive, skilled, dedicated work may be absolutely essential to the process, but its marginal contribution is or is becoming relatively small.

From this point of view the Japanese have a hinterland in Non-Communist Pacific Asia of possibly 200 or 300 million people, many of whom they will simply incorporate, by one device or another, into their economic superstate even while not moving them geographically. In effect, rather than importing the labour into Japan (or raising it indigenously), the Japanese will export the work to the enormous, talented labour force available in their Pacific hinterland. We will discuss later some of the ways in which this will be done and the implications of doing it. But I should note here that this adds 100 million or so people to the potential Japanese labour force – people who can be used with varying degrees of economy and convenience but who almost certainly will be available to the Japanese economy through the 70s and perhaps longer. If the Japanese can exploit this labour pool as well as it seems likely they can, they will have no serious labour shortages in the next decade or two. Then they may again get into shortages, but probably only because of the enormous success they will have had in utilizing this talented labour, thus raising its skill, average capitalization, and cost.

Let me consider the third and fourth items from our list together: the importance to the Japanese of allocating increasing resources to defence, as well as increasing resources to social, economic, and other public welfare purposes. Both such allocations are likely to be made. For the moment, however, let us take seriously the concept of a capital output ratio. We will accept the marginal capital output ratio of Japan's present economy as being roughly 3 or 4 to 1. If we diverted 10 per cent of the current approximately 36 per cent investment rate (i.e., 3·6 points) and then diverted another 10 per cent of the resources now going into consumption (thus sacrificing only one year's increase, after which things go much the same), we would free about 7 per cent of the gross national product. By the year 1975 (about the earliest time I would expect the diversion to reach this magnitude), the approximately 7 per cent of GNP would represent about \$20 to \$30 billion a year. That is a very large sum of money, certainly more than sufficient to meet any likely increased demands of defence, infrastructure, welfare, environmental planning, and so on – especially since the 20 per cent of the GNP that normally goes to the government will continue doing so and should itself increase by 50 to 100 per cent.

Having a large but to some degree controllable expenditure on defence and infrastructure could also give the Japanese a good deal of flexibility in controlling depressions by contra-cyclical programmes. Their previous almost total reliance on monetary policy as the main tool will probably have to be changed, since as the Japanese economy grows it seems to be less easily controlled by purely monetary means. (For one thing, new capital comes increasingly out of retained earnings and depreciation allowances and not through borrowing.) The Japanese will now have a large sector of public expenditure whose volume can, at least for a time, be varied to meet the contracycle needs of the economy. One can also believe that later in the decade they will want to put enormous sums of money into defence, foreign aid, and similar 'non-productive' expenditures; but in 1980 even 7 per cent of the likely $500–600 billion or so a year economy will be about $40 billion a year over what current allocations supply – a rather appreciable sum of money, and more than anyone has ever dreamed the Japanese might put to such uses.

The fifth point has to do with foreign trade. If the Japanese triple their economy in the next decade or so, their foreign trade will probably be about 10 per cent of world foreign trade (as opposed to the current 6 or 7 per cent). While 10 per cent begins to press pretty hard, it does not seem an absurd percentage to expect the Japanese to attain, particularly if about half of this 10 per cent is in trade with Non-Communist Pacific Asia. (We argue later that the latter will be feasible and that the Japanese will surely have an edge there over the rest of the world.) About half the remainder of the 10 per cent probably represents trade with the Western Hemisphere where, for a number of reasons, the Japanese should also be able to meet their goals without much fear of great and sustained indigenous resistance or other problems. The areas where the Japanese are most likely to meet with serious problems are the Communist states, Europe, and the Middle East. But probably less than one fourth of their trade will be involved in those areas – so that current prospects are very good.

In the long run trade issues are likely to become important, but as Japan grows economically, her leverage and opportunities to facilitate such growth in trade also grow. As a result, while one can expect many difficulties and frictions, it is hard to argue that the issue of trade will create any that are serious enough to slow down Japanese growth rates, though there will be problems of adjustment. The latter may slow down the growth of Japanese trade over the rate it would have achieved without them, but probably not in any dramatic – or from our point of view significant – fashion, with the possible exception of certain political issues to be discussed later.

The sixth and seventh objections I have listed can be considered under the rubric of social, political, and cultural changes. It is important to realize that, significant as these can be, a persuasive change in the 'work ethic' almost never takes place very rapidly, even though there may be great change in the rhetoric. Indeed, if one examines current changes in American cultural values, one notices that these really started – at least at the rhetorical level – in the period between 1920 and 1940, and then were reinforced subsequently by postwar affluence and other changes. In other words, in some sense, the actual 'work character' of a generation isn't really altered by these changes in such a way as to appreciably alter, on the average, visible productivity – even though that generation's mores are in a rapid state of change and the avant-garde is itself profoundly changed.

Thus Japan's modern 'dropout' may make no attempt to be productive, but it is not (as yet) a general Japanese problem. Of course, the generation after the current one may suffer much deeper and more fundamental changes, because the traditional values will have been transmitted by this current 'attenuated' generation. And competing values will also be transmitted, and with more authority, by their already changed parents. But it does seem to take about a generation or so for these processes to be important in a widespread behavioural and operational sense – and it also takes time for a change in generations to make its impact. Yet, for a number of reasons pointed out later, the significance, if any, of these negative influences on Japanese economic growth will probably be far less than expected. Thus, while many of the 'negative' influences may be of great importance in the twenty-first century, they are not likely to drastically affect the over-all economic growth rates in the next ten, twenty, and perhaps thirty years.

With regard to the eighth item on our list, it should be noted that one of the more spectacular recent political strains, the extraordinarily widespread, intense rioting and near revolt by Japanese college students, is probably now largely under control – or at least passing into a different phase. On the positive side of the house, the Japanese have initiated a number of reforms to make the universities more responsive to social needs (not necessarily as defined by the students) and to increase somewhat the communication between students and faculty. Basically, however, one can characterize their solution to this problem as being largely repressive. It might be interesting to very briefly go over what happened.

The school riots became significant in 1958. At first the police reacted rather roughly to them. There was also a very negative reaction on the part of other Japanese students, faculty, parents, most newspapers and the general public. As a result, perhaps for the first time in Japanese history, legislation in the Diet was strongly influenced by a grass-roots or 'populist' movement. The police bill that finally passed was quite restrictive. For the next ten years the students and the police fought each other with unbelievable ferocity, yet, except for the death of Miss Mickiko Kamba in the 1960 riots against the security treaty with the US, there have been no fatalities in these riots. There were large elements of what appeared to many Westerners as face-saving tactics and play-acting in this fighting, though I am in no sense trying to understate its intensity. There were also many bitter fights between student factions, which – to oversimplify enormously – can be divided into two main groups: the Yoyogi (for Japanese Communist Party) and anti-Yoyogi. (In many ways these factional fights were more bitter and more violent than the police–student battles.) The Japanese students became what might be considered the best student rioters in the world, the Japanese police the best containers of such riots. But the police acted with a great deal of circumspection, and at no point were really severe punishments meted out to the students. Finally, in 1968 the anti-Yoyogi (anti-communist) students had managed to alienate the faculty, their parents, the general public, and even the JSP (Japanese Socialist Party) as well as the JCP (Japanese Communist Party) and the newspapers. At this point there was widespread criticism of the police and the government authorities for not acting more decisively. This almost seemed to be the signal they had been waiting for. Appropriate legislation giving the government the powers they needed was rapidly passed. At the

University of Tokyo riots at the end of 1968, about four hundred students were arrested. Some two hundred are probably still in jail about eighteen months later. In 1969, student riots peaked; the government arrested 20,000 people. Since the most generous estimate of cadres and ringleaders was about 10,000, this was quite a complete round-up of most of the serious activists. Some thousands or so are still in jail today. However, that has not caused a sympathetic reaction for the rioting students: rather the opposite. In the late 60s more than half the University of Tokyo students tended to sympathize with rioters. I am now informed through private but reliable communication that less than 10 per cent do, and I believe that similar percentages hold for the rest of the school system.

There will undoubtedly be a great deal more rioting in Japan; in particular, the Zengakuren (pro-Yoyogi faction) has managed to penetrate some of the high schools. But, as near as I can tell, there is on the whole, a movement among high school students towards the traditional Japanese virtues and a disposition to tend to the business of getting an education – in fact, almost a movement toward the right.

It should also be noted that the government has many legal weapons for dealing with any problems caused by the academic establishment, whether students or professors. In particular, the government can now punish professors who do not cooperate in maintaining order. This raises the issue of academic freedom and independence, and under some circumstances it may even have counter-productive effects from the viewpoint of law and order. In the current milieu, however, the government is likely to enforce its desires.

In some ways, the last two points on our list of negatives may be the most important. They refer to Japanese organizational morale, spirit, and unity, and to management competency – both within the firm and for the economy as a whole. It is clear that as the firms get larger they become more competitive with each other, they depend more on their own resources, and they lose some of the quality of being members of one big family and the sense of themselves as being sub-familiar. Further, both the firms and the country as a whole have a bigger impact on other countries; as a result the familial, parochial attitudes have to yield before more statesmanlike, more broad-gauged. and more impersonal attitudes and techniques. It is too early to say whether the Japanese can carry out this transition without producing some or all of the problems of alienation, of rigidity, of caution, of conservatism, of confusion and the like that have been character- istic of other organizations grown too big for their original structures and practices. I myself would judge this exactly the kind of challenge the Japanese are most likely to meet well – indeed, with extraordinary skill and creativity. But only the future will tell if this estimate is accurate.

Let me now turn to several reasons for 'positive thinking' in terms of sustained high Japanese growth rates – starting first with some qualitative–quantitative remarks about these growth rates.

In the 50s the Japanese economy about doubled in size, going from small to medium. That was a spectacular but not an un- precedented performance. In any case, it did not have a great impact on the world. In the 60s the economy increased by more than a factor of three, going from medium to large. In the process it passed England, France, and West Germany to become the world's third largest economy. It now seems almost certain to attain the $200 billion mark in fiscal 1970. Various authorities predict that in the 70s the Japanese economy will increase by a factor of between three and five. Even if we picked the lower number, the economy ought to be at about the $600 billion a year level in 1980 (figured in 1970 dollars), and that means it will be gigantic – and according to some of these predictions, it may even be at the trillion (1970) dollar level. Further, even though Japan's economy in 1980 may be only a third of a half or so the size of the American and a half or two thirds or so the size of the Soviet, its impact on the international arena through foreign trade may be at least as important as the impacts of these two, and possibly more important.

In this enterprise of trying to estimate future Japanese growth rates, one can choose among several techniques. For example, one can do various kinds of input–output type studies, trying to identify where bottlenecks or other difficulties would occur and to assess whether the Japanese might be able to circumvent them.

We have done this several times at Hudson Institute, though admittedly not in a very thorough or deep manner. In fact, we do not have particular faith in such calculations and do not feel justified in allocating major resources to them. Rather, we use such calculations to check and discipline conclusions arrived at through other means. The most important of these is quite simple: to examine the Japanese society and economy today, its internal and external environment, in order to identify qualitative and quantitative reasons for the economy's very high growth rate, and then ask to what degree these seem likely to persist in the future. We find very persuasive our current conclusion to such an analysis – that high Japanese growth rates, rates in the neighbourhood of 8–12 per cent or so, are likely to continue for most or all of the 1970–1980 period and perhaps beyond. Among the many positive qualitative–quantitative reasons for this growth to continue are the following: *

1. High saving and investment rates (about twice those of the US);
2. Superior education and training (i.e., American quantity and European quality through high school);
3. 'Adequate capitalization';
4. Readily available 'risk capital';
5. Technological capabilities competitive with those of the West;
6. Economically and patriotically advancement-oriented, achievement-oriented, work-oriented, deferred-gratification, loyal, enthusiastic employees (probably increasingly so);
7. High morale and commitment to economic growth and to surpassing the West – by government, by management, by labour, and by the general public;
8. Willingness to make necessary adjustments and/or sacrifices;

* It might be worth noting that, more or less coincidentally, almost all these twelve points apply to Great Britain – but in reverse. They are all reasons why the British economy might grow more slowly throughout the 70's – and perhaps for the rest of the century – than the more dynamic European economies. This book, of course, is not on British issues, so I simply offer this as an interesting, if depressing, aside. Of course, if I had drawn up a list of negatives for the British economy I would have changed the order, grouping, and emphasis from the above.

9. Excellent management of the economy – by government, by business, and, to some degree, by labour; this results in a controlled and, to some degree, collectivist ('Japan, Inc.') economy, but still competitive and market-oriented (but not market-dominated) capitalism;
10. Adequate access – on good and perhaps improving terms – to most world resources and markets;
11. Almost all future technological and economic and most cultural and political developments favourable to continuation of the above;
12. Relatively few and/or weak pressures to divert major resources to 'low economic productivity' uses.

The above list seems to me so persuasive that I would argue that current (unofficial) estimates by several groups in Japan of a doubling or so of the GNP by 1975 and then another doubling or so from 1975 to 1980 is not an unreasonable prediction. The current official estimate of the Economic Planning Agency is 10·6 per cent a year, which corresponds to slightly less than a tripling of the GNP by 1980. It should be noted that all previous official EPA estimates have been low: they have consistently underestimated long-term growth rates. And they may have done it again. In any case, there is nothing on the horizon (despite our list of negative factors) that seems likely to interfere dramatically with these growth rates during the next few years. And the naïve prediction – based on previous performance and the apparent absence of bottlenecks or other evidence of 'topping out' – would be for *another increase in the rate of increase* – i.e., for Japanese growth rates in the next decade or so to be in the 12–15 per cent range, rather than the 8–12 per cent we tend to assume in this study.

The first and possibly the most essential factor in my argument – though by itself certainly not sufficient explanation for Japanese growth rates – is Japan's high saving and investment rates, which guarantee there will continue to be, both relatively and absolutely, enormous resources available for expansion. In recent years the Japanese have tended to save and invest about one third or more of their gross national product. This is the highest rate in the world (except for Kuwait's, which is technically higher – but that is a very special case indeed). Thus the Japanese today save proportionately about one and a half to three times as much as the European and North American nations do.

It is true that many foreign observers, perhaps thinking how difficult it would be for their countries to achieve, much less maintain, such saving rates, believe there must be great pressures on Japan's saving rate and a popular demand for more consumption. With regard to the mass of Japanese, such an assumption seems almost completely wrong. In the last five years the average Japanese worker has found his real income going up by about 10 per cent a year, or even more. (Part of this increase is a general increase in standard of living for all, and part is due to the individual's going up the ladder of seniority and promotion). Since he does not increase his saving rate, it means that each year he has 10 per cent or more available for consumption. Of course, if he decided to spend his savings he would have even more money available for consumption, but the Japanese have been a 'saving people' for hundreds of years and have already established what they regard as a reasonably high standard of living. Since the average worker is increasing that standard by about 10 per cent a year anyway, he feels little or no pressure to cut his rate of saving. In addition, there are certain peculiarities of the Japanese system, in particular the payment of a good deal – about one third – of the annual salary in the form of mid-year and end-of-year bonuses, that make high saving relatively easy. Furthermore, the lack of adequate pensions, the need to pay tuition for children in senior high school and college, and many other things make it almost necessary to save. Thus the individual who gets his money in a lump sum tends to bank it. One should also note that, despite the inflation of common prices, at least until recently the rate of return on individual savings has been satisfactory. Finally, and not unimportant, the Japanese know they are contributing to the growth of their country by saving, and they take a positive patriotic pleasure in doing so.

To have some conception of how important these high savings and investment rates can be, note the enormous tightness in savings and investments in the United States today. Imagine then that an extra $200 billion or so were available for loans and investment purposes – and that this was a genuine availability, because it came out of savings and therefore represented actual resources, not an inflationary creation of money. If such capital were available and easily invested, growth rates in this country, at least in the short run, would become fantastic.

Perhaps equally important for a sustained rate of production is the second factor on my list, education. Among the large countries of the world, only the Soviet Union and the United States compare with Japan in the percentage of their population with high school and post-secondary education of various kinds. One can even argue that the Japanese situation is probably better than that of those two countries. As far as 'objective' tests can tell, at least at the high school level the Japanese indeed seem to have achieved American mass education combined with European quality. (Japanese students generally surpass European in mathematics and science.)

The Japanese have also designed their education system intelligently; for example, they probably make better use of educational television than any other country does. And even where they have a failure, the failure may be partially deliberate (at least the continued existence of the failure may be considered more or less desirable). I am thinking here particularly of Japanese training in English. Almost all Japanese children today take six years of English in high school (grades seven to twelve) but relatively few become able to speak the language fluently or even usably. This is not surprising – the universities give no credit for such oral proficiency, and lack of that proficiency is traditional in Japan. As we mentioned earlier, when they borrowed language from the Chinese they borrowed only the written language, not the spoken. Many observers believe that this was a sensible policy. If the Japanese had made their children fluent in foreign languages, a tendency would have developed among them to leave the country. So the '*kanji* barrier' is at the most direct level: an inability to speak the foreign language. This continues to protect Japan's people from certain kinds of temptations, while leaving fully open to them the technical and other knowledge to be gained from written languages. However, now that the Japanese standard of living and of opportunity is approaching or even surpassing the West's, the need for this protection diminishes. And as Japan grows and makes a bigger impact on the world scene the need for oral fluency in foreign languages increases. I myself expect to see some dramatic changes in Japan's academic practice in this field.

Aside from language training the Japanese have done very well in the area of education. Since World War II they have opened some 750 junior and senior colleges, and they are well on their way to achieving an almost American-style mass education at the university level. The very top Japanese schools are probably not as good as the top American or the top European schools, but certainly their average schools are very good. Here again they have a great advantage. With an almost completely homogeneous population (the issue of the 650,000 Korean and 300,000 Chinese minorities does not really alter this point), they do not have to worry about disadvantaged minority groups or groups whose cultural outlook is so different that it is difficult for the majority's school system to deal with them. Furthermore, Japanese parents are quite willing to make enormous sacrifices if necessary to educate their children – in part because of advancement-orientation motives, in part because of family pride. These education-oriented attitudes often communicate themselves to young Japanese with an almost fantastic intensity, at least until the young Japanese get into the university. There it has been true, at least for a time, that they have felt a great sense of relaxation, which, combined with the general de-authorization of the older Japanese and of older values, in some cases caused an almost explosive outflow of frustrations. Of course, it is traditional that Japanese when very young are treated in an uninhibited and nurturant fashion; but society gradually clamps down on them, peaking in its demands for discipline and renunciation of self at about fifteen years of age until about forty-five years, and then it gradually begins to relax again. The difference here was that at the universities these restraints and requirements were suddenly, even if only temporarily, relaxed. It was understood by most of the students, though not all, that the restraints and requirements would be back on when they graduated. Most of these students are now gone from the universities, and in addition, the universities will in the future have a stronger sense of responsibility for student behaviour and much tighter discipline than they have had in the past. One likely result is that there will be less temptation or ability among these young Japanese to rebel. In addition, the recent phase of de-authorization of the older generation, which was produced by the loss of the war and the subsequent critique of authoritarian and totalitarian doctrines, is now largely over. This is a result of the passage of time, the revisionist histories of World War II, and, most important of all, the high level of prestige associated with the current generation of business leaders and the great pride in Japan's growth that is now communicating itself to the young.

It was necessary to put my third point, concerning available capital, into quotations, because there is so much controversy and misunderstanding about it. I mentioned in Chapter 3 that the debt-equity ratio of Japanese firms is incredibly high, often four or five and even ten to one. Many a Japanese balance sheet would, by technical US standards, imply that the firm was just about insolvent. Therefore, as the term 'adequate' is usually used by a Western accountant, the Japanese clearly do not have adequate capitalization in the sense of adequate equity capital.

From the viewpoint of productivity, however, it makes little or no difference whether the money used is debt or equity capital. The machines it buys are just as good. And from this viewpoint, the amount and quality of capital equipment behind each employee is, in the large companies at least, as good as in most European systems and almost as good as in the US – indeed sometimes better. Japanese labour can no longer be considered cheap manual labour; it surely is not. In fact, if we take account of all the fringe benefits and bonuses enjoyed by Japanese labour, even typical salaries and wages are quite high. A relatively low-paid foreman in a large American company making electrical machinery and equipment gets, say, $200–250 a week; his counterpart in Matsushita Electric Company now gets over $150 (fringe benefits and bonuses are included in each case). This is not coolie labour working with primitive equipment.

From the viewpoint of companies competing and expanding,

the high debt-equity ratio means that the Japanese firm gets its capital for expansion more cheaply than the American firm does. The money paid in interest on Japanese debentures is not only a tax deductible expense, but it is usually much less than the corresponding profits a US or Japanese firm would have to earn if it expanded by increasing its equity.

The next point, dealing with risk capital, again involves a phrase that does not mean quite the same thing in the Japanese context. But let me first set forth an anecdote without adding any caveats for the moment. I once attended a weekend meeting of American, Japanese, and European businessmen. During one of the informal discussion periods I posed the following problem: imagine that an opportunity became available to your firm, one that would require a fairly large piece of the firm's capital but also seemed to have an even chance of the firm's increasing its investment money by a factor of about five in a few years; there was also an even chance the firm would lose that money completely. What would you do?

The first reaction of the Japanese was that they would not believe the calculation. I then tried to make clear this was a so-called 'Gedanken question' – that they had to imagine they had checked and rechecked the analysis and convinced themselves that the opportunities and risks were as quoted. The Japanese felt, then, that they would simply have to take the risk. That is, they felt that believing this calculation meant that one had to make the investment. The Americans asked me if it would be *noticeable* if the 'investment' turned sour and the firm lost its money by having taken what would then – in retrospect – appear to have been a somewhat reckless gamble. I replied that they must assume that if such a loss occurred it would be very noticeable. One of the Americans then pointed out – and with the evident agreement of his compatriots – that if the *coup* were successful the firm would of course make some money, but this would not be as apparent as an outsider might expect, while failure was intrinsically more attention-worthy. From this point of view, then, an even money bet was not a good one, and almost all the Americans agreed that they probably would not take the risk. Several of the Japanese got very excited, one of them saying,

'But you Americans are the great risk-takers of the world.' I suggested that he was probably talking about the Middle West or South-west American, or the American in the oil business, or the fathers of the Americans here, but that American big industry – particularly staid, respectable, 'established' industry – had become relatively cautious. Many of the Europeans present felt that the issue would probably not even come up in their home companies, since nobody would seriously contemplate a situation in which there was an even chance of losing the firm's money.

This anecdote is not intended to imply that no American or European firms take great risks. One can find many that do. It does not even imply that the kind of very respectable American and European businessman who attends conferences in Japan may not also be a risk-taker. It does argue, however, that a surprisingly large number of them are not.

The reason I had to put the phrase 'risk capital' into quotation marks is that under present-day Japanese conditions – of 'Japan, Inc.', and of almost guaranteed rapid growth – the real risks are often actually low. The high growth rate usually cuts down the odds for loss, and often it also makes it easy to alleviate, make up for, or cover over any losses that do occur. Finally, a large Japanese firm in really serious trouble would almost certainly be bailed out by the government – either by arranging for a merger or for the banks to extend loans. In any case, the employees, stockholders, debtors, and other individuals involved would almost be certain of being taken care of. Thus one of the reasons that many large modern Japanese firms can afford to operate in a seemingly risky way is that they know their government and society stand behind them and that they will not be motionlessly driven to the wall unless there are other factors in the situation – (as is the case of 'obsolete' or small Japanese firms).

Of course, by American standards the Japanese seem to take too many risks. They are very expansionist, and they often expand even at the cost of some, at least temporary, diminution in net income. They also are often anxious to be in the most technologically advanced areas. In particular, as we have seen, if one Japanese financial group enters a new technological area, others often find it necessary, as a matter of prestige, to go into new fields too. While this emphasis on high production, new technology, and maintaining or increasing market shares can produce some mistakes, especially if carried to an extreme or done carelessly, they surely are the right kinds of mistakes to make. They are the kinds of mistakes that allow for high expansion rates and for overcoming the lethargy, inattention, lack of homework, and rigidity that often prevent the risk and expansion that are appropriate and desirable. The Japanese are also willing to take large risks because they are not as reluctant to suffer losses as American and European companies. One can argue that very few American and hardly any European companies would risk, say, 10–20 per cent of their capital on an investment that presented an equal chance of total loss or of tripling the money invested. Almost any large Japanese group would be willing to take such a risk.

Thus, partly as a result of the four points already mentioned, partly because they have been able to obtain American technology at advantageous rates and conditions, and partly because of the peculiar characteristics of the Japanese and of their economy, their technological capabilities are now more than competitive with the West. In fact, in many ways the Japanese are more advanced than the Europeans and the Americans. Furthermore, they seem increasingly creative and innovative. As a result there is now a reverse and increasing flow of 'payments for Japanese technology' in that about 10 per cent of the royalties the Japanese pay to other countries now comes back to them in the form of royalties for their own technology. Furthermore, in some ways the Japanese spend more than the Europeans for research and development – particularly when measured in terms of available manpower. If and when Japanese government research and development programmes become very big, one can confidently predict that Japanese research and development will in many ways be comparable to that of the United States and the Soviet Union. In any case, at all levels and in all kinds of areas, the Japanese are now technologically competent and sophisticated.

The sixth item, advancement-orientation, achievement-orientation, and such, is, of course, a classical explanation of Western industrialization and the West's high growth rates in the past. As a culture, the Japanese today seem to have virtually as many of these 'Calvinist' qualities as Northern Europe or the United States has had in the past, whereas in the West these attitudes and values seem to be increasingly eroding. They are probably eroding in Japan as well – although to a lesser degree and at a slower rate. But it is possible that this erosion will be stopped or even reversed in Japan and perhaps – though to a lesser extent – in the US too.

When we talk about advancement-orientation or achievement-orientation in this context, we should point out that it is a matter of advancement and achievement among Japanese as a group (or as a business commune), rather than a Western style of individualism. The difference between the US and Japan on these issues is one of those essential and important points about Japanese 'superiority' that may be hard for some Americans to understand, because they may not realize how great a difference lies between them and the Japanese.

Let me go back for a moment to the weekend gathering of Americans, Europeans, and Japanese businessmen I referred to earlier. I also asked the Japanese present how their families felt about their working on weekends. The answer was characteristic: Their families probably felt that the men must be very important, otherwise they would not be working on the weekend. In addition, their families have an obligation to them, since they had given up the weekend for the common good. Thus, when they returned home the families of the Japanese men present would treat them with special care and consideration – these men had made a sacrifice and, to the extent possible, their families were obligated to make it up to them.

I asked the Americans what the attitude of their families would be. To a man the Americans felt that their families, while acknowledging that working on a weekend might to some degree be necessary or reasonable, would also feel that it represented a form of selfishness by those men who sacrificed their families' weekend for relatively narrow and self-serving business interests. The men would be expected to make it up to their families.

Once again, as far as the Europeans were concerned, 'The matter would not come up.'

So, exactly as in Meiji Japan, the Japanese businessman can say to himself without any sense of hypocrisy, 'I serve the community' (or 'the government'). A Japanese still feels that his business's success is his country's success, and his country's success is his success. Most readers probably remember Secretary of Defense Wilson's unfortunately-timed remark in 1952 that was inaccurately quoted as 'What's good for General Motors is good for the United States.' The Secretary's actual remark was to the effect that he was not aware that what was good for General Motors was bad for the United States and vice versa. In that, it was not indefensible. I would not argue that in 1952 all the interests of General Motors and of the United States wholly overlapped, but it is clear – or should be clear – that one of the things that has made the United States the country it is, is the existence of organizations like General Motors. In 1952 it would have been hard to imagine General Motors economically healthy and the United States economically sick, or vice versa. This is somewhat less true today as we move closer to the post-industrial culture, but even now Mr Wilson's remark would not be outrageous, though many more would be willing to challenge it intellectually and factually. However, the fact that Mr Wilson was willing to make the comment showed that he possessed some degree of morale. Almost no Japanese businessman in similar circumstances would have any difficulty in making such a remark. Furthermore, few Japanese would think that such a remark deserved criticism.

Along this line we might examine a song that is special only in that it has been circulated around the world. Indeed it is typical of the kinds of songs Japanese management and Japanese labour sing every morning for five or ten minutes to start off the day. This is the Matsushita Electric Workers' song, and it is interesting to note that it is the Matsushita Electric Co. itself that has seen fit to reproduce the song in its worldwide advertisements.

I have often quoted this song in talks in the United States and Europe. It is a little dangerous to do so after lunch or dinner, because many Americans and Europeans literally find the song upsetting. They cannot imagine anybody seriously singing 'that kind of tripe'. I often ask them to go through the song line by line and note that for all practical purposes it is really a simple set of accurate and reasonable declaratory sentences that are not especially absurd, chauvinistic, simplistic, or exaggerated.

MATSUSHITA WORKERS' SONG

For the building of a new Japan,	(1)
Let's put our strength and mind together,	(2)
Doing our best to promote production,	(3)
Sending our goods to the people of the world,	(4)
Endlessly and continuously,	(5)
Like water gushing from a fountain.	(6)
Grow, industry, grow, grow, grow!	(7)
Harmony and sincerity!	(8)
Matsushita Electric!	(9)

The first line is certainly accurate: the Japanese double their economy every five to ten years, and one can clearly think of that as 'building a new Japan'. Line 2 is also meticulously accurate: the Japanese do put their strength and mind together in a way almost unprecedented in a modern industrial culture. (This is, of course, part of their characteristic social unity and communal harmony.) Line 3 is also reasonable – in fact, more accurate than one would at first think, since, as I have mentioned several times, the driving motivation behind the Japanese factory is often less to maximize profits than to maximize production; Matsushita certainly succeeds in doing both: it has had a growth rate of about 30 per cent a year until it is now the most profitable firm in Japan and the biggest taxpayer – items in which Mr Matsushita, the founder of the firm, takes great pride. It is also interesting to note that throughout Japan and at all age levels Mr Matsushita is considered an inspiration and a model.

Line 4, however, is not as accurate as most people think. In recent years the Japanese have exported less than 10 per cent of their Gross National Product to the peoples of the world. This is less than half the rate of prewar Japan, and about half the current rate of many European countries. In contrast to the usual image, the Japanese are less dependent on foreign trade than most Western European countries are, or indeed, than they themselves were before World War II. On the other hand, foreign trade is important to them and its importance is growing; their exports probably will become a greater percentage of future production. So, if one were to be accurate, line 4 would have to be changed to 'sending 90 per cent or more of our goods to our own Japanese people and 10 per cent or less to the peoples of the world.'

However line 5 is substantially unchallengeable. There is a sense of 'inevitability and continuity' about Japanese production. Line 6 is of course a metaphor, but it seems to me a reasonable image, one without marked exaggeration or self-praise. Line 7 is also meticulously accurate: Japanese industry often grows by 20 or 30 per cent a year. The 'harmony and sincerity' of line 8 is associated with line 2 and again is accurate. Line 9 simply concludes the song.

What I am suggesting is that the song is a series of straight-forward sentences without special excesses or gaucheries, and that there is no reason that any Japanese need be embarrassed or self-conscious about it. Nevertheless, most Western audiences, European and American, used to regard it with excruciating embarrassment. And, again at least until quite recently, most had a sense of great superiority over the 'simple-minded' Japanese who can take pleasure in singing this kind of thing.

Actually such songs were common in the United States before World War II, but most of the big companies – such as IBM – that once had song books burned them in the late 40s or early 50s.* We still have in the United States a few sales organizations that sing songs like these, but almost invariably off-key and tune-lessly. I am also told that three or four American companies, such as Lincoln Electric, maintain these old traditions (and that these companies are in fact incredibly productive). But most Americans

* The IBM anthem included such choruses as this:

> EVER ONWARD – EVER ONWARD!
> That's the spirit that has brought us fame!
> We're big, but bigger we will be.
> We can't fail for all can see
> That to serve humanity has been our aim!
> Our products now are known in every zone.
> Our reputation sparkles like a gem!
> We've fought our way through – and new
> Fields we're sure to conquer too
> For the EVER ONWARD IBM.

find it uncomfortable to work for such firms, despite the high salaries and lucrative profit-sharing bonuses that are also characteristic of them.

It should also be noted that in probably no place in the world but Japan are such songs sung voluntarily and for fun. Certainly not in China, where there is a grim compulsion about singing them and where pleasure and voluntarism are the last two words one would use to describe the situation. It was interesting to me that at one time in Vietnam, when the Viet Cong took over a village they often made the people sing such songs for an hour or two. And when the Saigon government took over a village they too made the villagers sing songs for a half hour or so. However, when the villagers were queried, 'What do you want?' the answer was almost invariably, among other things, 'We want to quit singing.'

The point I wish to make is the contrast between the high morale of present-day Japanese culture – in at least this matter of production – and the very low morale in the West on almost all issues.

In its own way, point seven on my list of reasons for expecting the Japanese growth to continue may be as important as all of the first six, since in some degree it can both substitute for them and reinforce them. It is generally believed that today there is worldwide commitment to economic growth. But actually the commitment is weak in many countries, where few people are willing to make tangible personal, business, political, or bureaucratic sacrifices for national growth – although they are perfectly willing to engage in rhetoric or polemics on the subject – and where most bureaucrats either do not understand what the requirements are or are not motivated to fulfil them. The contrary is true in Japan. Sacrifices are demanded as a matter of course, and they are admired when made with special zeal or skill. Everybody helps everybody else succeed, because to some degree – and despite the competition – the other's success is one's own success. We should also remember that in the nineteenth century the major avowed motive for economic growth was not to raise the living standards of the people but to achieve national security. A nation had to industrialize or risk losing its identity

– risk invasion or colonization. And even with this 'life and death' motivation, few nations modernized successfully.

For most nations today the commitment to growth does not affect the governing classes or other élites – or the masses, either – anywhere near as strongly as it did in the nineteenth century. But the Japanese public now seems more enthusiastic than ever before. They watch growth rates the way Americans watch baseball standings or football scores. Japan is a society and culture probably more interested in national prestige than any other in the world today, one in which national prestige issues arouse intense loyalty and commitment and tap deep sources of public identification. This situation creates a sense of common purpose among labour and management in a successful corporation, which in turn evokes public interest and applause. All of this helps reinforce point 8 on my list: an extraordinary willingness to make whatever adjustments and sacrifices are necessary for growth – by individuals in terms of family, time, and energy; by the corporation in terms of dynamism, risk-taking, and sheer hard work; and by the government in creatively accelerating and facilitating, as well as in protecting and governing.

All of these factors produce even better results for the Japanese, because, as indicated by point 9, they have reasonably good management at almost all levels and areas. By and large, management is not addicted to the fads, fashions, and ideologies that elsewhere have resulted in major contraproductive or wasteful activities. The future is likely to see this kind of good management even more favoured and rewarded. The Japanese government's fiscal policies seem ahead of any others in the world, both in terms of willingness to take stern measures to prevent imbalances before they become disruptive, and in terms of the sophistication of having time-phased short-, medium-, and long-term corrective policies.

Here again the Japanese have copied, understood, perfected, and then improved on Western theories. Part of this perfection and improvement is at the theoretical level, where on the whole they have gone to the greater use of simple phenomenological theories than the more complex analytic theories – a move which in the current state of economic science seems a wise one. (But they now seem to have some tendency to be going to larger, more complex, and computerized-type models. It will be interesting to see whether or not they use these well or are misled by them as so many have been in the West.)

More important than the analytic skill, however, is the fact that decision-makers take the obvious lessons and injunctions quite seriously. For example, everyone in the West is now generally willing to accept the idea that when there is a depression government spending should increase and monetary policy should be easier in order to encourage expenditures in both investment and consumption. But whenever it becomes necessary to draw the belt, to tighten, no Western government has been willing to do what the Japanese have done three times in the postwar period. In order to correct for bad balance of payment situations, they have artificially created three very sharp, very severe, but very short depressions (or if one wishes, recessions). It is true the Germans did something like that in 1966, but as near as I can find out the sharpness and intensity of the recession was not intended, so the Germans do not really get any moral credit for it, nor any theoretical credit either. But the Japanese may not deserve as much moral credit as I seem to be giving them. As one friend of mine put it, 'I will give them moral credit when I see real suffering among University of Tokyo graduates rather than among small business and people at the bottom.' And it is true that in many cases the cost of such adjustments has been shifted to parts of the population that have relatively little political power. But from the viewpoint of the over-all performance of the system, this willingness to have sacrifices made that are necessary for proper adjustments is enormously important – irrespective of which portion of the population bears the bulk of the costs. It seems quite likely that there will be a deterioration of the West's competitive position, and of its economic performance generally, as a consequence of the unwillingness of governments to ask any major group of people to make serious sacrifices – and/or to make groups wait, if necessary, for various 'goodies' or reforms for the sole reason that it is bad for the economy to try to get them at this particular moment or to get them all at once. The Japanese, on the contrary, have demonstrated a degree of skill and responsibility, in manipulating fiscal and monetary policies that would surprise many in the West, yet it goes largely unregarded.

I believe that this performance goes so unregarded partly because so many Japanese things have not been fully appreciated, but probably mainly because much of this performance has an essentially 'illiberal' appearance. In other words, if Japanese society tolerates slums, over-crowding, and such for a decade or so in order to be rich enough to really build, as described in the next chapter, a garden society for the rest of history, this is the kind of conservative wisdom that tends more to appal the West than to attract its admiration. Indeed, the general Japanese willingness to sacrifice almost any defective parts of their economy – or even of their culture – that would prevent their 'catching up with' or 'surpassing the West' is more appalling than attractive to most liberal and progressive observers.

Another thing that confuses Western observers is that the Japanese do not congratulate themselves publicly for any sacrifices or adjustments they make. In this they are starkly different from most 'revolutionary' or 'fanatic' régimes with goals to pursue, which tend to publicize sacrifices and adjustments so much that they typically overshoot severely or make them in extremely counterproductive ways. Thus, in revolutionary régimes there is often a certain tightening up for the sake of tightening up, a certain austerity for the sake of austerity, asceticism for the sake of asceticism. In many cases this gratuitous discipline grossly interferes with production, particularly with investment, with risk-taking, with motivation. One of the remarkable things about the Japanese is that, despite the enormous drive for production and growth and the emotion behind this drive, they have not allowed emotion to interfere with efficiency. In almost all other countries with this kind of fanaticism and emotion, one tends to find policies that produce results opposite to those intended, though they are policies that satisfy immediate emotional needs. The opposite has been true of Japan – when it seemed useful to tighten the belt they have tightened the belt; when it seemed useful to let the economy go, they have let it go. As a result, their fantastic growth rate has been fuelled less by sacrifices than by internal consumption on the part of a people who, as we have seen, typically live each year about 10 per cent (or more) better than they lived the previous year. (It must also be recalled that despite the great success of Japanese foreign trade, 90 per cent of the Japanese GNP is consumed domestically.)

This absence of hoopla about sacrifice and adjustment – this absence of government-staged demonstrations, special days, and the like – makes it almost impossible for the naïve foreign observer to detect the moral sacrifice when it is there, and to detect the iron discipline and enormous purposiveness of the whole process. But the Japanese do not need this kind of reinforcement. The fact that in the absence of Cuban and Soviet-type pageants, posters, and speeches the foreign observer cannot recognize purposive and popular drive and commitment is more his problem than Japan's.

Of course, none of the above factors would give Japan its present success if the country lacked sufficient access to essential resources. But fortunately for the Japanese their scarcity of indigenous material resources does not now seem to make much difference. They are tapping the entire world for raw materials, and because of the scale on which they do so and the technology they use, in some respects they enjoy cheaper raw materials than any other nation in the world. They also have more than adequate export markets to pay for these raw materials. Particularly with the current stress on world trade, low tariff barriers, the free movement of people and capital, the free access to markets, it seems reasonable to suppose that Japan's favourable status will, if anything, improve. Worldwide the costs of communication, transportation, and travel are going down, and this should contribute to making Japan's competitive position even more favourable. Finally, the onset of the 'post-industrial culture' also seems likely, at least in the next two or three decades, to favour Japan's competitive position.

Thus, it is not true that the Japanese export to live; they export in order to be able to buy imports. But under current trends the total of imports is becoming a smaller and smaller proportion of the economy, and essential imports are an even smaller proportion. This is to be expected as they go into a service economy, and even more so as they go into a post-industrial culture. (It is interesting to note that the Japanese are more conscious than almost any other people – at least at the government level – of this post-industrial culture and are beginning to have a sense of what it might mean for Japan.)

Furthermore, a good deal of Japanese investment overseas is designed to create a better import or export situation; and their import and export practices are designed not only for current gain but for long-term value to their importing and exporting position. This is also true of internal investments. For example, because of economies of scale and location, Japanese steel mills, which are located on the coast, can now get raw materials more cheaply than a US steel mill in Pittsburgh can – even when the Japanese are importing from the United States. They can also deliver their steel more cheaply to Los Angeles than the Pittsburgh mills can. (In some real senses American steel mills are mislocated.) In general the Japanese have made a virtue of their necessities and are now drawing their raw materials in the most economic and convenient fashion from the entire world. Because of the gains in shipping efficiency and other economies, as well as the future of new forms of transportation, and because of their future ability to invest vast sums of money in creating very large-scale operations, it seems quite clear that, if anything, costs for raw material will go down for Japan, not up. This does not mean, however, that there necessarily will be greatly weakened markets for Japanese exports. But one future problem has already reared its head – the Japanese will have too favourable a balance of payment and thus cause a currency drain in their trading partner. It is clear that the Japanese must not allow their favourable balance of payments to grow, and they might, for example, have to re-evaluate the yen (which would simply mean their having to work less hard for their imports). Doubtless that will be done in the next decade or two, but not immediately.

Another possibility is that a good deal of Japan's favourable export balance will start paying for capital investment in foreign countries, for tourism, and for luxury imports. (The Japanese have a great liking for prestige Western foods, prestige clothing, and the like.) This means that they will end up in a very good bargaining position. Not only will they buy essential raw materials from the West, but a good deal of their import volume will also be made up of tourism or dispensable consumer items or will accrue from their own overseas investments. Of course, some of their own exports will be luxury items, too, but possibly not quite as luxurious as their imports. In other words, if they are buying scotch whisky simply because they like the taste of imported scotch, they still always know that their own Suntory brand is a quite satisfactory substitute at lower cost. On the other hand, when they export a television set, the possibility for imported substitution by the buyer would involve a much more expensive and probably less reliable set.

Further, the Japanese have a very good, even if unstated, argument that as long as the world's resources and markets are opened to them for import and export on a competitive basis, there is no reason for them to become militaristic or even to risk nationalist or chauvinist popular feelings. However, if other (Western) countries should try to close them out in ways that are not really fair and not in accordance with the precepts of those nations, then the Japanese would have a right to be very aggrieved and to look around for other techniques by which to compete. In any case, as indicated by point 11, almost all future technological economic developments seem more likely to be favourable than unfavourable to Japan. Some cultural and political developments, as discussed later, may not be so favourable; but, as I have already argued, it seems reasonable that at least in the near and medium term their impact on Japanese growth rates is likely to be marginal and to take a long time to have a serious effect – if they ever will.

Let us now consider the last item in the list, the pressures to divert resources from growth to other uses. Many Westerners, even experts on Japan, do not realize how elated the Japanese are by their success. I am struck by the lack of insight of those Western observers who believe that some Japanese will want to kill the goose that is laying these golden eggs – that they will pose premature demands for distribution of the profits. It must be understood that almost all sectors of Japan today are improving in living standards, and though by US standards many would seem to have been left behind – at least relatively – this is not so according to Japanese mores and attitudes. There is very little special or intense concern in Japan for the bottom, for the least fortunate – and almost no guilt feelings about them.

Consider now a Japanese worker who every year earns 10 per cent more in real terms than he earned the previous year. He has a lifetime job with some factory. His union is very conscious of the need to keep the business competitive with other Japanese businesses, as well as the need to keep Japan competitive with the rest of the world. (The union is almost always a company union loosely affiliated with a national group, and since every union member's future prosperity depends on the company with whom he has this lifetime employment contract, he clearly must be conscious of the company's problems.) This labourer (or his union) is now expected by some Western observers to insist on having his income go up by perhaps 20 per cent, even though he knows that if it does it will cut down investment and growth for both his firm (to which he feels an intense familial commitment) and his nation. I suggest that the opposite will be true. After all, the commitment to catching up with the West goes back about a hundred years and actualizing it has now become feasible. Any Japanese individual, organization, or government arguing that this goal should be sacrificed for some proximate and – in Japanese terms – frivolous reasons is going to be in serious trouble. Of course, various individual Japanese may argue, 'These efforts are not worthwhile for me as an individual,' but they will not receive much acclaim. In fact, they are going to look like 'drop-outs' from what is to Japanese eyes the most charismatic and exciting project ever undertaken by the Japanese people.

One rather suspects that the productivity of this Japan, Inc. engine is likely to increase. Nor should we forget that the momentum itself is an important source of further momentum. For if an industry grows by about 25–30 per cent a year, more than half its machinery at any given time is going to be less than three or four years old, making the industry quite competitive. Further, many possible strains on the Japanese system, such as those that could result from lifetime unemployment, are automatically alleviated if the company is growing at great rates, since, rather than laying off people, the company desperately wants to hold on to them. Further, the company gets the habit of – and skilled in – being expansive. There are many people who work full-time at searching for new materials, designing new factories, investigating new markets, and the like. All this activity associated with expansion becomes a major profession rather than a once-in-a-while activity, and the people concerned gain great skill.

Also, the visible pace of change can alleviate an enormous number of social strains, and it can generate a sense of excitement that is almost completely absent in most of the West today. Indeed, at least for the next decade or so, Japan, Inc. looks much more like an accelerating than a decelerating locomotive, and it seems unlikely that even after that time it will decelerate very rapidly.

One result of the misunderstanding of this enormous momentum has been a great deal of misleading comment in the West, some of it based on biased perceptions. Consider two possible cases. If there were a small growth rate of 2–3 per cent per capita, this would be a very dynamic or exciting rate of change. If one interrupts this growth by diverting the resources from investment into consumption, the change in the growth rate is not dramatically noticeable. Of course, the day when one will become rich has now been deferred from say fifty years to one hundred years, but it is hard to take such deferment seriously – particularly when contrasted with the dramatic use and immediate value of the diverted resources in alleviating some widely perceived or publicized problems or even in raising the general standard of living of some very visible groups. That is not an uncommon situation in the West and in many of the under-developed nations. But now let us take a situation where the growth rates are on the order of 10–15 per cent. One can, of course, divert some major resources into consumption and lower the rate by only 1–2 per cent. But if one diverts so much that the growth rates are seriously interfered with, then in fact a very dramatic change in future prospects has been made. The day when one will get rich has been postponed from something like five or ten or twenty years to something more like fifty or one hundred. It is clear that under these circumstances few people would be willing to sacrifice such dramatic growth rates. This would be true if they had to defer some rather pressing needs. Further, when the economy is growing that fast, there is a visible – even dramatic – gain to be achieved by deferring such expenses to the future. Thus the Japanese will not take, say, 3–4 per cent from their savings and 3–4 per cent from consumption, they will drop their growth rate only 1 per cent or so, but the amount gained for whatever needs they are interested in will be about $14 billion. If they had done that ten years ago, it would have made only $2 or $3 billion available.

Thus, judging by Japan's recent performance and its historical capability for purposive, communal actions, one tends to place high confidence in their ability and willingness to apply the necessary remedies to any difficulties. And one expects them to continue doing this at least until there are basic changes in the Japanese national character that can effectively nullify these objectives and capabilities. But that is not likely to occur on a large scale for at least a generation, even though certain individuals have already raised the demand for such changes.

In the face of all the above considerations, it is hard to understand the widespread attention paid to the obstacles I listed earlier. And it is especially hard to understand the widespread insistence by many Japanese, particularly intellectuals, liberals, etc., as well as visitors (many of whom share these basic anti-capitalist, anti-business, anti-technology ideologies), on downgrading so sharply the Japanese ability to produce in the fashion I have described. Consider for a moment the comments made by a distinguished, and on other issues quite perceptive, recent visitor to Japan, Professor Jules Masserman:

In bold statement, many Japanese are in a psychological turmoil approaching chaos. Historically, Japan's threefold traditions of Shinto (the Way of the Gods), Confucianism (in which allegiance to the Emperor comes first, and to a friend last) and Bushido (the Way of the Warrior Samurai) were first rudely challenged by the intrusion of Commodore Perry in 1854. After this, in rapid succession, came the disruption of a millenium of feudalism by the restoration of the Meiji Emperors, their relegation in turn to a status of divine impotence by the success of the militarists in the Russo-Japanese War, the subsequent expansion of Japanese economic and political power throughout the East, the atomic horror and total defeat and disillusionment in World War II, the alien attempts at democratization enforced by the Mac-Arthur Constitution (which totally outlawed armaments and war, yet retained the Emperor as the 'Symbol of the State' and prescribed universal suffrage for a populace largely unprepared for it) and the highly uneven postwar pseudoprosperity which actually benefited relatively few, displaced farmers and fishermen from their lands into low-wage factories, and is already opening along the seams of major unemployment, inflation, political and labor unrest, and persecution of minorities (e.g., the ancient Ainu, and Chinese and Korean immigrants).

Bereft of the traditions of family discipline, the young of Japan, with a mocking veneer of Western dress and manners, contribute to a rate of delinquency among the highest in the world. But all ages and classes are disaffected: young couples, married or not, abort more pregnancies than come to term (2 million vs. 1·6 million births annually); the middle-aged long for their fancied prewar status as the Master Race of the East, and are joining fanatically religious and militantly aggressive 'patriotic' moves of explosive political power such as the Soka-Gakkai; many of the intelligentsia mix their science and philosophy with theological polemics and conundrums that sound jejune even to empathetic Western ears, and the elderly deplore the loss of honor and security previously accorded them as their due... To American psychiatrists, Japan offers a unique opportunity to study the cultural context of mental disorders, but to us as citizens of a world increasingly dependent on relative tranquility everywhere, we must regard the current status of Japan with some trepidation.[2]

Of course, Professor Masserman admits that he is no expert on Japan. He states quite candidly, 'I remained acutely aware that a week's sojourn makes no casual traveller an expert on any country – especially Japan, where the national watchword is *enryo*, meaning "be ever reserved!" However, since I was assured by Professor Burg and others that my experiences had been unusually rich, representative and meaningful ...'[3]

The quotation above, and especially the assurance by Professor Burg and others that Professor Masserman's experiences had been 'rich, representative and meaningful' (i.e., that his impressions were accurate and noteworthy), are characteristic of a number of impressions and comments about modern-day Japan.

Many experts and laymen trying to see behind the 'economic miracle' seem to believe that the Japanese are existing in some kind of a pressure cooker that is ready to explode, and that when this explosion takes place it will cause a very sharp discontinuity in Japanese growth rates. In particular, they expect the explosion to reveal a good deal of sham and make-believe behind the so-called economic miracle, or in any case to prove that this miracle had no serious staying power and was not particularly miraculous anyway.

I have, of course, argued extensively the other position: that the basis for Japan's economic growth is – at least from the perspective of further growth – both sound and extremely broad, that the economy and society which produce these high Japanese growth rates would, if tested, survive all kinds of economic and political vicissitudes but that in fact they are not likely to be subjected to such vicissitudes, at least in the next decade or two. If this is correct, then the so-called 'surprise-free projection' of continued or even increased growth rates is far and away the best bet.

It should be clear, of course, that there is some basis for the picture of a society under pressure and undergoing great changes and strains, even if it is not coming apart at the seams. The Japanese share with other modern societies the confusion and disruption associated with the coming transition to a post-industrial culture. They also had the shattering experience of losing World War II. There is a good deal of anger and confusion, a questioning of old values, indeed an erosion of old values, and an almost frantic search for valid meaning and renewed purpose that can be used as a basis for a new set of values. Yet it seems to me that although the Japanese will have to meet these questions along with the other emerging post-industrial societies of Europe, North America, and Australia, they are in a somewhat better position – at least in the short run – to do so. (It is hard to comment on the long-run problem of adjustment, since we do not know what this post-industrial culture will look like one or two hundred years from now. Our situation is very much like that of Dickens, who was able to describe with some accuracy the emerging industrial culture in nineteenth-century England but is not a particularly useful guide to late twentieth-century England.)

It would take us too far astray to attempt a systematic treatment of these issues here. But we would note that no serious body of opinion in Japan is likely to challenge the goal of economic growth either for its own sake or as a convenient 'wait and see' activity that would facilitate the pursuit of whatever goals are finally decided upon. As a programme in its own right, the 'completion' – or at least the continuation – of the Japanese economic and technological miracle will, in effect, have accomplished a one hundred-year programme to catch up with the West. The Japanese can feel that although they went through a most unfortunate digression in World War II, they can now take great pride in the fact that Japan in its relations with Pacific Asia, with the Pacific Basin, and with the world as a whole will have fulfilled any reasonable requirement that could have been laid on it, with the exception, perhaps, of the final step of achieving full superpower status. While it will not be clear to many Japanese exactly what this final step entails, it will be clear to them that it must be accomplished and that being wealthy and technologically superior will help.

It may be worthwhile for the reader at this point to look again at the quotation from Professor Masserman. He is, of course, quite correct when he argues that Japan's threefold tradition of Confucianism, Shinto, and Bushido are now badly eroded. The Japanese, however, have been a rather irreligious people for almost a thousand years – usually being perfectly willing to accept contradictory religions (using a Buddhist temple for the marriage of a daughter and a Shinto shrine for a funeral). The particular forms of religion that are now rejected developed from the early and middle twentieth century and were always quite artificial. There is still a great search for meaning and purpose, and there is some confusion among the younger generation about personal values, but the situation in Japan seems to be much better than in the West.

It is simply incorrect to dismiss the current prosperity as a shameful 'pseudo-prosperity' and as being extraordinarily and unhealthily uneven. Development in almost all countries has been uneven, and Japan is no exception. But it is not a great deal more uneven in Japan than in other countries, and at the present almost all Japanese share to a degree in the prosperity.

Much of the rest of Professor Masserman's indictment is equally misleading. When he argues, for example, that young couples use abortion excessively, so much so that there are more pregnancies aborted than come to term, he is simply criticizing a Japanese custom. The Japanese do not like to use foreign objects (e.g., intra-uterine loops or other contraceptive devices) in their bodies, nor do they use drugs loosely (i.e., the pill). Therefore, as a matter of personal, family, medical, and state choice, they have selected abortion as one of their chief methods of birth control. There does not seem to be any evidence that in their culture this was in any serious way an unfortunate choice.

All in all, everything that Professor Masserman states does indeed exist, but with a much smaller impact than he indicates, and the total is grossly exaggerated and misleading in terms of the frustrated, seething cauldron portrayed. The Japanese have a very important problem. They are becoming an incredibly successful economic, technological, and financial power, and this will give them a large number of choices. They may also have many grievances, some of them also unprecedented in the modern world. But wherever one goes in Japan one finds the Japanese satisfied or pleased with their success. They feel they have participated in creating it, that it reflects credit on them, their companies, and their country, and that whatever new problems it gives rise to they will be able to deal with as they come up. That is not to say there are not great uncertainties; nor is it to say that the Japanese are necessarily on the right course. For example, in the last twenty-five years or so something like a third of the Japanese people have moved from the countryside to the city. Even if these cities were not as overcrowded as they are, and even if they had better than the very primitive amenities they possess, this would be a jarring experience. But other nations have gone through similar experiences without much unrest, and the Japanese have done it with the benefits of extraordinary prosperity.

It is particularly simplistic, and perhaps peculiarly Western, to see a beginning of the end in such unprecedented success and in so many breakings of Western moulds of social and industrial conduct. We would perhaps do better in understanding Japan if we were to consider judging our own mistakes in the light of another country's successes, rather than automatically assuming that cause and effect relationships common in Western industrial cultures must of necessity exist elsewhere. Though we may have set the industrial revolution in progress, we cannot be certain that we readily understand its transmutations in another culture. As I have suggested in the case of the high abortion rate, what one might assume to be an index of social decay is actually largely a result of deep-seated cultural antipathy to Western practices.

Japan is very much a phenomenon in its own right. Some aspects of this phenomenon may be measurable enough with our standard economic and political indicators, but our continual mistakes in using these indicators to project the Japanese 'economic miracle' should caution us that there is a gap to be filled between the accumulation of data and the understanding of it. While I do not claim to be able to fill that gap (just the opposite, since Hudson Institute is now starting a major new study of Japan), most of the current scepticism of the Japanese 'Economic Miracle' seems to me to reflect, indirectly or directly, ideological or ethnic biases or just plain misinformation. Indeed, I have noticed that a number of current changes in Japanese society that I would judge important or useful to continuation of the economic miracle as it faces new challenges (such as a necessary change of the 'familial' and parochial attitudes of Japan, Inc. to more individualistic and cosmopolitan attitudes suitable to Japan the Superstate) are often taken by these sceptics as signs of immediate decay and disruption.

Chapter Five

The Emerging Japanese Superstate

As I mentioned in the Prefatory Note, the term 'superstate' had been chosen with care, leaving open the issue of what kind of a superstate: whether a 'low posture' state in possession of an enormous economy but otherwise neutral – or a power as well, and if so what kind of power. In this chapter I would like to focus primary attention on those issues that arise from Japan's just being a state in possession of enormous economic, technological, and financial resources, introducing other issues in a relatively peripheral fashion or deferring them to the next chapter.

This is a very artificial thing to do. One of the problems of a growing economic power is its attendant entrance into the political sphere. It is probably as impossible to seek to become one of the top economic powers of the world, much less number one, without eventually becoming entangled in international political problems as it is to become an Olympic swimming champion without getting wet. Therefore, if, as I argue, Japan continues to grow at rates comparable to those it has achieved in the last twenty years – and does so for at least another decade – Japan surely will deserve to be judged the third most important international power in the world. It should far surpass in national power – in influence and political significance – its giant neighbour China. While experts differ in defining importance, power, and influence, and in how they measure these related qualities, they are still likely to agree with this ranking. This 'super' Japan will present the rest of the world with opportunities and challenges. In fact, many Europeans in the late 70s are likely to feel that Japan presents them with the same kind of upsetting economic and technological 'pushes' and 'pulls' they now feel from the United States.

Japan will be even more important in what we will define later as Non-Communist Pacific Asia. The Japanese have already demonstrated in this area a peculiar paradox of the post-World War II period. Their participation in the war was at least partially an attempt to expand a cramped Japanese economy by resorting to an openly military imperialism. And though the goal may have been to set up a mutually advantageous 'co-prosperity sphere', hundreds of thousands of Japanese had to be scattered over the Pacific to maintain political order. Yet ironically, the Japanese now – or soon will – draw far more from Pacific Asia than a successful establishment of their projected World War II empire might have brought them.

The Japanese believe that their deliberate 'low-profile' foreign policy and their de-emphasis of the military in the 1950s and 1960s are largely responsible for this success. We assume in this chapter that the Japanese will try to continue into the 1970s this remarkably successful policy. But as Japanese economic interests grow, they will inevitably affect more often – and more intensely – other nations with similar or conflicting interests. The problem today is becoming particularly important as Japan finds itself caught up in a dilemma brought about by its success – a dilemma viewed with some anxiety by many Japanese, as well as by many observers. Is it possible for Japan to become a top economic power in the world without an increased commitment to military and political influence? If so, will it be willing to do so? Should it be willing? Or to quote some common current Japanese clichés, 'Can Japan be a technological and economic giant while remaining a political and military pygmy?' 'Is this desirable?' Or, more bitingly, 'Should Japan continue to be an economic animal?' 'If the answer to any of these is negative then what should Japan's goals be?' 'How are they to be achieved?' And so on.

Let me assume that Japanese growth rates continue as I have described through the 70s and perhaps even into the 80s but that the Japanese do not make any special effort to convert their economic, technological, or financial capabilities into political or military advantages – indeed that they even try, to some extent, to avoid such conversion. It should be understood that despite much jubilation in Japan at its current success, this economic success is likely in the short run to re-raise all kinds of anxieties and self-doubts among Japanese élites. One such reaction will probably be exactly as suggested above: 'Let's retain the low posture, continue the economic growth, and move very gradually and carefully, deferring as much as possible all of the more controversial, or dangerous, decisions and programmes.'

It of course seems inevitable that even in this low-posture policy the Japanese would play a somewhat more active role than they have over the past twenty years. And some growth in political and military power is also almost inevitable. But I assume in this chapter that there will be only incremental changes in these variables or incremental effects from the changes made. Thus, the ties with the United States could be loosened somewhat to provide for greater independence and more competition – but nothing serious. There could also be a gradually strengthened military posture, but I assume here that the Japanese will eschew, at least for the time, the acquisition of nuclear weapons – or that if they do get nuclear weapons they will do so in a severely restricted form, e.g., just a small number for symbolic purposes or solely for anti-ballistic missile defence and as part of a low posture.

Four Japanese Economic Scenarios

In order to be more specific, let us consider four economic projections for the Gross National Product of Japan. We will start each of these scenarios with an assumed 1970 gross national product of $200 billion and anticipate growth rates such that by the end of the century Japan's GNP could be as low as $1½ trillion or as much as $4½ trillion.

The table opposite gives four representative 'surprise-free' projections.

The 'official' column is not really official, but it assumes over the next decade the same growth rate (10·6 per cent per annum) as that assumed for the next five years by the most recent official estimate of the Japanese Economic Planning Agency.[1]

The low projection assumes that in the next five years Japanese growth rates will average only 8·5 per cent – a drop of about one third from recent experience – and that these rates will decrease

Some Assumed Average Annual Growth Rates (in '70) for Japanese GNP 1970–2000

Fiscal Projection Period	Low	'Official'	Medium	High
1971–1975	8·5	10·6	11·8	14·9
1976–1980	7·5	10·6	11·4	13·4
1981–1985	6·5	8·5	10·8	11·6
1986–2000	4·0	6·0	7·5	8·7
1971–2000*	5·9	8·8	9·4	11

*i.e. An average growth rate for the entire period of next thirty years that gives same GNP in 2000 as the assumed pattern in the column above.

further until they reach an average of 4 per cent in the last fifteen years of the century, averaging 5·9 per cent over the period of 1971 to 2000. For the Japanese these would be low indeed, yet with such rates they should still achieve a GNP of $1·5 trillion in the year 2000. We can think of this first column, then, as being quite low but within the range expected by some Japanese experts.

The high projection is quite high, as it assumes that during the next five years the Japanese will average 14·4 per cent growth rates, or slightly more than their record in the last five years. But it is also what respectable and competent experts believe or accept as well within the range of serious considerations. The medium projection, which starts off at 11 per cent, I would consider the 'best guess.'

All four projections assume drops in the growth rate as time passes. Thus, it is thought that some of the factors mentioned as possible obstacles to growth will, in fact, begin to take effect – but mostly during the 80s and 90s and without having a decisive effect on the next five to ten year period.

The corresponding projections of Gross National Product in billions of 1970 dollars are given below:

Some Projections for Japanese GNP: 1970–2000*

Year	Low	'Official'	Medium	High
1970	200	200	200	200
1975	300	330	350	400
1980	450	550	600	750
1985	600	825	1,000	1,300
2000	1,500	2,000	3,000	4,500

*In 1970 dollars.

It should be noted, however, that the premise of the above table, that – with the single exception of the first five years of the high projection – future growth rates will not surpass the rates of the last five years and indeed will turn down in the near future, is, in fact, only an assumption. Indeed, the data would seem to suggest an increase before there is such topping out and more of a flattening than a turning down. Thus, while the high projection is relatively 'optimistic' (perhaps it might better be termed 'neutral') in terms of the maintenance of high Japanese growth rate to the end of the century, the other three projections are decidedly 'pessimistic' in assuming a pronounced dropping-off from current growth rates.

Thus, as mentioned, we assume that the initial 8·5 per cent in the low projection drops to 4 per cent in the last fifteen years, averaging 5·9 per cent over the entire period of thirty years; the initial 10·6 per cent in the 'official' projection drops to 6 per cent, averaging 8·8 per cent; the initial 11 per cent in the medium drops to 7·5 per cent, averaging 9·4 per cent; and the initial 14·9 per cent in the high drops to 8·7 per cent, averaging 11 per cent.

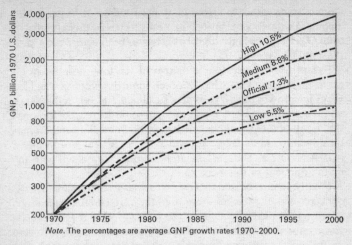

Some Scenarios for the Growth in Japanese GNP, 1970–2000

I believe that these four 'surprise-free' projections constitute a range that is probably wide enough to cover the reasonable possibilities – that is, despite the data indicating that all four projections are conservative, most serious observers of the Japanese economy would be a little surprised if Japanese performance were very much outside the indicated range. Our major interest, of course, is in the next five to fifteen years, where the high and low scenarios differ at most by a factor of only slightly more than two in 1985 (as opposed to a factor of three by the year 2000).*

As mentioned earlier, if I had to choose a best estimate, I would choose the medium one. In that scenario Japan probably passes the United States in per capita income around 1990 and probably equals the US in Gross National Product by about the year 2000.

In the 'official' scenario Japan is likely to catch up with the Soviet Union in Gross National Product, but not with the

---

* Since all projections are calculated in terms of 1970 dollars, if there is any inflation the actual numbers in current dollars, of course, would be higher.

United States either in Gross National Product or in per capita income. In the low scenario Japan fails to pass either country in total GNP; in the high, it probably passes both before the end of the century.

Except for the last decade or two of the low scenario, in all cases Japan grows by what in other countries would be judged very high growth rates if they were sustained. Indeed, in that sense all the scenarios are optimistic, even, to some degree, the low one: that is, all of them assume there will be no immediate and dramatic downturn in Japanese growth rates to typical European or American levels. Thus, *all the projections* are consistent with the main argument of this book.

Finally, it must be said that *all are 'scenarios'* – they are 'artists' conceptions' or sketches more than they are careful projections based on detailed calculations. However, I feel that I am experienced enough in these kinds of calculations to say that, if it were useful to do so, I could provide detailed arguments based only on reasonable and defendable assumptions which, used in numerical studies, would show how one could produce the results indicated in any one of the above scenarios. That is why I label all four as being 'surprise-free' projections.

There are a number of calculations – or elaborated scenarios – one might wish to carry through in a really thorough study of the implications of these scenarios. For example, one would be very interested in getting some sense of the 'mix' of Gross National Product able to give rise to the above, the possible changes of imports and exports, the way Japanese growth rates might influence the growth rates of other countries, and the interactions of the above with all kinds of political situations and political changes. In most cases high Japanese growth rates are likely to increase the growth rates of other countries by supplying them with both advantageous markets and cheap goods. In a few cases they might interfere with another nation's normal trade patterns by taking its markets, or with a nation's foreign imports by driving up prices through competitive buying. In almost all cases – even where Japanese growth is, on balance, beneficial, it is likely to cause much disruption and turmoil and to hurt individual groups and persons. Most important of all, as discussed in the next section, the Japanese hope to have their enormous future economic growth without disastrous effects in the home islands in terms of pollution, ecological destruction, and so on.

Japan's New Comprehensive National Development Plan

One of the most interesting things about Japan's current growth rate is that the Japanese are probably more aware than the rest of the world that their growth is lopsided and in many ways 'misleading' – or at least the Japanese make more references to it. I have argued earlier that the case is often overstated – that so many Europeans look at Japan with European spectacles often tinted with Marxist or certain liberal progressive biases, that the Japanese intellectuals definitely have these biases, and finally, that the well-known 'Japanese inferiority complex' causes excessive agreement by the Japanese with such comments from outside visitors. None of this denies that there are serious deficits in Japanese living conditions (which are about on a par with those of the Soviet Union) – in public utilities of all sorts, overcrowding, pollution, and so on. The Japanese now feel that they are rich enough to do something about all this. And since it is worth doing, there is nothing odd in their decision to start focusing attention and resources on the physical and social environment. However, insofar as this decision was motivated by a drive to still criticism, I suspect that it was motivated as much or more by the negative remarks of visiting Western intellectuals as by indigenous pressures. Whatever the reasons, the Japanese have decided to stop their relative neglect of these issues.

The new Comprehensive National Plan, adopted in May 1969 and now being worked on, is intended, as far as I can see, to make Japan into a kind of a garden spot. If it succeeds, the Japanese will not only be able to enjoy the results by the end of the century, they will be able to say to the rest of the world, 'Not only can we equal you in economic development, but we can do it without wrecking the country, the environment, and the general amenities of living.' This will double their enjoyment of the plan's results.

The new plan is designed to show 'the basic direction of general land development' and the 'allocation of social capital' through 1985. More specifically, it seeks to 'maintain harmony between humanity and nature' by promoting more effective utilization of land and greater regional development. It is a blueprint for the rational and efficient de-centralization of the entire country, tying all areas together into a rather closely knit but de-centralized unit. For example, the Japanese expect that no place in the country will be more than six hours by train from any other, even without introducing new super-high-speed trains. And with such trains that time may be cut in half.

After these new railroads and other amenities have been constructed, the Japanese, who currently use about one third of their available area, will be able to use all parts of Japan quite intensely. And while they will not redistribute themselves uniformly, they will redistribute themselves enough to reduce current densities and still maintain very civilized travel and communication systems. And if some of the present systems are any harbinger, these will be substantially more civilized than anything available in the West.

Probably something on that order is their only remedy to the tremendous problem of urban congestion. The Comprehensive Plan notes that roughly 63 per cent of the total population and nearly 84 per cent of the industrial output are concentrated in only 31 per cent of the nation's total area, primarily around the nation's two biggest cities, Tokyo and Osaka. This, of course, is not uncommon; almost any Latin American country has a higher concentration – and usually around only one city. But in Japan's case, the problems have become really crucial. Tokyo, in particular, offers a dismal prospect for the future. It is already the largest city in the world and while probably not the most densely populated, it is grossly overcrowded by civilized standards. Under current conditions, Tokyo's population may very well reach 25 million by 1985, an astounding figure even by today's norms.

As always, if the Japanese display their 'unsurpassed capacity for purposeful communal action', they will probably carry through their 'national network for systematized integration of central management functions and of physical distribution structure'. Indeed, their solution to all these current problems of civilization are likely to be an aesthetic and cultural delight as well as an economic, technological, and engineering miracle. They are now preparing actually to install, not just to talk about, a modern communications, transportation, and distribution system using the latest available technology that will facilitate and encourage a greater dispersion of both population and industry throughout the country. The plan and visions of these new systems will be extended by the development of a number of new regional urban centres to provide the surrounding areas with the same convenient services offered today in the major cities. This will involve nationwide, real time data transmission systems – i.e., reliable and practically instantaneous communication networks, improved inner-city and intra-city transportation, and all kinds of new port facilities on both coasts. It is quite possible that if these objectives or some equivalent are not achieved, the Japanese economic growth might be significantly affected, because the industrial sector will literally be running out of inexpensive, usable room for expansion. But under this plan all four islands will be contributing heavily to the Gross National Product as well as to better amenities and a higher standard of living generally.

I emphasize again, however, that the economic and technological aspects are only part of the plan. Virtually every other area of national activity, from the aesthetic through the cultural to the recreational, is covered. The plan seems far more ambitious and daring than anything in the United States or in any other country that I am familiar with. Further, I suspect that unlike the situation in most other countries, this one will be taken quite seriously. It really is a kind of a blueprint – not necessarily a precise blueprint of the future, but one that supplies good guidelines as to what the Japanese can expect. Naturally, as time passes, the Japanese will adapt, modify, and generally be creative. But this plan is a broad overview surveying the country as an integral unit and mapping out in flexible detail a reasonable and attractive future course for the country.

Japan and Non-Communist Pacific Asia (*NOCPA*)

The term 'Pacific Asia' seems first to have been used by Prime Minister Eisaku Sato at the Fourth Ministerial Meeting of the Asian and Pacific Council, ASPAC, held June 9, 1969. If we modify the term by adding 'non-Communist', then it includes the non-Communist parts of East Asia, South-east Asia, Australia, New Zealand, and the Pacific Islands east of the 180° longitude line and includes, as given below, fourteen countries. If we were to add China to this group we would have substantially the old East Asia Co-prosperity Sphere as it was defined in wartime Japanese policy.

I have already mentioned that economically the Japanese probably draw more today from Non-Communist Pacific Asia (or NOCPA for short) than they could have reasonably expected to gain from the success of the old Japanese war goal of establishing a Japanese-dominated co-prosperity sphere. In particular, Australia almost certainly will supply, if it does not already, more coal and iron ore (or its equivalent) than Japan could have expected from a puppet China – and supply them very inexpensively through modern large-scale mining techniques, the economics of mass ocean transport, and the Japanese predilection for oceanside plants.

We therefore must note at the start that not only have the Japanese achieved in NOCPA at least the economic equivalent of their old co-prosperity sphere, but they have done it without serious exploitation of any country in NOCPA. Indeed, Japan today has about one third of its foreign trade with NOCPA (exports and imports) and has attained that volume of trade (about $10,231 million annually) without, as yet, stepping severely on any toes or getting mixed up in serious quarrels, though there have been many incidents and rising currents of anxiety. Such rising anxiety is almost inevitable as the area awaits, almost fearfully, the enormous expansion of Japanese economic and financial influence – and, of course, some degree of political and military influence.

Despite the enormous diversity represented by these fourteen countries, it will sometimes be useful for us to look at them as an aggregated group, and at other times to think of them in three separate groups. In this latter case we can think first of the eleven countries in 'developing NOCPA': Burma, Cambodia, Taiwan, South Vietnam, Hong Kong, Indonesia, South Korea, Malaysia, Philippines, Singapore, and Thailand. These are in a very good position, in most cases, to furnish not only raw materials to Japan, but even more important, relatively inexpensive and skilled labour for the labour intensive portion of the Japanese productive cycle (and perhaps also for those activities which result in excessive pollution or other undesirable by-products for a highly advanced and concentrated nation). The second group of nations, New Zealand and Australia, is basically European in culture. But rather interestingly their major relationship with Japan is likely to be that of supplying raw materials and perhaps the early stages of manufactured products, i.e., improved raw materials. Then finally, of course, there is Japan itself.

I give below one conceivable scenario of how these three areas might develop in terms of the standard gross indices of population, GNP per capita, and GNP itself.

DEVELOPING NOCPA

Year	Population	Per Capita Income	Total GNP
1970	310	200	62
1980	400	400	160
1990	500	800	400
2000	600	1,600	960

For Australia and New Zealand we have a similar optimistic but not implausible economic scenario, while for Japan we will assume medium projection.

AUSTRALIA AND NEW ZEALAND

Year	Population	Per Capita Income	Total GNP
1970	15	3,000	45
1980	18	4,500	81
1990	21	7,000	147
2000	25	10,000	250

DEVELOPING JAPAN

Year	Population	Per Capita Income	Total GNP
1970	103·5	1,950	202
1980	114	5,000	570
1990	122	10,000	1,100
2000	128	20,000	2,500

I have deliberately kept the numbers rough, in order to emphasize the largely intuitive and subjective element in these projections. However, they are all consistent with some of the more detailed scenarios which we have done elsewhere. However, the scenario for that part of NOCPA which we call 'Developing NOCPA' is somewhat more optimistic in terms of GNP per capita than the relatively detailed scenarios for this region given in the appendix. (The two scenarios assume basically the same population growth until 1980 and then there is a somewhat more rapid tapering off of the population growth in the one given above, as well as a somewhat more rapid increase in total GNP.)

The economic scenario for developing NOCPA seems to me to be a perfectly reasonable one, in fact very much a surprise-free projection, given the likely impacts of Japanese and other investment in this area, of Japanese and Western managerial techniques generally, and of other plausible stimuli to economic development. In fact, it also seems quite likely, as discussed later, that the Japanese trading companies might tie the entire area together into what would be basically one economic unit – stimulating economic activity everywhere (but raising all kinds of other issues as well).

Thus, there is nothing fantastic in assuming that both Japan and the area as a whole grow in gross national product by about 7–8 per cent a year. In our calculations such regions as Hong Kong were assumed to attain growth rates of greater than 10 per cent; such areas as Taiwan, Thailand, South Korea, and, eventually, South Vietnam and Singapore were assumed to grow at approximately 10 per cent; while the rest of the region was mostly assumed to be between five and eight per cent.

We have indicated that the above projections are relatively optimistic in terms of economic growth, but it is also clear that they may still turn out to have been almost grossly understated, particularly if we have underestimated the full potential impact of the various stimuli. In particular, Indonesia might do a lot better than we have assumed (about 4 per cent from 1970 to 1975, 5 per cent from 1975 to 1980, and 7 per cent from 1980 to 2000). A large increase in Indonesian performance would make a very great difference since Indonesia contains about a third of the population of the region and important human and material resources.

It would also be relatively easy to imagine that Australia grows substantially more rapidly than projected above, particularly if she allows a certain amount of immigration from other Asian nations. This might be done in such a way as to keep any particular minority group rather small and, given the likelihood that these groups will rise to the top rapidly, it seems quite plausible that Australia would keep its largely European character and not generate any special kinds of minority problems. On the other hand, one can easily imagine that adding about 50,000 or so hard working, diligent, thrifty and dynamic Asians to the population every year (one or two million over the 30 years) would really spur economic development enormously and allow the Australians to partake much more fully and fruitfully in the economic and cultural life of the area.

Japan also has a large shortage problem, but is even less likely than Australia to be interested in allowing, much less stimulating, any kind of Chinese immigration no matter how controlled. It is thus easy to imagine that Japan ends up as a country with a high per capita income but at the same time with a corresponding expensive labour force so that within the next thirty years there is a great change in one of the most basic characteristics of Japan – the availability of high quality, inexpensive labour for industry, commerce, and personal services. This last, by itself, may encourage a large-scale migration, or at least make temporary overseas assignment very desirable, for those Japanese who would like to live – even temporarily – in a grand style which may seem almost impossible in Japan itself. (The US, of course, has already gone through this change and Europe is doing so currently. Developed Europe, of course, has large sources of inexpensive labour available from relatively undeveloped European areas. And, indeed, European nations are encouraging, at least for the time being, a relatively large-scale movement of such people.

One of the most important issues of the future – as discussed below – and one which current Hudson Institute studies are focusing a special effort on, are the various kinds of political, economic, social, cultural, and even personal issues that are almost certain to arise as a result of this kind of potential Japanese economic predominance and pervasive presence in NOCPA.

On the one hand, the leaders of NOCPA would like to keep their relations with Japan strictly economic and cool, fearful of getting too deeply involved with this future economic giant – particularly given their memories of the Pacific War and the war-time co-prosperity sphere. On the other hand, they complain of insufficient Japanese aid, arguing over and over again that there really is no Japanese aid programme, only a 'foreign trade promotion campaign'.

Yet it should be emphasized that from many reasonable economic and administrative points of view, current Japanese arrangements with NOCPA are substantially more viable and sensible than the wartime co-prosperity sphere, and therefore it would not be too surprising if there were little or no pressure in Japan to 'take over' the area. In World War II, it took a large navy and several million men to garrison and protect the wartime empire. The economic contribution of the inhabitants was often delivered resentfully and at a very low rate of efficiency. In the 70s and 80s, by using normal contractual and quid pro quo arrangements, Japan presumably will possess substantially the same access to these resources and raw materials. Obviously the terms will be somewhat different, but from the viewpoint of the Japanese businesses involved and of the Japanese economy as a whole, they will really be much better terms; they will provide much greater returns and efficiency than could have been the case through wartime conquest, or possibly even through a successful development into a political empire. Under current conditions, the Japanese will have to make many concessions, but they also have powerful bargaining levers, since the relationship really is a two-way trade. In fact, the Japanese will be making these areas quite wealthy at the same time they are making themselves superbly wealthy. If the Japanese operate in sensitive areas mostly through joint enterprise and with local capital (or with various other kinds of local participation), they are likely to find at least this aspect of their operations relatively acceptable to all the nations concerned – as long as they follow local standards, do not throw their weight around too much, and are not too pervasive and ubiquitous.

The history of the NOCPA area since the war has been one of violence and turmoil, and it seems quite likely that this violence and turmoil will continue. In many ways, it is one of the most explosive areas in the world. However, despite the great general interest in the area and despite the enormous investment of the United States in South Vietnam, there are probably no vital economic or strategic interests in this region for any of the large nations of the world, with the possible exception of Japan. (There are, of course, many important, if not vital US political, moral, and morale interests.) For this reason, the conflicts in this area are not as escalation-prone as they might be. But troubles may arise.

I made the point earlier that the Japanese will probably be much more intimately involved in local economies in the NOCPA area than the Americans are likely to be. First of all, it is traditional for the Americans to avoid dealing directly with small firms; rather, they generally deal through middlemen. Not only do the Japanese often act as their own middlemen, but they even participate directly in the operation of final outlets. In many cases they buy into local firms, using either joint ventures or total purchase, and try to get a very firm foothold in the day-to-day economy. Sometimes this method of operation makes them less visible and more acceptable. However, if they do not go to great lengths to use indigenous personnel at all levels of operation and management, then the use of local firms and joint enterprises if pushed very far may make their physical presence, their perceived presence, and their vulnerability to the details of every local regulation much greater than that of the Americans.

In any case, it is very likely that the Japanese will soon be dominating much of the region economically in many of the same ways as the overseas Chinese used to dominate some of it. For example, once a large trading company such as Mitsui or Mitsubishi has offices in every important part of the region, it might use its offices for intra-regional and international transactions that have no other direct connection with any Japanese firms and for furnishing services to non-Japanese.

One should note that if the Japanese trading companies get to have a pervasive influence and centrality to the economy of NOCPA (in some cases just in the internal trade of these nations and in other cases in their foreign trade), this is likely to give the Japanese opportunities for enormous economic leverage and influence on the firms and countries in the NOCPA area. And that is a leverage and influence the Japanese would do well not to abuse – or possibly not to use at all except for the most straightforward and legitimate of purposes. Indeed, Japanese trading companies, combined with small Japanese entrepreneurs, might eventually acquire monopoly positions in almost all trade and commerce in many areas and/or activities. That is particularly likely – and intolerable – if, as has been customary, the Japanese tend to be clannish and work closely together against all competitors. I have already mentioned how irritating the clannishness of the overseas Chinese has often been to their host countries. A similar Japanese clannishness in this case could be much more aggravating or disquieting. The local Japanese could easily find themselves as exposed and disliked as the traditional Chinese merchant has often been in these areas and, therefore, they could possibly be, even if unfairly, obvious scapegoats for all kinds of issues. And it should be noted that the Asian origin of the Japanese will not alleviate this problem much, if at all.

Of course, many Japanese hold the theory that because they are Asians they understand the Asian mind much better than Westerners do. The fact seems to be that they do understand well those aspects of Asia in which practices are very similar to those in Japan. But in matters where the Japanese differ markedly from other Asian societies, which are at least as numerous, the Japanese seem to know less than those Westerners who have some knowledge. In part, this is simply because of their misplaced confidence in their being able to learn anything about Asia by simple introspection and without having to make any special effort. The state of Asian studies in Japan is, on the whole, rather low, and this shows up in a good deal of Japanese discussion of Asian issues.

The Japanese may try to create some kind of exclusivity or preference in the NOCPA trading area, perhaps a customs union of some type, or something modelled on, for example, the European Economic Community, or at least a free-trade or near free-trade area. Unlike the EEC, this area would be, of course, almost completely dominated by its leading economy – i.e., Japan. But the formal language and the formal institutions could pay a great deal of lip service and even lend some reality to the concept of relative equality among the members, thereby making it much more acceptable politically. But no matter how it is done, NOCPA is almost certainly going to be an economic hinterland of – and workshop for – Japan, yet most likely one that will not be seriously exploited in the pejorative sense. Indeed, it will probably be rewarded for its efforts and be largely politically free to make its own choices – as long as those choices do not disturb the basic stability and prosperity of the area.

It should be noted that political influence can accrue even if it is not desired – for example, simply because the Japanese will be important. People will be interested in Japanese views and attitudes and in getting more accurate expectations about future Japanese behaviour. That in turn means they will be consulting the Japanese, and the Japanese will often be listened to with respect. Such situations can involve the Japanese to some degree in the political consequences of their advice, even if it was given only on request and with no intention of getting involved. And of course it is most unlikely that the Japanese will always be this self-restrained and self-disciplined.

One thing that might make an enormous immediate difference to many countries in the area is a Japanese concession on opening up their domestic market to rice from other countries. Under the current situation the Japanese subsidize their domestic rice production at a cost of several hundreds of millions of dollars a year. One of the main reasons for subsidization has been that voters in the rural areas tended to vote for the Liberal Democratic Party and it made political sense to support them. But many of them seemed to shift their allegiance when they went to the cities. And the disparity of opportunities and living standards between the countryside and the cities has become so great that many more of these voters are quite anxious to move to the cities. In addition, the last election indicated that the trend toward the Japanese Socialist Party is somewhat weakened or perhaps even no longer present. Under these circumstances, the Japanese can afford to make 'a concession' that would look very generous to the other nations of the area. In fact, however, it would make complete economic sense from their own point of view – making needed labour available for their industries, saving a great deal of money in government subsidies, and at the same time creating new trading opportunities with important countries in NOCPA.

Further, if Japan takes some interest in the welfare of the area as a whole, its position in NOCPA may turn out to be something like the position of the United States in South America. There are, however, important differences. First of all, the probable NOCPA fear of a potential or eventual revival of Japanese military aggression is likely to be much greater than the corresponding South American fear of the United States, although the fear of various other kinds of illegitimate interventions may be lower. Secondly, the large and continuing presence of the United States, China, and the Soviet Union in Asia, and the level of industrial advancement and modernization in Pacific Asia as compared to Latin America, are likely to make the Pacific Asian nations more resistant and self-confident in dealings with Japan than most Latin American countries have been in their dealings with the US.

It now seems reasonable that if nothing intervenes to disturb the stability of the area, the Japanese in the 70s and early 80s will invest a great deal of money, certainly a few billion, more likely something in the region of $5 to $10 billion, and perhaps much more, in NOCPA. One result of this enormous investment will be a very close tying of this area to Japan (and, to a somewhat lesser degree, vice versa). In fact, I would guess that by about

1980, from 40 to 50 per cent of all Japanese imports and exports will be with NOCPA. That is, in the same way that Japan is now tied to the US because we buy and sell about 30 per cent of her imports and exports, so Pacific Asia is likely to be tied to Japan.

It seems clear that in any case the Japanese foreign aid programme will grow, although Japanese aid now is more in the form of hard loans and normal commercial credit than the kind of thing usually thought of as foreign aid.* There seems to be no particular reason why most of this aid should be given on substantially better terms than it is today, but some of it probably will be.

It seems likely, then, that with or without aid programmes – and even without major rearmament – the Japanese will become the overwhelmingly important power in the area. There will still be a large US economic presence in Pacific Asia and possibly a dominating US military presence. There will also be an economic and political, and perhaps even military, presence of Europe and to some degree of China and the Soviet Union as well. But the Japanese presence will predominate. It might not be as pervasive and suffocating as the US presence has sometimes been in Latin America, or it may be even more so. The Japanese are likely to be less scrupulous, and more skilful, than the American government in using economic power, including the ability to exploit existing corruption and carry out other local financial interventions.

Further, in the past the Japanese trading firms and other businesses have been quite responsive not only to the need and objectives of their co-nationals, but also to the Japanese government in general, and they have often helped other Japanese businessmen – sometimes to the detriment of non-Japanese customers, suppliers, or competitors. If the trading companies

---

*One can make an argument that these 'hard-headed' Japanese aid policies are often better for both sides than the softer loans (and gifts) that have been characteristic of US, French, German, and British foreign aid. Their policy forces a much closer examination of the project, in particular the ability of the project to repay the loan. One of the real problems in many other aid programmes is that even though aid is often granted on very soft terms, the projects are so poor from the economic point of view that they cannot repay even the soft loans.

do attain such a commanding economic position and yet continue a policy of almost always acting in the narrow Japanese interests or those of their clients, rather than in the interests of the area as a whole, then they are likely to arouse enormous animosity even though they perform extremely useful economic functions. Therefore, despite the traditional Japanese emphasis on personal relationships and on not looking at situations in terms of clear-cut standards and rules, it will be of extreme importance for Japanese trading companies in particular to behave as good world and regional citizens – or at least as non-ethnic businesses. There are, incidentally, signs that various Japanese businesses are beginning to do this – it is likely to be more a question of degree than of kind.

Given all the possibilities for friction and concern, it is more than conceivable that some NOCPA nations – or even local areas – will rebel against Japanese economic domination or at least attempt to restrain the Japanese. And the Japanese may find this extremely irksome. For example, the Australians now furnish both coal and iron to the Japanese. At some point they may decide to process these commodities in their own countries and perhaps export only iron pellets to the Japanese; or they might even wish to export finished steel. If this were done suddenly or without coordination with the Japanese, it might cause the forced obsolescence of a good deal of Japanese capital in the steel industry. If the Japanese believed, correctly or incorrectly, that they had been misled about the assurance of supplies from Australia, they would feel very aggrieved.

There could also be incidents between Japanese businessmen and tourists and the local inhabitants. And it is possible that countries like North or even South Korea will create *Pueblo*-type incidents involving the Japanese. The Japanese are not likely to take this as calmly as the Americans (and the Americans did not take it very calmly – one poll indicated that 50 per cent of all Americans expected to go to war). In particular, the Japanese cannot be expected to accept offences against honour or 'face'. And if they did not obtain immediate revenge, it would be in the Japanese tradition for the wrong to 'bear interest' so that when it is finally righted it could be a very large 'righting' indeed.

It is clear, then, that there are all kinds of potential problems that could arise out of Japan's economic and technological domination of NOCPA – in particular, that it could easily result in political and perhaps military domination by the Japanese too, even in the absence of any threats from the Chinese or others. In the case of such threats, the Japanese might take actions that are welcome to the country concerned but that later lead to an undesired presence of Japanese military power or of economic and military advisory programmes.

Certainly any 'classical' analyst looking at this situation would conclude, therefore, that unless countervailing powers appear this region is designed for Japanese domination. However, many of the things we have studied at Hudson Institute about the 70s and 80s lead me to argue that this is by no means inevitable. Conditions really have changed. It is both more possible and more likely than most would imagine that the Japanese will find desirable and feasible a basically commercial quid pro quo relationship, and that the rest of the powers in NOCPA will want to cultivate such a relationship and take care not to tempt or provoke the Japanese into rocking the boat.

Another important possibility for alleviating the impact of the Japanese presence is for Japan and/or the United States – perhaps intentionally, perhaps accidentally – to make Pacific Asia into an integral part of a larger entity that we can think of as the 'Pacific Basin Community,' composed of states bordering the Pacific Ocean. This Pacific Basin Community, even excluding the USSR, Communist Korea, and China, contained as of 1967 something like 22 per cent of the world's people and something like 44 per cent of the world's GNP. If one adds the Soviet Union into the Pacific Basin Community, that would increase people to 29 per cent and GNP to 58 per cent, giving it at least economic leadership.

The Pacific Basin

Interestingly enough, in the 70s and 80s the three dominant powers in the Pacific Basin are also likely to be the three dominant powers in the world. They may find that in the Pacific Basin they have almost no interests in serious conflict – that all can work together in a remarkably smooth manner, emphasizing the rule of international law and regional stability. This working arrangement in the Pacific may not extend to the rest of the world, but on the other hand, except for potential US–Soviet conflicts in Europe and the Middle East, there have been few points of intense conflict that are likely to remain so in the 70s and 80s. In any case, it is clear that this concept of a Pacific Basin may seize the imagination of many.

A concept that might well dominate Japanese thinking would be the argument that the age of the Pacific has arrived – that just as the centre of world power and dynamism once moved from the Mediterranean to the North Atlantic, it now has moved to the Pacific Ocean. I am reminded of a story about a Japanese taxi driver who told an American scholar, 'We democracies must stick together.' When asked which democracies he meant, the taxi driver replied, 'Japan, the US, Canada and Australia.' This is not as idiosyncratic a position as might be imagined. Many Japanese think quite naturally in these terms. If to this is added Latin America, we have a most impressive area of the world. From the viewpoint of the Japanese, although they will do a good deal of trade with the Middle East (for oil) and with Europe, this Pacific community could seem exactly the proper focus of ambitions and identity.

One can imagine a fairly complex trading community here with long-term assurances – on which all parties can rely – of satisfactory terms of investment, tariffs, trade, etc. Undoubtedly some kind of programme could be worked out to include the Latin American nations, which should encourage a great increase both in US and Japanese investment in Latin America. (That would also probably be accompanied by German and other European investment, so in effect the Latin Americans would have three or more centres of power to play off against one another.) In any case, it seems to me almost certain that by 1980 or soon afterward the United States will be displaced, at least in Brazil, by the Japanese as the major outside investor. One could also imagine the Japanese playing a major role in financing the Choco Valley Canal through Colombia, thus supplying themselves with an alternative to the Panama Canal. It seems clear that the Japanese will eventually make themselves responsible for the development of some major areas and industries (including recreation and exploitation of natural resources) in Alaska and Western Canada, and no doubt they will do similar things in parts of Latin America.

Japanese tourism could also be important in developing the Pacific Basin Community. With the further development of airline traffic, long-distance fares across the Pacific will probably go down by a factor of two or three; supersonic airplanes will bring the time for these trips down by a factor of two or three, and connections will no doubt become more frequent and convenient. Under these circumstances air travel is likely to increase enormously – literally by factors of ten to one hundred – and the Pacific Basin may become a new Mediterranean Lake.

If, in addition to this, the Japanese–Soviet Economic Commission manages in the next few years to be very successful (and they have already started a number of projects, including building a seaport in Siberia and development of Siberian forestry resources), the Japanese may become heavily involved in Soviet Siberian development. The Japanese are then likely to think of themselves as a bridge between the United States and the Soviet Union and, in fact, the arrangement might well serve in this way. The Japanese could then feel that they are a member of the superpower club – but not quite a full member. Or, if they manage to use their unarmed or limited armed condition as an asset and take initiatives in arms control measures or regional measures of various sorts, they could turn their nuclear innocence (or nuclear weakness or nuclear restraint) into an asset in political relations in the Pacific. Thus, this 'new Mediterranean' might be a fantastic new culture or civilization – a creative and dynamic union between the East and the West.

Hybrid cultures have often been very vigorous, and we can imagine an especially vigorous Japan, which is its own mixture of East and West. From the East would also come other influences and ingredients – a basically Chinese and Indian culture, with the Chinese elements coming less from mainland China than from Japan, South Korea, Taiwan, Hong Kong, Singapore, and

so on. The West, of course, is represented by a very new West –
Canadians, Australians, North Americans, and Latin Americans,
rather than Europeans. To some degree, the Soviets can also be
added to the pot, perhaps being, say, 10 per cent in and 90 per
cent out, but adding and getting a very important culture influence. The 'new Mediterranean', then, might well be in the twenty-
first century the creative centre of the post-industrial culture and
civilization: a true worldwide cosmopolitan culture that would
put Europe and Africa into a peripheral position. Given the probable nature of modern communications and the expected very
high economic growth rate among all the Chinese culture areas
outside mainland China, something like this seems inevitable.
Even Honolulu and Hong Kong may in their separate ways
represent much more the wave of the future than anyone has yet
dreamed.

Many people may object that I leave mainland China out of
this fascinating new centre of activity. It is not by neglect but by
intention that I do so, and not because I want mainland China
to be absent. In some ways, I admire Chinese culture even more
than Japanese culture. But I believe the Chinese would choose to
be left out of this Pacific community. And this raises the question
of the future relationships between the Chinese People's Republic
and Japan.

Chinese (CPR)–Japanese Relations

We must note at the start that many Japanese feel a basic affinity
with the Chinese, often making the point that there is really only
'one alphabet, one tribe.' They refer to the fact that traditional
Japanese culture is derived from China, much as Western culture
is derived from Rome and Greece, and that the Japanese use
Chinese characters in their language. In addition, many Japanese
claim to have a sense of guilt about the way Japan treated China
before and during World War II. Finally, many Japanese are
entranced by the sight of a united and powerful Communist
China that demands and gets respect from much of the rest of the
world.

Despite these affinities, the two countries today are barely on speaking terms and technically are still in a state of war. A formal peace treaty has never been signed by the two governments, nor have they succeeded in establishing diplomatic relations. The only formal contacts have been on a semi-official basis, and these discussions have been primarily confined to bilateral trade. On the average of once a year, a delegation of Japanese politicians journeys to Peking to negotiate the annual trade agreements and inevitably to hear the latest Chinese political conditions for an improvement in Sino-Japanese relations. The Japanese government, however, has refused to accept the Chinese view that politics and economics are inseparable and has consistently maintained that trade is only possible on a completely non-political basis. The Chinese have accepted this in principle but not in practice, so the same political demands are raised each year when the trade agreement is re-negotiated.

One of the major demands has involved credits and deferred payments. For political reasons, the Japanese government has refused to allow the Japanese Export–Import Bank to subsidize large Chinese purchases of sophisticated machinery and equipment, which has frustrated Peking's attempts to import ships and entire synthetic fibre plants. This has certainly inhibited the growth of Sino-Japanese trade somewhat, but not entirely. In fact, between 1962 and 1969 trade between the two nations increased by 750 per cent, from $84·5 million to $625·0 million. In 1969 alone, trade increased by 20·2 per cent. Yet in the Japanese fiscal year 1968 trade with China represented only 2·5 per cent of total Japanese exports and 1·8 per cent of Japanese imports. Inevitably this trade was far more important to the Chinese. Roughly 12 per cent of China's total exports were shipped to Japan in 1968, while approximately 22 per cent of its imports came from Japan. Over-all trade with Japan represented about 15 per cent of China's total trade for 1968. Japanese exports in 1968 were mostly steel and iron products, in addition to large-scale chemical shipments. Japanese imports consisted mostly of coal, pig iron, rice, and other agricultural products. A more comprehensive account of Sino-Japanese trade 1962–9 is offered in the Notes for this chapter.

The statistics, however, do not tell the entire story. In recent years, for example, most of this trade has been carried on outside the official trade agreement, by the so-called 'friendly firms' who deal directly with the Chinese. Until 1965 their share of Sino-Japanese trade was about 50 per cent, but in 1966 it increased to 67 per cent and then in 1967 to 72·3 per cent. Many of these 'friendly firms' have been set up by the huge Japanese conglomerates for the express purpose of dealing with China. And until the late 1960s when the Chinese attitude began to change, this arrangement was quite satisfactory to all concerned. The Chinese, however, were determined to make some modifications in the nature of the trade so as to introduce some political element into their relations with the Japanese and thereby put the Tokyo government at a disadvantage.

The Chinese employed several tactics to achieve this goal. They continued, of course, to demand outright political concessions, which the Japanese predictably rejected. But the Japanese were less able to resist certain unilateral moves by the Chinese, as in 1968 when the original agreement of 1962 formalizing trade between the two nations came up for renewal. The Chinese deliberately downgraded the status of the new agreement and refused to extend it beyond one year, which added considerably to their leverage over the Japanese. For one thing, it meant that the Japanese would have to return to Peking each year – and then only when they received some form of invitation – to negotiate an entirely new agreement, enduring the familiar hardships of negotiating with the Chinese in their own capital. At the same time – and this also tended to detract from the importance of the new trade agreement – the Chinese began to place increasing emphasis on trade with the 'friendly firms' – but with new conditions. In what seemed to be an attempt to invest the political attitudes of the major Japanese firms trading with China, the Chinese made new demands on the 'friendly firms' and on the participating firms they represented by insisting that representatives of the participating companies themselves come to China. Thus, the situation became increasingly difficult for many of these firms, so much so that the Daichi Trading Company, a 'friendly firm' subsidiary of Mitsui, was forced to cease operations entirely.

Such attempts to use trade for political manipulation – to influence both Japan's domestic and foreign policies – seem certain to continue in some form so long as the character of the Chinese régime remains as it is today. Nor is it clear that the kind of change in China that Mao Tse-tung's death is likely to bring will alter this aspect of Chinese conduct, for the Chinese attitude reflects certain basic elements in the ideology between the two states. China is big, poor, traditionally isolationist and xeno-phobic, politically radical, and austere. Japan is rich, an ocean-going trading nation, closely tied to the capitalist economies of the West, and rapidly 'Westernizing' in important ways at all levels of society.

Despite all this, and despite its increased strength, status, and pride, Japan probably will remain – at least for the immediate future – quite anxious to get along with Communist China – to get along at least as well as it has got along in the recent past, and possibly better. But there are many complexities to this relation-ship. Among them are some issues of Chinese People's Republic–Japanese rivalry in which the initiative seems likely to come from the Chinese. I will focus on these issues not because I think they necessarily will be the most important ones in determining future relations between Japan and Communist China (though they may well turn out to be important) but because I want to raise some almost undiscussed matters that seem to be worth emphasiz-ing.

In some ways the Chinese are one of the proudest peoples in the world, almost as anxious for prestige as the Japanese. Tradition-ally they have thought of themselves as the 'Middle Kingdom,' the centre of civilization and culture, and Communist China definitely reflects this concept. Yet today, the Japanese have an economy probably twice the size of that of Communist China – or more – and are growing at about two or three times the rate of the Chinese People's Republic. It is soon going to be increasingly clear, at least to foreigners, that Japan, not China, is the big power of Asia.

Communist China, therefore, may simply choose not to com-pete in these terms with such a formidable opponent. (They may attempt the same solution to their similar problem in relation to the Soviet Union and the West.) Communist Chinese leaders may argue out of a centuries-old Chinese concept that the important criteria by which a culture, a society, a nation is measured are not the crude indices of GNP or general use of Western materialistic technology, but the quality of human life, of culture and society. From Communist China's viewpoint, it is possible that a good Chinese government may judge that all it owes its peasants is adequate food, adequate clothing, adequate shelter, adequate medical care, and a reasonably good chance for bright people to obtain an advanced education. ('Adequate' refers, of course, not to American but to Chinese standards.) All of these are probably now available to the mainland Chinese – or will soon be – and are likely to continue to be available.

From this point of view, then, the pressure may not be for accelerated growth rates, but towards issues and criteria of another sort. The Chinese may want to suppress what they see as the artificial values and decadent demands of Western industrial society. They may want – or need – to emphasize that China is lean, hard, purposeful, dedicated, austere, ascetic, and *serious*, and that the capitalistic nations (and 'revisionist', Soviet-style Communist states) are decadent, corrupt, and materialistic. They may wish to continue the slogans of the Cultural Revolution: 'Ideology and production, but ideology before production'; 'Red and expert, but red before expert'. Indeed, the Chinese government may want to add to the list of items the government owes the average peasant a very important one, 'protection from the corruption of the West'.

It may seem particularly important to the Communist Chinese to make this argument with regard to those enclaves in Southeast and East Asia that enjoy a better economic performance than theirs. The Hong Kong Chinese today have a per capita income of around $500 and seem likely to rapidly increase that. The Chinese in Singapore are doing very well. Such countries as South Korea, Taiwan, Malaysia, Thailand (with about 3 million ethnic Chinese) are growing at a rate of about 10 per cent per year and are also likely to continue doing very well – particularly, as we have indicated, if the Japanese have large capital resources available and invest in these countries.

Thus, capitalist Japan may play an increasingly important role in accelerating the economic growth and general prosperity of these countries on the east, south-east, and south rim of China. It may then become important to the Chinese to single out the Japanese as the 'corruptors' of Asia – as the agents of the neo-imperialist West and perhaps even of a revisionist Soviet Union. The Japanese then will be subject to condemnation as 'lackeys of the West', 'running dogs of the Americans', 'renegade exploiters of Asia'. In short, there may develop in Asia a conflict of values far more subtle than simple politics and economics. And China may serve as a powerful inciter and organizer of indigenous and international forces of reaction against a simplistic view of modernization or Westernization that equates 'progress' with materialist affluence and technological competency.

China already has explicitly rejected these values, at least as overriding, and has put forth its own claims to represent a unique and superior form of modernity. This may be generally persuasive – at least the Chinese can attempt to exploit the 'anti-progress' emotion around the world that already is reflected by the New Left and in such Western issues as pollution, destruction of the environment, depletion of natural resources, and reaction to the general strain and aberration of much of modern life. The mere fact that this position is likely to attract – in one form or another – a great deal of worldwide support is likely to give it increased validity in China itself, and to some degree in Japan and in the East, South-east and South Asia area as well.

If the above political-ideological-cultural strategy is followed, the Japanese leadership may again assume an important place in the Chinese hierarchy of devils (and, to some degree, among the radical, the disaffected, and the alienated of other countries – including Japan). All this is likely, to put it mildly, to poison Sino-Japanese relationships, as well as to have an impact on the Japanese people's own view of themselves.

This last may be very important indeed. After all, as we showed in Chapter 2, in the traditional Japanese cultural hierarchy, which is still deeply imbedded in Japanese life, the austere, dedicated, cultured, faithful Samurai warrior is at the top of society, even though he is relatively poor, and the mercantile class, while relatively rich, is at the bottom of the social ladder. In effect, what the Chinese would be saying to the Japanese is that 'It is we, the Communist Chinese, who are the modern equivalents of the Samurai class and possess all of its virtues, and you, the Japanese, have become traitors to your own scale of value. You have become an even more corrupt modern equivalent of the old Japanese mercantile class, with all of its associations of softness, materialism, sloppiness, depravity, and general selfishness and egoism.' I have noted, for example, that even today many Japanese remark that there was no such thing as a fat Japanese before World War II, but now there are many. Older Japanese in particular view this development with alarm, but doubtless many young Japanese show – or will acquire – the same attitude. It may also be worth noting that many Japanese who visit mainland China come back with a very strong emotional reaction: 'Well, at least they have lean, hard, purposeful faces.'

The prevalence of such attitudes in both the Chinese and Japanese societies, as well as among many foreigners, may take a good deal of pleasure out of affluence for at least some Japanese. It may move others to a serious questioning of the materialist and technological 'mercantile' values that are likely, at least superficially, to seem dominant in Japan; and it may create in still others defensive, resentful, and/or philistine attitudes. One Japanese friend has even pointed out rather ruefully that the Japanese today are not only about five inches taller than they were before World War II, but they are also remarkably Western in appearance and general physique. In effect, he said, 'The Chinese can accuse us of having sold out physically.' It is easy to imagine that these 'towering Japanese' – particularly if they let their success lead to patterns of behaviour that seem arrogant and rude – could become very unpopular in many areas of the world, but particularly in their *truncated* 'New Co-Prosperity Sphere'. Indeed, if all of these developments were combined with certain other irritating or threatening traits, practices, and events, then the 70s and 80s could produce considerable resentment and 'backlash' against the Japanese in various Asian and other areas.

Chapter Six

The Japanese Challenge

An Overview of the Main Issues

I have mentioned earlier the commonly voiced Japanese view that Japan is a technological and economic giant but a military and political pygmy. This is a very reasonable description of the current situation, but it is likely to soon be inappropriate – except relatively. That is, relative to its status a few years ago, Japan is now considered one of the five or six most important powers; relative to its current and anticipated GNP it is still a political and a military pygmy. I have tried to demonstrate, or at least to make plausible, that though this condition might continue through the 70s, it almost certainly will not persist into the 80s. In any case, the 70s will be a period of transition.

To some degree, prestige, influence, and power come because other nations concede that one is entitled to them. Yet despite its impressive record in World War II, for various reasons, Japan has not been regarded in the post-World War period as quite comparable to such nations as West Germany, France, and England. Even now, despite the fact that it has had the world's third largest Gross National Product * for several years, there is still a tendency not to think of Japan as the third-ranking state. This tendency is shared to a remarkable degree by the many Japanese who look at the GNP per capita criterion and note that in this variable Japan is still nineteenth or so (though even by this criterion it is moving up rapidly).

Of course, increased GNP by itself does not necessarily bring

* Most people, even knowledgable ones, are surprised to hear that the Japanese have attained this status – indeed, have had it since 1968.

commensurate increases in political or military power and prestige. However, some years ago Anthony J. Wiener and I argued in our book *The Year 2000* that Gross National Product and a nation's state of technology were, in most cases, the two most useful indicators of *potential* power, influence, and general performance. We understood, of course, that the caveat 'potential' was an important one. We also understood such other variables as population, morale, ideology and ideological zeal, esprit, military and political capability, internal discipline, prestige, authority, various kinds of skills, leadership, the quality of the planning analysis and decision-making processes, and so on, all must be considered in trying to judge existing or potential power or influence in any specific situation. We also understood that very often quite poor but dedicated or disciplined countries have demonstrated to richer but more complacent and 'soft' nations that Gross National Product and technological virtuosity are not always the crucial yardsticks in a confrontation or dispute. In other cases wisdom, prestige, and cultural superiorities have outweighed technology and GNP. Nevertheless, under the usual modern conditions for most nations the two variables most likely to make a country powerful and influential are the total 'heft' of its economy (i.e., the Gross National Product) and the quality of its technology.

However, the terms 'power' and 'influence' cover a lot of issues and it is conceivable that the Japanese might continue to be a relatively minor military power – at least as compared to the United States and the Soviet Union and perhaps even in comparison to the Chinese – and still have a role in world affairs rather close to that of a political as well as an economic superpower. Indeed, self-restraint in the military sphere, and to a lesser extent even in international politics – if either continues to be feasible and appears compatible with perceived Japanese needs for prestige, independence, influence, and basic security – might at least for a time be an enormous economic and even political advantage to them. It would not only make it much easier for the rest of the world to accept spectacular Japanese growth rates and many of its consequences, but it might give the Japanese some worthwhile opportunities to display leadership and creativity in search for arms control and world peace – in particular, it might be possible for the Japanese to make a political and economic virtue out of its intentional military weakness.

All this is possible, yet given likely Japanese attitudes, I suspect it is almost completely unrealistic to expect either the 'low military posture' or the 'low political posture' to be maintained very far into the 80s and perhaps not even through the 70s – unless, perhaps, the programme of making a virtue out of such restraints turned out to be eminently successful, in itself a rather unlikely eventuality.

Indeed, if Japanese growth rates do continue to average around 10 per cent, it is almost certain that Japan will be under many 'external' pressures to take a 'more active role' in world affairs. However, these external pressures are likely to be important only as a transition force or in supplying a rationalization, as the Japanese themselves are almost certain to insist on superpower status. And despite argumentations and pressures to define this 'full superpower status' as not necessarily requiring nuclear armament, the Japanese will insist on some degree of independent nuclear status – though not necessarily under simple Japanese national control.[1] Nor is it necessary or likely – at least early in the game – that the Japanese forces, either nuclear or conventional, would be of a size to compete with the United States or the Soviet Union, though they may. The Japanese will have or have easy access to enough nuclear and conventional devices and equipment so that all will concede Japan's right to full superpower status; this may require only symbolic and/or preparatory forces, rather than actual capabilities. The important thing is likely to be having nuclear status, not the objective capability of the forces.

As discussed in Chapters 1 and 2, it is exactly this issue of the 'proper place' of the Japanese and how they get there that is the essence of Japan's challenge, a challenge both to the Japanese and to the rest of the world. To America it is in part a trade and an economic challenge, in part a question of both cooperation and countervailing power in Non-Communist Pacific Asia, in part a matter of internal economic adjustment, and in part one of helping, in effect, to 'guide' this new Japanese state – particularly avoiding the unnecessary creation by its own actions of false or dangerous pressures or temptations.

Such pressures or temptations, of course, are especially likely if the United States and Japan become engaged in a trade war, if there is a precipitous abandonment of Non-Communist Pacific Asia by the United States, or if US policy is such that it appears particularly blundering, insensitive, immoral, or otherwise unworthy as a leader or guide.

To China and the Soviet Union the Japanese challenge is likely to mean the frustration of some of their fondest hopes and expectations. Particularly in the Soviet Union, a spectacular growth of Japan can be expected to have an exaggerated psychological impact, at least on some of the intellectuals. The revolution and the following fifty years of struggle, pain, and sorrow were not intended to put Russia in third place. Khrushchev once said that Russian Communism is 'goulash plus ballet' but this will not be accepted by many of those who suffered so many hardships from 1917 to 1947. In any case, while the ballet is very good in the Soviet Union, the goulash is only so-so. And the fact that the Japanese form of goulash is superior in both quantity and quality is going to hurt (not to speak of the potentialities of there being quite good Japanese ballet as well). Despite these disturbing effects, it is not unlikely that the Soviets and the Japanese will generally get along with each other – in fact, one can easily imagine some kind of *ad hoc* or other combination among all three superpowers.

Such coordination, even if it arises out of purely benevolent considerations and restricts itself to relatively innocuous economic and public welfare issues among the cooperating powers, would probably be viewed with the deepest suspicion by the Chinese and by many European states. I have already discussed in Chapter 5 some other aspects of the dramatic and disturbing challenge that the Japanese will present to the Chinese. US–Japanese–Soviet cooperation will simply be taken as confirming their deepest suspicions about the Japanese.

The Japanese challenge to Europe will be more complex. As yet, only 5 per cent or so of Japanese trade is with Western Europe, but this is probably going to be one of the most rapidly growing aspects of Japan's trade. Europe's first reaction is likely to be protectionist against Japan. But despite the current protectionist movement, such things as the existence of General Agreement on Trades and Tariffs, America's desires for free trade, and Europe's own interest in trade, etc., will probably prevent a serious programme of discrimination. Of course, it is likely to take the Europeans some time before they understand that Japan is really a superstate and possibly a superpower; now they are just too preoccupied with China and caught up with their (partly wishful) thinking of the pressures the Chinese will be putting on the Soviet Union. (From the European point of view Chinese pressures on the Soviet Union are more beneficial than not.) Also contributing to distract Europeans from the question of Japan is a concept most Europeans and many Americans have – that the United States and the Soviet Union will eventually have to get together against China. That is, the Europeans not only overstate the likely Chinese pressures on the Soviet Union, but they generally hope they can exploit those pressures for European ends and are worried the US will interfere.

Another very important reason for the systematic European underestimate of Japan's economic growth and its consequences in addition to the common love affair with China is the general Marxist approach of many European intellectuals. This leads them to underestimate or underrate the technological and economic success of 'capitalist' Japan – in many cases even to sneer at this success as simply productive of more pollution and the other ills of modern society. I discussed earlier the extraordinary degree to which many American and European intellectuals impute desperate social strains to Japan that really only exist in their own countries – if at all – and the general failure to understand either the enormous kick the Japanese get from their economic success or the profound roles that national pride and, indeed, ordinary nationalism still play in Japan.

One important result of the further growth of Japan is that it may put China into a perspective in which it is judged the fifth, sixth, seventh, or even eighth most important power from the economic and military point of view, and not the third (as is so common today). This in turn should make clearer to the

Europeans that the pressures on Russia, if any at all and if important, are likely to be internal pressures. Further, a rather close cooperation between the Soviet Union, Japan, and the United States will create new kinds of European nightmares of a superpower hegemony of the world. And this in itself is likely to push the Europeans to do some uniting or to otherwise try to deal with this perceived superpower caucus, hegemony, consensus, or whatever they care to call it.

Japanese trading companies operating in both East and West Europe and in the Soviet Union (they are already unbelievably well established – at least as compared to other capitalist groups – in Moscow and in Eastern European capitals generally) might accelerate many of these trends. And in doing so, they are likely to have another enormous advantage over the typical Western firm in dealing with many socialist countries, in particular with the Soviet Union. The groups that do the buying in the Soviet Union and in some of the other socialist countries often like to deal on a very large scale. In particular, they like to make a contract that satisfies a major portion of their needs for any particular item. This means that they wish to deal on a scale that is practically impossible for most private companies, but well within the scale of the Japanese trading company, if not today then in the not too distant future. Indeed, these Japanese trading companies may be big enough to sign contracts for almost any size without making many very special arrangements to meet the terms. In any case, Japanese firms of all kinds now seem to be extremely successful in negotiating deals in Eastern Europe and the Soviet Union, and have already established a much greater presence than the Europeans have.

The same trading companies may also be a useful mechanism for the Japanese in establishing a close coordination of overall Japanese commercial policies and liaisons with various European nations, with the European Economic Community as a whole, or with large firms in Europe. This coordination, of course, would be in addition to that of individual firms and the now common practice of joint ventures, the setting up of joint companies, and other examples of cooperation and coordination.

To summarize briefly, what I am suggesting here is that to a remarkable degree, the large Japanese trading firms may be the answer to a number of problems of multinational trading in the 70s and 80s, in part because they are likely to be so successful at related and complementary activities. They may find themselves soon operating on such a scale and in such a manner that they necessarily become imbued with a certain political and public-interest character that has been mostly absent from their past operations but that could have a significant influence on future trade.

One problem the Japanese may have in continuing their economic and technological growth is possible counter-reactions. Of course, there will always be issues related to terms of trade and standards of behaviour, but, particularly in what we have called NOCPA (Non-Communist Pacific Asia), there will also be emotional and political issues. The traditional model of inter-national relationships in which the kind of trade and investment domination Japan seems likely to achieve in Pacific Asia – particularly if there are aggressive Chinese pressures on the region which have to be resisted – is almost inevitably followed by political and/or military interventions by the leading power, as well as by some degree of commercial domination. And that is traditionally followed by something between 'fraternalization' and informal hegemony – or perhaps even by legal acquisition of some or all of the territory by the leading power. The more the Japanese can reassure the various countries of NOCPA that this will not happen, the less likely is it that these countries will take drastic measures early in the game to prevent or limit Japanese infiltration and influence. Of course, such measures, even if suc-cessful, would not necessarily prevent eventual Japanese domina-tion, but at the least they would throw up roadblocks to immediate Japanese commercial and political influence. In the traditional model of expansion, such resistance generally gives the threatened country a better chance to maintain its independence. Thus it would seem to make sense for the Japanese to go a great distance to maintain at least the appearance of a 'neutral low posture'. Up to now Japan's foreign policy, with its relatively passive attitude and almost total disinterest in foreign intervention, has been quite successful in this respect, but, as the quotations in the Appendix show, not completely successful.

Even though in principle a continued low-posture Japanese policy is possible, and even though I will further investigate some of its implications, I would judge it to be a rather unlikely alternative. Premier Sato noted in his November 1969 address to the National Press Club in Washington: 'I find the shape of a new Pacific age, where a new order will be created by Japan and the US, two countries tied together by common ideals.' In contrast, Mr Nixon in mid-1969 said that the US intends to reduce its military presence in Asia and leave the basic responsibility for security to the Asians themselves. The long-run implications of the two positions should be clear. I noted that in an earlier speech on Asian security made in September 1969, Premier Sato said: 'It is Japan that is gradually going to play the leading role, while the US will be cooperating from the sidelines.' In part this remark simply reflected Japan's current economic and technological success and its growing confidence. In part it also constituted a reasonable and even essential reaction to the problem of filling or, better, preventing a potential vacuum in Pacific Asia. If the US really intends to withdraw as much as possible, it will be important for the Japanese – and the other countries of Pacific Asia – to prevent a vacuum from developing which the Russians or the Chinese may rush to fill. It will be very important to have an orderly transition. For the Japanese to be there first, consequently, would imply a more or less continuous transition of responsibilities from the US to Japan.

If this is the policy, then it would seem clear that from the point of view of almost every nation in NOCPA – as well as the United States and Japan – a relatively slow transition would be better for all concerned. While it would then be generally understood that at the minimum Japan was planning to play an increasing part of the role given up by the United States, and while many would worry about possible Japanese attempts to eventually establish a hegemony of some appropriate type, the issue would remain open. Further, it seems that the more slowly this transition is effected, the more likely that useful but not disruptive countervailing powers will be created, that expensive frictions will be decreased, and that the potential will be greatly increased for relatively acceptable give and take arrangements with a good deal of collectivity and mutuality. Such arrangements would be not only between Japan and the separate countries of the region, but among these countries as well – with perhaps limited US and/or European participation.

The Japanese should not be in a hurry for another reason. Their high priority postwar objectives, such as the restoration of their economy and physical security, the regaining of status and prestige, the rebuilding of internal morale and confidence, the liquidation of 'war guilt' and the other political consequences of World War II (including reconciliation with their former enemies and with the other superpowers) all will have been attained. There would seem to be little reason to risk any of these to effect some major acceleration of some foreign policy goals as yet unrealized or unrealizable on the domestic scene.

It is also important to note that the Japanese may prefer a relationship to NOCPA much like that of the US to NATO or like that of the US to the Organization of American States, even if it were feasible to achieve more. While NATO and the OAS are clearly organizations in which the US still plays a role somewhat more than that of first among equals, it is a role relatively acceptable to most of the other members. There are many who will agree that for both Japan and NOCPA this kind of arrangement would be much more satisfactory than most of the classical forms of hegemony or imperialism. In any case, current Japanese anxieties and uncertainties about the new role of Japan are so great that a continuation of the low posture and a 'wait and see attitude' are almost inevitable for the next two or three years.

Thus, so long as their relative strength is increasing, particularly in respect to China, the Soviet Union, and the United States, and, to a lesser degree, to the nations of NOCPA, the Japanese may feel that playing a waiting game, even if unconsciously or without deliberate plan, may be the safest and in some ways the most expeditious route to whatever final state they wish to achieve. It is also a relatively safe way to defer many major decisions about which the Japanese themselves are still uncertain.

However, despite their caution and good intentions, the Japanese may be tempted, in a way most Americans abroad usually are not, to indulge in excessive interference in the internal affairs of those developing states in which 'graft', 'corruption', and other unofficial transactions and arrangements are considered more or less legitimate. Japanese businessmen, and even their government officials, seem to be much more familiar than Americans with how to operate in such an environment. This could easily lead to excessive Japanese influence in that environment. In fact, such influence could become so excessive that it turns out to be counterproductive, because it could eventually touch off counter-reactions, or it could result in a Japanese 'takeover' and all the attendant problems and costs. Of course, the Japanese might be quite willing to exploit these characteristics if they wished to have control of such a state – or to weaken the ability of its bureaucracy to function in a 'normal' manner: to do so may be dysfunctional only when judged by narrow economic criteria or as compared to an economic situation with a more objective and normal quid pro quo relationship.

This issue of the independent growth of the separate states of Pacific Asia is an important one. Many of these states, particularly those in the Chinese culture area or that have large Chinese populations, are growing economically at a rate of about 10 per cent a year. And Australia is growing at about the same rate. If their growth rates continue, these states will have some real vitality and internal strength and are likely to soon develop an ability to resist the kind of gradual takeover that was so common in the seventeenth, eighteenth, and nineteenth centuries when Europeans made their initial commercial and cultural penetrations of Asia and then subsequently acquired political control. Thus Norway, Denmark, Finland are all small states, but they all look very indigestible as political areas for imperialism.

Partly for this reason, partly because of the continuing presence of the US, partly because of a quite basic if recent change in international behaviour, and partly because of basic changes in international and within national society, conquest and colonization in the traditional imperialistic sense may no longer seem justifiable economically, politically, and/or militarily. Certainly given the success of Japan's normal commercial quid pro quo relationships during the past twenty-five years – and their likely future success – there is a real chance that Japan, while dominating NOCPA economically, will do so, as I suggested, in a manner quite similar to the US's 'dominating' of Canada and Latin America, and thereby be more of a stabilizing than a disrupting force in Asia.

In addition, one should note that there are a number of internal restraints on the development of excessively aggressive or nationalistic tendencies in Japan. There is, after all, a genuine and quite general fear of a revived militarism, especially one of the sort that appeared in Japan in the 20s and 30s and had such manifestations as 'government by assassination'. The right, the centre and the left have shared this fear, and it is perhaps the most powerful restraint. But the right and the centre are beginning to give it up as unrealistic under current conditions in Japan.

In addition, the Japanese defeat in World War II and the success and prestige achieved within the present system might both be perceived as a failure of imperialistic policy for Japan. Then there is the absence of any recognized external danger and the fact that current attitudes, along with the past experience of extreme nationalism, have created and sustained an atmosphere very hostile to extremist ideologies. One must also take into account the greater dependence of Japan on trade and good relations with advanced industrial nations than with its Asian neighbours, as well as the current tendency to subordinate foreign policy to domestic issues and to calculations and analyses done by businessmen or from a business point of view. And finally, there is the enormous anxiety, the feelings of prudence and caution, and the general good sense of other Japanese élites and even of the 'masses'.

Yet under quite plausible conditions none of these or the other mechanisms we have mentioned are likely to be strong enough to prevent the classic pattern of political domination following commercial and/or cultural penetration. Among the notable possibilities are that Japan could go through one of its traditional cycles of enthusiastic accommodation to foreign standards followed by an intense nationalistic and xenophobic reaction.

Although a limited reaction of this sort seems almost certain to many observers, we are talking about something much more intense than most of these observers currently expect. Or there could be a step by step process in which the Japanese find themselves ntervening in various internal issues and local situations, resulting over a number of years in a sequence of small takeovers or concessions. Or China could initiate a policy of actual threats, aggressions, or subversions which require Japanese intervention, possibly initially welcomed by the local people but eventually resulting in Japanese domination. Or a precipitate American withdrawa l from Asia could be so unsettling to the area that the Japanese would feel compelled to move in firmly and decisively, even if reluctantly.

Further, many will argue that even if Japan becomes an economic and technological superpower, but continues in the 70s and 80s to follow the equivalent of its present 'low-posture' policy militarily – and in particular if the Japanese do not get nuclear weapons – then no matter how well they do in the two central variables of Gross National Product and advanced technology, they will not be a superpower in quite the same sense that the US and the Soviet Union are superpowers. For all of these reasons the coming defence debate in Japan may play a central role in influencing the future development of these issues.

The Defence Debate in Japan

Let us turn now to current Japanese defence issues as a step towards further analysis of the future possibilities. The recent election has been publicized as setting the nation's course for the 1970s. If so, the results reflect a movement towards 'revisionism' and 'normalization' of Japanese defence policies and internal politics; Premier Sato promised partnership with the United States to safeguard the stability of Asia, and he pledged to retain the Security Treaty under which the US maintains bases as a deterrent to war in Asia. His ruling Liberal Democrats won 288 seats in the 486-seat House of Representatives on the strength of their past performance – mostly the Japanese economic success and the successful Sato–Nixon talks of November 1969 regarding complete reversion of Okinawa. The neutralist opposition Socialists remained divided and lost some of their strength, going down from 144 to only 90 seats. The militant Komeito became a strong third party with 47 seats, and the moderate Democratic Socialists won 31 seats (no change from previous elections). The Communists, who broke with the Chinese Communists in 1965, increased their seats from 4 to 14.*

There was more apathy evident in this vote than in any previous postwar election – so that 32 per cent of the 69·7 million eligible voters did not bother to cast their ballots. Nonetheless, the defeat of the neutralist Socialists, accompanied by the rise of Komeito and the Communists, mutually antagonistic but both assertively nationalistic, suggests that idealistic unarmed neutrality may be dead as a political issue in Japan. The Socialists will have to abandon doctrinaire Marxism and obsolete programmes (as their German and Italian counterparts have already done) and consolidate their ranks before they can hope to retain the number two party position. In the 1970s and 1980s the major opposition to the Liberal Democrat policy of partnership with the United States is likely to come from proponents of armed neutrality, be they leftist or rightist, and of a 'Gaullist' approach to international relations.

Given the successful outcome of the December 1969 elections, Premier Sato was able to postpone the power struggles within the

*The revival in the strength of the Japanese Communist Party, with some 200,000 members, and commanding 2·5 million scattered votes, was significant. Autonomy helped its image, as well as the charge levied against it by Maoist and Trotskyite student groups of being part of the Japanese establishment. As extremist student groups stormed universities, the JCP-related Minsei student organization proved to be campus 'moderates.' As a result, the JCP-related organizations are in a better position to control *Zengakuren* and campuses than ever before. The organization has been expanding its activities to senior high schools, and now claims chapters in one out of every five high schools. This activity has yet to be translated into votes in national elections, but some analysts argue that this could develop into a situation in which the Communists might become as significant an element as they are in some important Western European countries. While I find this implausible, the situation clearly deserves continuing observation and analysis.

ruling Liberal Democrats. The heir apparent to the leadership appears to be Finance Minister Takeo Fukuda, but he has a strong rival in the secretary general of the party, Kakuei Tanaka. At present Fukuda has more supporters in the new cabinet, including the controversial agriculture minister, Todao Kuraishi, who had been forced to resign in 1968 after a speech favouring atomic weapons for Japan. A significant upgrading of defence was marked by the appointment of party faction leader Yasuhiro Nakasone as director-general of the Defence Agency. He is generally regarded as being relatively hawkish and he advocated a 'revision' of the Security Treaty by 1975 and an autonomous defence.

By the 1980s long rule and intra-party struggles will probably have produced a decline in the conservative majority, while the Komeito will have steadily increased its ranks. With forty-seven members elected to the House in December 1969, Komeito is now a significant element in politics and at least a possible coalition partner for the ruling Liberal Democrats if their fortunes slip. At its 1969 annual convention, Komeito did not back a 'positive' nationalist action, but instead a composite of every generalized aspiration of leadership with safety that has appeared since World War II. Komeito thinks the Security Pact with the United States should be phased out in the 1970s, beginning with the elimination of unnecessary bases and going on to complete but armed neutrality. It thinks Communist China should be won over by taking a strong 'one China' stand and by sponsoring its admission to the United Nations. Japan should play a stronger independent world role, and Komeito advocates the opening of an Asian headquarters for the United Nations in Tokyo. The UN police force should be expanded to preserve world peace. Komeito would change the Self-Defence Force (SDF) into an autonomous National Guard with no other duty than to protect the home islands and maintain law and order within Japan.

The legal limits for Japanese rearmament are set by Article 9 of the Constitution, according to which

... the Japanese people forever renounce war as a sovereign right of the nation and the threat or use of force as a means of settling international disputes.

In order to accomplish the aim of the preceding paragraph, land, sea, and air forces, as well as other war potential, will never be maintained . . .

Postwar governments have interpreted Article 9 as renouncing the use of force only as a means of settling international disputes, but not in the exercise of self-defence. In their view, the constitution rules out the acquisition and development of offensive weapons, as well as the dispatch of Japanese forces abroad. A legal barrier to nuclear rearmament is embodied in Article 2 of Japan's Atomic Energy Act, which confines research, development work, and applications in the field of nuclear energy to peaceful uses of the atom.

Japan's Self-Defence Forces are composed entirely of volunteers and are organized on the principle of civilian control. Their administrative direction is entrusted to the Defence Agency, an organ attached to the office of the Premier and headed by a director-general with the rank of minister. The education of the future officers corps is carried out primarily by the three-service Defence Academy, while advanced training is offered by the National Defence College. All three services are over-officered, a feature which would facilitate their expansion at short notice.

The current defence budget totals $1·35 billion, somewhat less than 1 per cent of the GNP (0·84 per cent). The new Sato cabinet aims at gradually increasing this figure in the early 1970s to about 1·5 per cent. Given the present annual average growth rates, 1·5 per cent of GNP could mean a leap to $5 billion or so in arms spending in 1975.

The National Defence Agency has requested a $280 million budget increase for 1970. The defence industries are beginning to taste large-scale profits as the government gradually shifts to domestic procurement after two decades of major reliance on the US. They place great stress on research and development in a constant attempt to keep a very high level of sophistication in their weaponry. In 1969 Japan was making 97 per cent of its own ammunition and 84 per cent of its airplanes, tanks, guns, and naval craft.[2]

According to statistics of the Defence Agency,[3] defence contracts grew from $311 million in 1964 to $673 million in 1958 and

are estimated to have reached $1 billion in 1969. Defence indus-
tries currently plan to promote joint research and development
programmes with American firms under which Japan would get
advanced aircraft engine technology in return for helping US
concerns through 'related' research in electronics.

The Japanese Defence Agency recently announced its fourth
Five Year Programme, to start in 1972, aimed at creating a
'system capable of effectively dealing with all armed aggression
involving localized or minor warfare and the use of conventional
weapons'.[4] It is interesting to note that 'localized' is not defined.
Does it, for example, mean that Japanese forces would intervene
to help repel an attack on South Korea or Taiwan, both of which
are now considered to be within Japan's defence perimeter?

I have emphasized throughout this book that in the 70s Japan
will be a great power in almost all the ways that count, except for
military strength and on issues that derive from military strength.
But even here, as one can see from the above, its current stance
is by no means inconsiderable. Most American bases in Japan
have been taken over by the SDF. Japan's level of defence spending is about seventh in the world; so is Japan's population. The
defence expenditure is out of line only in terms of Japan's
enormous production. But even the present level of defence
spending, assuming it is augmented to incorporate the responsibility of Okinawa and then kept proportional to the GNP, will
make Japan a significant military power – not in land forces,
where the lack of a military draft and insular security make it
unnecessary, but in the more expensive and technologically
advanced aspects of naval and air armament. Japan's technological superiority and economic potential over her Asian neighbours will give her maximum advantage in these areas.

Postwar pacifism is increasingly being tempered by the realization that the giving up of military force by one nation does not
automatically produce conditions for peace and that existence of
defence forces is not to be equated with militarism. The kind of
utopian idealism and rigid dogmatism espoused by the Socialists
has been rebuffed at the polls. They are giving way to detached
study and hardheaded analysis of Japan's problems, to pragmat-
ism, and to intellectual flexibility in approach.

Until recently a candid discussion of military power was un-thinkable. Thus, agriculture minister Tadao Kuraishi resigned under public pressure in 1968 because he had casually suggested that Japanese fishing vessels would be protected from harassment by Soviet trawlers 'if we had atom bombs and a 300,000-man army.'* Although no responsible Japanese politician would publicly advocate nuclear armament today, the whole subject of military security has been thrown open to intense public scrutiny. As a result, there are mounting pressures both inside and outside government circles for transforming the SDF into a force for projecting Japanese power in the world.

A draft copy of the government's first white paper on national defence, which was leaked to a Tokyo paper,[5] makes a clear-cut admission that Japan is in the dangerous position of being sur-rounded by 'superior military powers'. A survey conducted by the Prime Minister's office in 1968 indicated that 81 per cent of the Japanese favoured 'defending the country by themselves', with only 4 per cent content to rely on US military guarantees. One impetus for greater defence efforts comes from the business world, since 90 per cent of SDF's military hardware is made in Japan. Many now believe that Japan has an influential military-industrial complex which lobbies effectively for greater defence efforts. They note that in the autumn of 1969, Kenzo Okubo, president of the Japan Ordnance Association, urged the government to produce nuclear armaments and devote 4 per cent of the GNP (about $8 billion in 1970) to defence. While there were some negative comments made about this kind of lobbying by the 'Japanese military-industrial complex', it appears that few if any people were really outraged.

Japan and Nuclear Weapons

I have pointed out that the highly publicized Japanese nuclear allergy is not a simple thing, and in particular does not represent a firm commitment to nuclear pacifism by a majority of the Japanese people. In addition, I have argued that if annual growth

* As noted, he is now back in the Cabinet.

rates continue at about current levels and the Japanese attain the kind of economic and technological stature that some (including myself) think that they will, most Japanese will almost inevitably feel that Japan has the right and duty to achieve full superpower status and that this means possessing a substantial nuclear establishment. The Japanese might also feel, as many people in Western Europe do, that Japan will be able to get away with much less manpower in their armed forces if these forces are based mainly on nuclear weapons or at least have an appreciable nuclear capability. This reduces sharply the serious problems modern governments have in attempting to maintain conscription or even large volunteer armies.

We should note that from the economic point of view the Japanese should have a GNP of $300 or $400 billion in 1975. If they allocate from 2 to 5 per cent to defence this should be between $5 and $20 billion a year. The lower figure is about equal to the defence expenditure of a major European power. By comparison, the US with a 4 per cent GNP growth rate and 8 per cent allocated to defence (the 1965 figure) would in 1975 be spending about $90 billion a year on defence.

On the technological level, just because of their nuclear electrical power industry alone, the Japanese by 1975 or so will have a capability to produce enough plutonium for several thousands of small nuclear weapons a year. Much of this could be done without cutting back sharply on electrical production and by increasing the cost of a kilowatt hour by only a modest amount.

Japan has also become the fifth nation to orbit a satellite. By 1975 it should have readily available all the technology necessary to produce a series of modern weapon systems, including some roughly equivalent to the early Minuteman and early Polaris.

I have predicted elsewhere that within the next five or ten years the Japanese are likely to unequivocably start on the process of acquiring nuclear weapons. Since such things tend to cast long shadows, their entering into this process will probably lead the Japanese to encounter some of the pluses and minuses of nuclear power long before they have any appreciable nuclear military capability. However, as I have tried to indicate, not only am I uncertain of my prediction, I even hope that I am wrong. One can set forth very persuasive arguments for why such a nuclear policy would be wrong, or at least premature, from the Japanese point of view. Thus the Japanese may indeed come to feel that they can improve the prospects of both their own country and the world generally by restraint in this area. Accordingly, there is a good chance that national acquisition of nuclear weapons will be judged a mistake.

Will, then, Japan build nuclear forces? One of the critical variables will be Japan's long-run expectations about the future of nuclear weapons. If the Japanese felt, for example, that in the not too distant future there will be a comprehensive worldwide arms control programme in which they would no longer have an 'invidious position' with regard to the other two superpowers, or even if some of the disparity between these two superpowers and Japan was – or was soon going to be – decreased or eliminated, they might well be content to wait. If, however, they felt that the tradition of non-proliferation was getting so strong that they faced the prospect of remaining non-nuclear for the 'rest of history,' and that with, then, only five nuclear powers they themselves would be irretrievably 'second-class' in some very important senses, including political and military ones, their desire to get nuclear weapons might be accelerated.

In the latter case, it is possible that the Japanese would feel that the best time to take the first nuclear step was in the immediate future; that if they waited much longer they might find that when they did wish to act conditions were much less propitious. For example, there could be some kind of crisis – perhaps between them and China, or perhaps involving Russia or the United States in such a way that there would be no fear of a counter-threat from either of the two superpowers to deter China or another power from threatening Japan.

The Japanese clearly have to look to one or both of the superpowers – presumably the United States – for protection during their acquisition period, or find some assurance from China that the Chinese will not be 'provoked' to some serious actions by a Japanese nuclear programme. They might also feel that the safe and prudent policy would be to first achieve a nuclear option, which would not be as provocative as a serious programme to immediately procure a large actualized capability. In effect, they are getting this option right now, but it would still be relatively easy – and probably safe – to accelerate or broaden the current more or less 'accidental' programme.

There are of course, a number of variations on this. In particular, the Japanese could, at least in principle, start a missile defence system using conventional high-explosive warheads. The efficiency might be extraordinarily low against sophisticated attacks, but still appreciable and perhaps sufficient against many plausible Chinese attacks – attacks with relatively unsophisticated penetration aids and tactics and with a small number of missiles. The Chinese might then no longer be able to make highly confident and/or credible threats about their own capabilities against the Japanese. The world and China would also take note that the Japanese were prepared to go into the nuclear defence business and that the Chinese should not provoke them into doing so.

It is also important to understand that a Japanese nuclear ABM system need not necessarily be followed soon by offensive nuclear capabilities. They might well consider that to be a completely separate decision and even choose to emphasize the separation of the two decisions. Or there might be strong moral and political pressures generated in the outside world on the Japanese to keep the two decisions separate; for example, if for all the reasons we have mentioned the Japanese committed themselves not to get *offensive* capabilities, the world might still be distressed at even a limited Japanese decision restricting themselves to a *defensive* nuclear weapons system. Nonetheless, a limitation to solely defensive capabilities might alleviate some of the troubles a nuclear decision would inevitably cause.

Having said earlier in this book that under current conditions it is not unlikely that the Japanese in the early or mid-70s will make definite steps toward the acquisition of nuclear weapons or will actually acquire such weapons, I would like now to present some of the arguments for their not doing so – or if they insist on doing so, for their doing so in ways that do not excessively rock the nuclear boat. To rock the boat, even by a simple acquisition of nuclear weapons, may be a very bad policy indeed, not only from the world point of view but also from a narrow and direct

Japanese point of view. There can be little doubt about the enormous animosity towards Japan that such a move would raise.

Thus if the Japanese do get nuclear weapons, it would be best for them to obtain them in some special form or manner – possibly as a combination of active air defence and active ballistic missile defence but with a very small, or negligible, possibly even zero, offensive force. In effect, the possession of these nuclear weapons might put them more in the position of a Great Britain than that of a France or China, much less a Soviet Union or a United States. They would have nuclear weapons, and with this possession would come a certain prestige, a certain confidence, a certain kind of knowledge, a certain entrée into world conferences and other kinds of discussions, a certain kind of independence of the United States, but with care the acts leading to this acquisition need not rock the nuclear non-proliferation boat.

Perhaps most critically, the Japanese would then have a very real defence against Chinese threats plus a deterrent against major threats. Of course, the Japanese would severely limit the range of their defence missiles; unless so limited, even ABM missiles could have a range of many hundreds of miles – and a very real retaliatory capability against China. Indeed, such a system might be effective against all but quite large and sophisticated Soviet attacks. Such a posture would be consistent with the last twenty years of Japanese 'low posture' or even 'isolation' policies.

In effect, until 1952 the American Bakufu (military occupation government) made all the basic decisions and set the initial goals for Japanese foreign policy. The continuing American guarantee after 1952 and the low posture of Japanese foreign policy encouraged the Japanese – both the government and the people – in a policy of positive non-involvement and non-responsibility almost as a way of life. Of course, this policy fitted very well with their particular requirements of focusing almost entirely on economic growth and getting along with everyone. And the Japanese are quite aware that this kind of uninvolvement and disinterest cannot be maintained indefinitely. Until now, the Japanese have indeed got along with both Koreas, both Chinas, both Vietnams, both Germanies, both the United States and the

Soviet Union, India and Pakistan, the United States and China, and so on. But as I have indicated in the preceding chapter, it may not be possible for them to continue doing this even if they try to de-emphasize the political and military areas. The expected hostile reaction of China to these Japanese developments will be a major force that Japan itself must react to. Recent indications of a Japanese willingness to accept some responsibility for the defence of South Korea already 'endanger' Japan's 'isolationist' policy.

China and the Japanese Challenge

China's policy in the 70s will be a major factor modifying US–Japanese and Japanese–Soviet relationships, the attitudes of various countries in Pacific Asia towards the growing Japanese giant, and even Japanese interests and defence arrangements. Current Chinese extremism at home and militant rigidity in international affairs tend to bring home at least to some Japanese the risks of going it alone. And they enhance appreciation of the United States alliance. But it should be remembered that many Japanese still do not accept this position. If the Chinese continue with their current policies, and possibly even if they don't, it may become gradually clear that Japan and China are in the future going to play the role of rivals in Asia.

Given increasing Chinese militance and pressures, the US and USSR may in the long run prove unwilling to stabilize conditions for any protracted period. Growing Chinese power combined with a waning of the US commitment in Asia will not only generate uneasiness in Japan and stimulate a desire to build up her military strength, but it can also make many in Pacific Asia more pleased than apprehensive about such a Japanese build-up.

It should be noted that in the present circumstances neither the Chinese nor the Japanese seem to expect serious threats from each other. In fact, the situation seems to be very much the opposite. From the viewpoint of most Japanese today – or at least until very recently – the only scenario that can be written for an attack by the Chinese on Japan involves some 'provocative' or 'attractive' aspect of current US bases in Japan. For this reason many Japanese think that by permitting these bases in Japan they are extending a favour to the United States, not actually increasing their own security.

It is true that many Americans argue to the Japanese that the Communist Chinese represent a serious threat, and they receive at least a pro forma agreement from the Japanese. But as is well known, the Japanese are a very polite people and therefore may be willing to agree with the Americans in their formulations while still not accepting them. And, indeed, if one pursues this topic in any depth, one soon finds that most Japanese consider the current threat from China to be minimal and do not anticipate any rapid increase in it. Also, while the Japanese are beginning to understand that the growth of Japan's strength and prestige may change their relationship with China, few feel that it will bring them to the point of escalation-prone confrontations.

Despite the fact that the Chinese are probably going to think of the Japanese as 'agents of American imperialism' and as the 'corruptors of Asia,' most Japanese seem willing to argue that this attitude and animosity will remain consistent with a basically peaceful orientation towards Japan.

It therefore is possible to argue that the most likely way for military tension to rise between China and Japan, as opposed to a political and emotional tension, would be as a result of some distinct Japanese initiative, say the procurement of an ABM system, an attempt to establish control over some part of Pacific Asia, or the creation by the Japanese of an anti-Chinese alliance in Pacific Asia. Any of these acts might be received by the Chinese as a signal that the Japanese have a much higher estimate of the probability of war or of serious crises between the two nations than they had thought. Presumably, they would impute most or all of this activity (and the corresponding estimate that had led to it) to a Japanese desire to be aggressive, and even a Japanese defensive reaction against Chinese aggression in some parts of Pacific Asia would be thought of by the Chinese as Japanese aggression. In any case, even if we ascribe a specific Japanese initiative (e.g., deployment of an ABM system) to a Japanese desire to gain international status, the Chinese are likely to feel that such deployment must still indicate, whether intended as such or not, a much more active role by Japan in Asia – probably either a containment or rollback policy against them.

Finally, and of course most important of all, the Chinese are almost certain to view any defensive Japanese system, whether an active defence or an alliance system, as an inevitable precursor of an offensive capability. This picture of a strengthened Japan, perhaps backed up by the United States – or even the Soviet Union – would become an additional nightmare in Chinese eyes and could cause the Chinese to begin thinking of Japan as their most serious immediate enemy. In effect, a Japanese decision to deploy a ballistic missile system or to organize some kind of Pacific Asia security system could have the same effects on Sino-Japanese relationships as the creation of the German Navy had on Anglo-German relationships in the 1890s.

Many but not all of the above arguments would be reversed if the Chinese were already in an aggressive or otherwise hostile mood regarding the Japanese. Again, everything depends upon timing, contexts, and details. Thus if the Chinese were, for various reasons, contemptuous of the US and confident that the Soviets were going to allow them a free hand in Pacific Asia, one could imagine that the creation of a ballistic missile defence network in Japan or a regional security force or other such arrangement could improve the situation markedly – in much the same way as the creation of a serious French or British military capability might have quieted Hitler if it had been achieved in the mid-30s. Thus, China may play a key role, perhaps *the* key role in the orientation of Japan and of the Pacific Asia area.

As in the 1960s, there will probably exist an enormous disparity between the aggressive tone of Chinese propaganda and the actual military risks that the Chinese – even with a limited nuclear arsenal – will be willing to run. But there is also fairly convincing evidence that the Chinese will not hesitate to use force if they feel genuinely threatened and think they can get away with it without unreasonable risk. One has only to point to the Chinese intervention in the Korean War and to the border conflicts with India and the USSR. Assuming a resolution of the Vietnam conflict along lines acceptable to the Chinese, Peking will probably continue in the 1970s a policy of careful support of Communist insurgency movements in South-east Asia and of minority insurgencies such as the Nagas in India. Japan would be particularly sensitive to the status of South Korea and Taiwan, which strategically flank it. Korean developments are surely of greater strategic concern to Japan than developments in South-east and South Asia, although for commercial and various other reasons Japan cannot afford to ignore a degree of Chinese political primacy in South-east Asia that went beyond the neutralization of the states flanking China. Therefore, any major Chinese moves in East Asia could be regarded as having a high probability of stimulating definite changes in Japanese policy. This may be one of the most likely ways in which such changes are induced.

Japan and Its Relations with the United States

Following their meeting in November 1969, President Nixon and Premier Sato agreed that it was in the mutual interest of the two nations to continue working closely together in an effort to stabilize and develop the Pacific area. Many have interpreted the agreement as a shifting of responsibility from the US to Japan. On the American side a rising concern with domestic needs and disillusion with overseas efforts at peacekeeping have combined with an awareness of Japan's wealth and power and produced a desire for greater Japanese involvement in the security and the economic development of East Asia. On the Japanese side a new sense of confidence stemming from economic power and enhanced world standing has produced the desire for a more autonomous policy and, in a less polarized world, a more influential role.

Further, the growth of the Japanese economy has had an inevitable effect on certain sectors of the American economy. In the 1960s, for example, the United States had quite a flourishing industry in the manufacture of pneumatic tapes for various types of entertainment systems. Much the same was also true for the manufacture of many kinds of radios. However, both these industries, with some important exceptions, are now largely based in the Far East and usually, but not always, under Japanese control or management. The United States is still the leading force in the television and phonograph industries, yet most observers seem agreed that in the next decade these industries will join the migration.

Here again, Japanese competition is an important factor to the Far East, but actually it is not the decisive one. With increasingly higher overhead costs reducing their profit margins significantly, many American companies have simply found that it is far cheaper to establish manufacturing subsidiaries in South Korea, Taiwan, or Hong Kong than to continue production in the United States. And it would seen to me that this movement of American firms to the Far East should be greatly encouraged, despite the short-term unfavourable effects it may have on our international balance of payments. For one thing, it will create new sources of competition with the Japanese. More importantly, it will establish a firm and, one hopes, dynamic American economic presence to complement the US political and military presence in the area. This in turn will result in greater economic competition for the Japanese and thus provide the other nations of Non-Communist Pacific Asia with increased flexibility and bargaining power in dealing with the major powers.

In the next two decades certain political and security goals will continue to bind together Japan and the US. The friendship of each is likely to continue to be the other's single greatest concern in its Pacific policy. But autonomy and independent policy – which Americans profess to want for the Japanese – gain meaning and conviction as they are exercised away from, or against, US policy. Real partnership and equality may be even more difficult to achieve between the United States and Japan than between the United States and Western Europe. Unless and until the Japanese go into a major nuclear armament programme, neither side will be able to forget that Japan owes a good deal of its strength and safety to US power.

Yet the areas of shared interests and values that tie the United States and Japan together are sufficiently pervasive to provide the basis for an alliance that should continue to serve both parties well – at least for the next decade or two, and perhaps indefinitely. Indeed, I would be willing to say that it is now obvious that the

United States has opted for an arrangement by which American might and Japanese economic power will be combined to rule the Pacific area. A critic noted recently that this amounts to nothing less than an attempt to establish a Japanese–American Co-Prosperity Sphere. Such an arrangement could prove very advantageous to the United States. From a military perspective, the United States has gained valuable flexibility from her bases in Japan. After Okinawa is returned to Japan in 1972, American forces based there may be used to fulfil security commitments in Taiwan, South Korea, and other Pacific areas. The Japanese are to build up their forces to a point where the US will be able to limit greatly its bases and troop concentrations in Japan itself. This increased Japanese military strength benefits the United States in two ways: the defence budget is reduced and fewer dollars are spent overseas.

Alternatively, any significant change in the present Japanese–American set-up would have serious impact upon Japan, the most drastic effect being the need to assume full responsibility for its own security. The United States would have to rely upon nuclear deterrence to protect itself, and upon bases closer to home to contain China. In the absence of the Security Treaty, the cost of defence to Japan might prove quite annoying although not wholly onerous to Japanese businessmen.

Japan and the Soviet Union

Another set of major issues revolves around the attitude and intentions of the Soviets. I did not include Siberia in my description of Pacific Asia even though from many points of view it should be so included. As far as the Japanese are concerned, Siberia is potentially an especially important area because its energy (natural gas and oil) and raw material resources exactly complement the Japanese economy. A Soviet–Japanese economic commission has for many years attempted to arrange major co-operative economic efforts. If such an effort ever succeeds in getting under way in a major fashion, the political implications would be highly significant. But the economic possibilities are by no means insignificant. There is, potentially, a very solid base of mutual economic interest for Japanese–Soviet collaboration in Siberia.

Japan's trade with Russia in 1969 was estimated at $703 million[6] and it is expected to rise to $720 million in 1970. The growth of trade, however, can perhaps be better appreciated by the fact that between 1957 and 1968 trade increased by more than thirty times. The only significant agreement reached by the Japanese–Soviet Joint Economic Committee prior to 1970 was for Japan's importation of 8 million cubic metres of lumber over a five-year period beginning in 1969, in return for $150 million worth of machinery, facilities, and consumer goods needed for the development of the Soviet's forest resources. Other Russian proposals have been unacceptable to the Japanese. According to the *Far Eastern Economic Review*,[7] for example, the Russians were seeking Japanese assistance in developing the Udokan copper mines, but agreement was not reached because the Japanese refused to commit the funds the Russians sought. The Russians estimated development costs at $1,900 million and wanted the Japanese to invest $900 million; but the Japanese estimated that only $400–$500 million was required for a planned 400,000 tons of copper, and of this they were prepared to commit only about a quarter of the development costs.

While the Russians seem to feel that Japan's need for raw materials close to home gives them sufficient leverage to make hard demands, the Japanese have not yet been willing to commit themselves and their money to unfavourable development projects. They appear very reluctant to grant the Russians export credit, a matter of importance to the Kremlin. The Japanese have argued that Japan has never given export credit to an advanced nation like the Soviet Union.

The most recent meeting of the Japanese–Soviet Joint Economic Committee took place in February 1970. This was the fourth meeting and its outcome was a pledge to develop Siberian forestry resources, a promise of continued studies on development of Siberian natural gas, iron ore, and coal resources, and mention of an agreement to build a new seaport at Vrangelya, near Nakhodka in Siberia, 'through Japan–Soviet cooperation'. The final communiqué of the meeting put development costs of the new port at $300 million, with Japan's share yet to be negotiated. In addition, it mentioned Japan's interest in joint projects to exploit Siberian natural gas resources, Soviet Siberian coal and iron for supply to Japan, and Siberian timber.

The other side of Russo-Japanese economic cooperation is the competition Japan offers to Soviet efforts for increased influence in Asia. The clash between Moscow and Tokyo over their respective roles in Asia is only beginning. Although no formal peace treaty has been signed with the USSR and the issue of the Kurile Islands awaits resolution, negotiations about trade and development find Japan with considerable ability to manoeuvre in the setting created by the Sino-Soviet split.

It would be very natural for the Japanese to think in terms of an American–Japanese–Soviet equilibrium through which the two-way cold war détente may become a triangular entente. Thus, some Japanese currently envisage a Soviet component gradually being added to the present Japanese–American alliance to form a somewhat looser but more comprehensive arrangement. Such a future would probably be characterized by fairly intense Japanese friction with China, but the Japanese might well be willing to pay that price. In fact, the price might still be compatible with a good deal of trade with China. The picture this presents – of a US and a Soviet Union relatively distant from each other over most issues but still able to include some arms control agreements – should both encourage the Japanese to take a major role in stabilizing Pacific Asia and, in particular, to act as a restraint on the Chinese.

All of this could be combined with a sense of separateness and apartness. That is, the Japanese might well feel that neither Western democracy nor Soviet communism provided any more important answers to the basic issues of Japanese society than did those of any other Asian or European society. These attitudes might easily be reinforced by more intimate experiences with these ideologies, and thus, while they were willing to work very closely with the US and the Soviet Union economically to coordinate aid and other international programmes, there is not likely to be any ultimate growth of intimate entente, and certainly no kind of formal union. Rather, the Japanese would have confidence in the fact that they were rapidly outgrowing both of their superpower partners in economics and would eventually do so in technology, which at some point might give them some important kinds of leverage – but that there is no rush, and certainly no compelling short-run reason to challenge either of these two nations.

As far as a reaction to potential Chinese challenges is concerned, the Japanese could well adopt the attitude that they might be willing to help either the Soviets or the Americans in a very junior capacity but that the bulk of the effort would have to be borne by either the US or the Soviet Union. It is not likely that the Chinese will be able to exploit this attitude of restraint on the part of the Japanese, since presumably the Americans and the Soviets would indeed feel compelled to act first. It would only be because of complete abdication of responsibility by the US – and possibly the Soviet Union – that one could envisage the Japanese being forced to take the initiative to preserve stability. Such an initiative presumably would be accompanied by a massive rearmament programme; indeed, there would then be every reason for a massive rearmament by the Japanese.

It is also possible that the Japanese might well develop feelings of real community either with the Pacific democracies or with the Soviet Union, or perhaps just with the United States itself. This sense of community might grow to the point where, in effect, the requirements of *giri* applied. This would be a most unlikely development but not a completely impossible one; if it were to arise it would generate a true feeling of community – since it is almost certain the United States (or other members of the 'Community') would, in its own way, reciprocate the attitude.

It is even conceivable that this rather curious bloc of three superpowers could develop some really high levels of cooperation and coordination, the Soviets, the Japanese, and the Americans generally acting together on almost all issues affecting the Pacific Basin while remaining independent or even competitive in the rest of the world. Even though the unity of the three superpowers was incomplete and even weak, it would almost certainly force at least a weak coordination between the Europeans and Chinese; they might not only trade intensely with each other but also act in other ways as a generally passively cooperating yet counter-vailing power to what, they would judge, would otherwise almost surely be a US–Soviet–Japanese hegemony over the world. Certainly, from a financial point of view such close cooperation of the US, Soviets, and Japanese (or even part of those two 'capitalist giants', the US and Japan) is probable and reasonable, yet it is going to be regarded very suspiciously by the Europeans. Particularly if the Soviets are added to this ongoing de facto Japan–US combination, then paranoiac Europeans at least (as well as paranoiac Chinese) are likely to attribute the most sinister intentions to any joint enterprise of the three superpowers.

Threatening and frightening as this tri-power cooperation might appear to many Europeans, it is not likely to appear threatening or frightening enough to force political unification. In particular, the West Germans have and need to continue having a special relationship with the United States. In addition, morale among Europeans would probably be low enough to prevent their quite being able to envisage themselves as taking on the rank of superpower or even being willing to make the necessary sacrifices. If, however, the Europeans did form a Euro-pean political community or did act as a unit in their relationships with the Russians, Japanese, and Americans, then we would have something very close to Europe's old balance of power, in which there were four undeniably great powers (UK, Germany, France, USSR), a near-great power (Austro-Hungary; the current analogy is China), and some intermediate powers big enough to make a difference, such as Italy. In this case it might still be Italy, or it could be such countries as India, Canada, Brazil, etc.

Some Special Problems and Issues

There are at least four nations with whom the Japanese have some very special and important relationships or issues which we should consider, even if only briefly. These are India, Indonesia, Aus-tralia, and Canada.

In the case of India, it may well turn out that Japan (and per-haps some European countries) will play a greater role in furnishing useful economic and technological assistance, and otherwise helping to develop the subcontinent, than either the Soviets or the Americans. For a whole series of reasons, the Americans and the Russians have not done well in India (with the exception of the 'Green Revolution' and supplying the new wheat), and it seems to me they are not likely to do well in the future. While the Japanese do not get along easily or well with the Indians, by and large neither does anyone else, and the Japanese are more willing to make the effort – or at least make some kind of effort, which the Americans are not. In the immediate future the Japanese might make a major impact on India by jointly setting up fertilizer plants or many light industries (particularly, cheap labour might be exploited by Japanese investment, perhaps organized through joint ventures); Japanese missions have already made an impact on improving Indian farming practices, and this work could be greatly increased; and finally, the Japanese might well be, at least from the Indian point of view, ideal military advisers, being obviously competent but neutral in the cold war and increasingly anti-Chinese. From one point of view Japan's situation as an Asian state is an advantage, since it may raise the confidence level of some of the Indians. From another it is not, since most Asians do not like to defer to other Asians. However, no Indian need feel that he is deferring unnecessarily, because, after all, these Japanese are economically very advanced Asians indeed. One can even imagine some eventual kind of joint Indian– Japanese nuclear force to which the Australians, Indonesians, South Koreans, and others might contribute, but whose main purpose is to satisfy the immediate nuclear ambitions of the Indians and the Japanese in a way (under multinational auspices) that does not rock the nuclear boat – particularly as far as West Germany and Italy are concerned. This could fulfil some important sub-objective of arms control and European and world stability.

The possible Japanese relationship to Indonesia also deserves some comment. Here again, we find an almost perfect complement between two economies. However, we note that the Indonesians have badly mistreated their Chinese merchants, because they resented that group's virtual monopoly on certain commercial activities within Indonesia. It seems quite important that in attempting to develop Indonesia the Japanese take care not to overwhelm the Indonesians with their presence. They must also be certain that they do not develop an attitude of superiority and arrogance towards the Indonesians, an attitude many Indonesians claim is already developing. It should be quite possible for the Japanese and Indonesians to work in partnership without creating inordinate strains so as to accelerate enormously Indonesia's rate of development. One favourable factor will be the assistance of a number of competing countries, European and North American, thus diluting to some degree the Japanese presence. Even so, it will take great self-restraint and careful planning, creativity, and the 'social imagination' of Japan, if both sides are to benefit as much as they should from this very natural economic 'marriage.'

The problem of Australia will also require real tact and creativity, and on both sides. It is going to be very important that the Australians not feel they have been left alone in NOCPA to face – or even to work with – the Japanese. It will be a continuous and perhaps overwhelming requirement in Australian policy to maintain close connections with the Americans. Subject to this caveat, it seems likely that the Australians will develop a very deep and broad economic exchange with the Japanese. This would probably to be very good for Australia, not only economically but socially and cuturally as well. In many ways the Australians live a rather parochial and inbred life. As a result of their current economic success and a close relationship to the Japanese and to the rest of Pacific Asia, they are likely to be forced into a most stimulating and cosmopolitan existence. The biggest issue for them to face will be the extent to which they wish to go along with, participate in, or even initiate various kinds of defence and security arrangements.

Australia is one of the few countries that has consistently been able to maintain a favourable balance of trade with Japan. So favourable, in fact, that for at least the past three years the Australians have managed to export roughly double what they imported, while becoming in the process one of Japan's major suppliers of primary products and raw materials. Prior to World

War II Japan's main supplier was mainland China, but since then Japan has been forced to rely increasingly on the United States, which is now its major supplier, and on Australia, which has gradually become Japan's second largest supplier. Australia's abundant natural resources and relative proximity have made it an ideal trading partner. In the last twelve years, for example, trade between the two nations has increased by approximately 400 per cent. In the past five years alone trade has increased by about 50 per cent to well over $1·3 billion. In terms of the Japanese economy, this amounted to 7·5 per cent of Japan's total imports in the Japanese fiscal 1968 and 3·1 per cent of its exports. Owing to the different size of their economies, the percentages are even more impressive in terms of Australia's economy. Over 24 per cent of Australia's exports were sold to Japan and nearly 12 per cent of its imports came from Japan, which represented about 18 per cent of Australia's total trade.

But these statistics alone do not reflect the full measure of Japan's importance to the Australian economy and its domination of the Australian mining industry. For example, Japan purchased 60 per cent of Australia's total mineral exports, and in some commodities it virtually monopolized the market. In fiscal 1967, for example, Japan purchased 88 per cent of Australia's iron ore exports, 97 per cent of its coking coal exports, and approximately 50 per cent of the crude copper exports.

Yet until now Japanese investments in Australia were extremely small, almost insignificant in comparison with those in North and South America or South-east Asia. Since 1951, Japan has made about 29 per cent of its investments in North America, 27 per cent in South America, 19 per cent in South Asia, but only 3 per cent in Australia and New Zealand.[8] Instead, they made long-term commitments for minerals and industrial raw materials that totalled several billions of dollars, covered ten- to fifteen-year periods, and produced the desired result. On the basis of these commitments, American and Australian interests invested a great deal of money to develop these natural resources. From the Japanese point of view, this arrangement was practically ideal. Their investment in these projects, and therefore their risk and capital outlays, were negligible, yet they were still able to satisfy their requirements. This situation will not last, however, as many Japanese have begun to realize after even a short visit to Sydney or Melbourne. Quite naturally, many Australians were offended by the Japanese reluctance to make any major investment in the Australian economy while 'exploiting' the nation's resources. As one Japanese magazine reported, 'A certain Australian intellectual openly wondered whether it was advisable for Australia to remain "a quarrying ground for Japan" – especially in the field of iron ores.'⁹

Admittedly, fears of Japanese hegemonial ambitions in Southeast Asia still exist among Australians and that may explain part of their reaction. One probable result of the increasing 'presence' of Japan in Pacific Asia, beside the possibility that it will be tempted to establish a hegemony in Pacific Asia, is that the Australians will become more anxious than ever to maintain an American involvement in Pacific Asian affairs.

Another area in which the Japanese are likely to become important and in which there will be major Japanese investment is Alaska and the West Coast of Canada. In addition to the normal commercial type of investment and development, here the Japanese are likely to concentrate substantial sums on developing recreation areas for their use. Relatively early developments in air transportation will probably bring about rapid, convenient, and inexpensive access to these areas for the Japanese. At the same time the need for recreation by the affluent Japanese will soon become enormous.

Actually, the Japanese might develop a whole series of 'special relationships' in addition to their current one with the US. These special relationships could be regional, as for example with the NOCPA community I have described earlier, or with the Western Pacific South-east Asian Group of the old Co-prosperity zone. A third special relationship could be with the Soviet Union, where the focus of attention would presumably be the joint economic development of Siberia. This possibility would have important political implications for the Japanese, both in bridging US-Soviet differences, and probably (though, from the viewpoint of the Japanese, reluctantly) in contributing to the development of bad relationships with China.

Finally, the Japanese could try to dilute their relationships with both the United States and the Soviet Union by merging them into a single 'committee'.

Japanese National Goals

Irrespective of what policies the Japanese pursue, one must assume they will feel a very deep and abiding concern about where they stand in the international hierarchical structure. In the 70s the answer will be deceptively simple. They will clearly be the third power in the world – well above China or any single European competitor. But at least at first it will not be clear whether they are likely to be considered the first of the five (Japan, West Germany, France, China, and the United Kingdom) or the third of the three (United States, Soviet Union, Japan).

On one of my early trips to Japan, I had prepared a lecture in which I indicated my belief that by the mid or late 70s Japan would be the first of the five. I did this despite objections by several American experts on Japan that the Japanese simply wouldn't know what I was talking about – that they were so used to thinking of themselves as being number twenty or so that this idea that they would be considered first of the five large powers would leave them incredulous and perhaps even angry. However, on my first presentation one of the Japanese misunderstood my statement and thought I was talking about the year 2000. He asked me why Japan was the first of the five rather than the third of the three. During the whole trip no Japanese seemed to have any trouble thinking of Japan being at least the first of the five by 1980 or a little earlier. This is an issue for the short run – at most the next decade or two. It seems likely that sometime in the mid or late 70s it will be important to at least some Japanese to be thought of as the third of the three. That in itself may make for certain kinds of initiatives and programmes, the most obvious and constructive being to give increased foreign aid on a scale befitting a superpower.

The Japanese often assign an 'assimilated rank' to a nation – or at least let their treatment of foreigners be greatly affected by their ranking of their countries. Thus, the ranking by the Japanese of themselves might have important effects on the relationships of individual Japanese with individual foreigners, particularly if the Japanese insist on foreigners rendering to them the deference to which their new rank entitles them. But Germans, Englishmen, Frenchmen, South Americans, Australians, various South-east Asian nationalities, and so on may not easily yield such respect and deference to individual Japanese. Such tensions, combined with the anticipated spectacular increase in tourism and commercial travel, could give rise to all kinds of incidents.

This will probably be particularly important in Pacific Asia, where the Japanese are likely to think of themselves as very much the leading power in their relationships with the other nations of the area. And unless the other nations give them this kind of deference, some Japanese can be expected to react, at least on occasion, quite badly.

It should be clear that in the longer run (the next two or three decades or even more) the Japanese will continue to be dedicated to their first priority and major national goal – surpassing the West, at first economically and technologically but later in other ways as well. But within the next decade their economy will go from large to gigantic. Almost all the postwar objectives will have been fulfilled. Their confidence will be buoyed not only by this but also by a growing world respect – even awe – for their economic and technological performance.

Finally, there will be an increasingly widely held belief – first in Japan and then elsewhere – that Japan will actually surpass the United States in GNP per capita and possibly in total GNP by the year 2000. This will lead to a further increase in confidence, a kind of confidence associated with people who firmly believe that time is on their side but who do not intend to allow this belief to cause any relaxation in effort. All of these will give the Japanese a new sense of freedom to seek new objectives.

In the West, on the other hand, there is a seeming 'loss of nerve.' While this 'loss of nerve' takes different forms in the US, in many Western European countries, and in the Soviet Union, its impact in all these areas is quite dramatic and noticeable. Further, in the leading country of the West, the United States, there seems to be, at least to many outside observers, a growing anarchy and disunity, an overwhelming explosion of domestic problems, and a failure in international performance, particularly regarding Vietnam.

Actually, many Japanese believe that these factors are greatly exaggerated but that where there is so much smoke, there must be a reasonable amount of fire. None of this implies that the Japanese will necessarily become chauvinistically and nationalistically excited about the 'decadence' of the West, or that they will aim once more at building an Asian or world empire. It does mean, however, that there will be a real sense in Japan of uncertainty of choice and a concern about which of the old values and objectives still apply. The Japanese will certainly feel that there ought to be some important and exciting way to capitalize on their growing affluence and technology, but it will not be quite clear to them how – or whether – the old rules apply.

One thing seems certain. In addition to their economic and technological performance, the Japanese intend to make their environment into a work of art and a marvel of engineering. In the last twenty-five years, they have, by other nations' standards, underspent on almost all aspects of their infrastructure. However, in part for its own sake and in part because this seems to be the way world attention and interests are being focused, they have decided to take in hand the problems of pollution, overcrowding, traffic jams, and all the other consequences and contradictions of the modern, affluent technological society. As discussed in Chapter 5, the Japanese have a twenty-year programme during which they intend to 'fix Japan'. I would guess that before the twenty-year programme is over they will have succeeded in doing so. They will be able to say that not only have they become the first truly post-industrial culture but they have achieved their advanced status in style – that the islands of Japan have become a truly worthy environment for the Japanese people. In fact, since a more attractive and liveable environment cannot be found anywhere in the world, if the Japanese are persuasive enough I may move there myself.

Twenty-five years have now passed with Japan living under a constitution consciously adapted from American models and in a form of modern industrial, economic, and social competitiveness and mobility widely regarded as American in style. It is not unreasonable to believe that the rule of the 'Showa' generation will continue essentially unchanged. A convenient generation difference is noted in Japan between those born before and those born within the rule of the present Showa Emperor. Over two thirds of the population now belong to the Showa generation, which – on the surface at least – feels little if any responsibility for prewar militarism and nationalist excesses. It seems to many observers that the Showa generation's postwar ethos has so consistently substituted economic for political gratification and personal for national gratification that internal dynamics of nationalist ambitions are lacking. I disagree, however. It does appear that the Showa generation will carry forward – with added confidence – essentially those policies that made Japan the world's third economic power; but it is not unreasonable to think that the 1970s may also produce a reassertion of nationalism and an attempt to redefine Japanese national and cultural identity, rather than pursuing the adoption of foreign models that has characterized the twenty-five years since the end of the war.

There is an astronomical phenomenon that I think has some relevance here. When a celestial object such as the rising sun is near the horizon, it appears to be a great deal larger than when it is at its zenith. But the observer should be cautioned that that is an illusion. It would be a great mistake in the case of Japan to assume that the rising sun has reached its zenith. Rather the opposite; it has just begun its climb. How brightly, where and when and how long it is going to shine are all open issues on which I hope I have shed some light but do not feel I have in any way settled. Indeed I hope that the current Hudson Institute Study, or some other study, will do that – or at least give some guidance to the West on how to live with this incredibly apt student of and partial convert to Western industrialization, science, and technology. Perhaps equally important, but presumably more difficult, will be to give some guidance to the Japanese themselves.

Appendix

Introduction

These charts represent an approach developed by the Hudson Institute in its seminars for senior members of business, government, and the professions. As used in these seminars they are somewhat more complete and comprehensive than in this appendix, but I have included enough material here to be representative of the technique and to gain for interested readers some of the advantages.

The separate pages on any particular subject are designed to provide a highly compressed over-all treatment of a group of related issues and their context without using long discursive passages to connect them. The approach is designed to be rather like the *pointillistic* style of the French Impressionist Georges Seurat, as the elements of each module are intended to form their most meaningful pattern of relationships when combined in the mind of the reader. But even aside from such holistic effects, the synoptic presentation of appropriate topics in carefully formulated and grouped charts has a number of values. In many cases just presenting a list of the major points can be useful. In most cases if the reader does not understand the charts as presented, he can refer to the text for further elaboration of the same issue or theme.

For all these reasons I thought it might be useful to append this series of abbreviated 'Chart Pages' to *The Emerging Japanese Superstate* as a highly selective recapitulation, elaboration, and background (and possibly introduction if the reader wishes to use it that way) to the issues and problems discussed in this book.

Two Useful Chronologies

Chart 1 provides a standard chronology of Japanese history, emphasizing political and military events. The most interesting thing to note is that Japan developed in relative isolation from continental Asia, and that most of the contacts which took place were on Japan's initiative. Only twice were there serious attempts to invade Japan, both by the Mongols during the Kamakura period, and both attempts, of course, failed.

From our point of view an equally important chronology is that in *Chart 2*, which begins with Commodore Perry's arrival and the weakness of the bakufu. In signing the treaty of Kanagawa the bakufu did not really intend to accept a resident minister from abroad but found they had to. The chagrin of the Japanese at these contacts with the US and at the 'unequal treaties' was demonstrated by the assassination of the Japanese who signed them. Yet signing these treaties probably gave the Japanese the breathing space, the time and freedom they needed in order to assimilate the experience of these first contacts and make themselves sufficiently strong to prevent Western domination.

The next three items take note of the Satsuma and Choshu clans' initial antagonism to the foreigner. Reprisals were swift and painful, yet rather than becoming angry, the Satsuma clan in effect invited 'to dinner' the British and French who had bombarded them so as to find out more about the foreigners' weapons and methods. Subsequently the Choshu also established a liaison with European forces. In short, episodes that would have caused bitterness in most

cultures brought the Japanese to admire and emulate their enemies.

1869 notes the surrender of the *daimyo* fiefs to the emperor, probably the first and only occasion in history where an upper class voluntarily resigned its privileges in order to accelerate modernization. Modernization was subsequently carried through by the upper class, often to their benefit but often at their cost as well. Thus, compulsory education of the masses followed almost immediately. Soon afterward came the elimination of Samurai privileges. The subsequent violent suppression of a Samurai revolt by a conscript army eliminated the last formal vestiges of Tokugawa class society and made it clear that any Japanese could fight well, that the Samurai had no monopoly of military talent.

From the rest of the material in the chronology we note the significance of the Versailles Conference's rebuff to the Japanese in 1919 and the passage by the United States Congress of the Oriental Exclusion Act of 1924 as factors embittering the Japanese towards the West. Despite Japan's incredibly successful modernization process, under the strain of the depression Japan went militaristic and by 1936 had entered an almost manic phase described as 'government by assassination.'

And finally, the last three lines conjecture about the future – taking note of the likelihood that student unrest had peaked by 1969, that after 1970 the Japanese will no longer talk 'poor mouth,' but that it will take five years or so before Japan's new political status really begins to be widely recognized and accepted.

Two Useful Chronologies

Chart 1

A CHRONOLOGY ON JAPANESE CULTURE AND SOCIETY

by Kosaka Masaaki

I. The Age of Aesthetic Culture (c. 700–c. 1200)

552	Introduction of Buddhism to Japan
592–628	Reign of Suiko Tennō; Shōtoku Taishi, Regent
604	*Seventeen-article Constitution*
645	Taika reform
710	Establishment of the first permanent capital, Nara
712	*Records of ancient matters (Kojiki)*
720	*Chronicles of Japan (Nihongi)*
752	Dedication of the great Buddha at the Tōdaiji in Nara
c. 770	*Manyōshū (a collection of myriad leaves: an anthology)*
794	Heian-Kyō (Kyoto) becomes the capital
c. 990–1020	*Tale of Genji (Genji Monogatari) and Pillow Book (Makura Sōshi)*

II. The Age of Religious Culture (c. 1200–c. 1600)

1192	Founding of Kamakura Shogunate
1232	The Jōei Code (collection of maxims and rules for administrators)
1262	Shinran (1173–1262), founder of the True Pure Land Sect (Judo-Shinshu)
1274	First Mongol invasion
1281	Second Mongol invasion
1338	Ashikaga Takauji becomes *Shogun*
1467	Onin war. Commencement of Endemic civil wars throughout Japan
1568	Oda Nobunago controls the capital
1571	Nobunaga destroys the Enryakuji on Mt Hiei

III. The Age of Politics (c. 1600–1860)

1582	Toyotomi Hideyoshi succeeds to power
1598	Death of Hideyoshi
1603	Establishment of Tokugawa Shogunate
1637–8	Shimabara revolt
1640	Europeans excluded
1648	Nakae Tōjyū (1608–48)
1685	Yamaga Sōkō (1622–85)
1688–1704	Genroku period (Saikaku, Chikamatsu, Bashō, and Ukiyoe prints)
1705	Itō Jinsai (1627–1705)
1801	Motoori Norinaga (1730–1801)
1858	United States–Japanese commercial treaty

IV. The Age of Enlightenment (c. 1860)

1868	Meiji restoration
1912	Death of Emperor Meiji
1920	Prewar liberalism (Taishō democracy)
1925	Universal male suffrage
1931	Manchurian incident
1941–5	Pacific war
1952	End of military occupation by allied forces

Moore, Charles A., ed, 'The Status and the Role of the Individual in Japanese Society', *The Japanese Mind: Essentials of Japanese Philosophy and Culture* (Honolulu: East-West Center Press, 1967), pp. 259–60.

Chart 2
A CHRONOLOGY OF MODERN JAPAN

1853	'Black Ships' arrive — Bakufu seeks advice
1854	Treaty of Kanagawa
1855	First of 'Unequal Treaties'
1858	Four Unequal Treaties
1860	Assassination of Ii Naosuke
1862	Killing of Richardson by Satsuma
1863	Attacks by Chosu on foreigners — reprisals against Satsuma
1864	Reprisals against Chosu
1868	Meiji restoration ends Tokugawa period and inaugurates modern Japan
1869	Voluntary surrender of Daimyo fiefs to emperor
1872	Compulsory education
1876	Samurai forbidden to wear two swords; conscript army set up
1877	Suppression of Samurai revolt by conscript army
1878	Children's civilization song

1890	Imperial rescript on education
1894–5	War with China, conquest Korea, Formosa
1900	Joint European expedition force for relief of Peking during Boxer Rebellion
1905	War with Russia, penetration of Manchuria
1912	Death of Meiji emperor
1915	Twenty-one demands on China, war with Germany
1919	Versailles Conference refuses to include a racial equality clause in League of Nations covenant
1920	Prewar liberalism (Taisho democracy)
1924	Oriental Exclusion Act passed
1925	Universal male suffrage
1927	Showa reign starts
1929	Depression; 1932: rice crop failure in Japan
1931	Manchurian incident
1932	Shanghai incident
1933	Japan leaves the League of Nations
1936	Period of 'government by assassination' culminates in a military-dominated cabinet
1937	War with China
1940	Axis pact
1941	War with the United States
1945	Occupation starts
1952	Occupation ends
1958	First serious student riots
1960	Security treaty riots
1969	Peak of student unrest (?)
1970	Osaka Exhibition – end of current 'poor mouth' attitude (?)
1975	Japan is a technological and economic giant but a political pygmy (?)

More Historical Background

Chart 1 indicates some of the aspects of Tokugawa Japan that were important in preparing the country for the subsequent modernization. Tokugawa Japan was not only an example in its own right of social engineering but a very important historical transition period. Japan developed much of the necessary background for creating a modern culture during this period. A good deal of this was bound up with the so-called Sankin-Kotai system in which the great daimyo had to live six months a year in Tokyo. This had an influence on secularization, the creation of a monetary economy, the strengthening of the merchant class, and so on.

Chart 2 provides a rather succinct and yet very explicit and clear description of the changing Japanese mood during the early part of the Meiji restoration.

The enthusiasm of the Japanese for Western culture is illustrated in the Children's Civilization Song of 1878, given in *Chart 3*. The children count from 1 to 10, at each number reciting a desirable object of civilization.

Chart 4 suggests how dramatic and shocking was the Japanese victory over the Russians in 1905. We are told that people in central Africa who had never heard of Russia or Japan nonetheless knew that a non-European people had defeated Europeans in war.

Charts 5 and 6, excerpts from twentieth-century Japanese poems, suggest the ambivalence of Japanese reaction to the West. The 'heretic' confesses his admiration of the 'red hairs' — the foreigners. But in the second excerpt the poet asks how to restore the lost wholeness of Japanese society.

Chart 1

TOKUGAWA JAPAN

1. Two hundred years of almost complete isolation of an already relatively homogeneous country
2. 'Hostage system' forces:
   A. Travel, roads, communication, centralization, etc.
   B. Growth of monetary economy

C. Enrichment of merchant class
3. Impoverishment of Samurai
4. Growth of literacy
5. Centralized nation-state
6. Basis laid for 'Puritan ethic,' 'work orientation,' and 'commercial society'
7. Orientation towards 'duty,' communalism, hierarchy, etc. firmly laid

---

Chart 2

THE MEIJI 'RESTORATION' (GUIDING PRINCIPLES AND POPULAR SLOGANS)

'Honour the Emperor, expel the barbarian.'

Popular slogan of the anti-Shogunates

'Knowledge shall be sought from all over the world and thus shall be strengthened the foundation of imperial polity.'

Charter oath, Emperor Meiji, 1868

'We shall take the machines and techniques from them, but we have our own ethics and morals.' *

Hashimoto Sanai

* Note similarity o f these positions with ninth-century slogan, 'Chinese knowledge, Japanese spirit'.

'A rich country and a strong army.'
'Western science, Eastern ethics.' *

Popular slogans of Meiji modernizers

'Lay aside the principle of dependence [on Europe], improve our internal government affairs, make our country secure by military preparation . . . and then wait for the time of the confusion of Europe which must come eventually.'

Viscount Tani

* Note similarity of these positions with ninth-century slogan, 'Chinese knowledge, Japanese spirit'.

Chart 3
CIVILIZATION BALL SONG

A popular children's song composed in 1878 in which children counted the bounces of a ball, reciting ten desirable Western objects – gas lamps, steam engines, horse carriages, cameras, telegrams, lightning conductors, newspapers, schools, letter-post, and steam boats.

G. B. Sansom, *The Western World and Japan* (London: The Cresset Press, 1950), p. 401.

Chart 4

'I, your humble servant, an obscure student, having had occasion to study new books and new doctrines, have discovered in a recent history of Japan how they have been able to conquer the impotent Europeans. This is the reason we have formed an organization . . . We have selected from young Annamites the most energetic, with great capacities for courage, and are sending them to Japan for study . . . Our only aim is to prepare the population for the future.'

Leaflet distributed in Annam, *c.* 1905

Chart 5
SECRET SONG OF THE HERETICS (1909)

I believe in the heretical
  teachings of a degenerate
  age, the witchcraft of the
  Christian God,
The captains of the black ships,
  the marvellous land of the red
  hairs,
The scarlet glass, the
  sharp-scented carnation,
The calico, arrack, and *vinho
  tinto* of the southern
  barbarians . . .

– Kitahara Hakushū (1885–1943)

Chart 6

The road that has newly been
  opened here
Goes, I suppose, straight to the
  city.
I stand at a crossway of the
  new road,
Uncertain of the lonely
  horizon.
Dark, melancholy day.

The sun is low over the roofs
  of the row of houses.

The unfelled trees in the woods
  stand sparsely.
How, how to restore myself to
  what I was?
On this road I rebel against and
  will not travel,
The new trees have all been
  felled.

Hagiwara Sakutaro (1886–1942)
The New Road of Koide

National Character and General Remarks on Some Social Attitudes

These pages review much of
the material in Chapter 2: Some
comments on the Japanese
Mind.

Chart 1 draws upon Ruth
Benedict's outline of the
complex and seemingly
contradictory nature of some
aspects of the Japanese
national character. Many of
these contradictions, of course,
are resolved when one
understands that there are
specific circumstances when
one or another adjective
applies.

Chart 2 focuses on the
individual male Japanese,
rather than on the culture as a
whole, and is, of course, even
more controversial as a
generalization. However, it is
not at all controversial in being
reasonably typical of what
many Japanese think of
themselves.

Charts 3 and 4 describe the
Japanese personality, as they
see themselves and as
compared with Anglo-
Saxons.

Chart 5 tries to sum up, in
twelve phrases or so, some of
the major characteristics of
traditional Japanese culture and
character. Like any such
generalization, it is somewhat
sweeping and simplistic, but it
does give a useful perspective
on our topic.

Topics in *Chart 6* have been
discussed in some detail in
Chapter 2. The following pages
add to this discussion by
quoting extensively from the
views of various authors. I
would draw particular attention
to the quote from the young
Kamikaze pilot Kyokji Vehara,
which illustrates the very special
form patriotism and loyalty can
take among the Japanese.

Chart 1
ACCORDING TO RUTH BENEDICT JAPANESE ARE:

1. Aggressive and unaggressive
2. Militaristic and aesthetic
3. Insolent and polite
4. Rigid and adaptable
5. Submissive and resentful of being pushed around
6. Loyal and treacherous
7. Brave and timid
8. Conservative and hospitable to new ways

Chart 2
INDIVIDUAL MALE JAPANESE OFTEN DESCRIBE THEMSELVES (OR OTHER JAPANESE) BY SUCH ADJECTIVES AND PHRASES AS:

1. Egoistic
2. Emotional
3. Introspective
4. Illogical
5. Stoical
6. Diligent
7. Persevering
8. Disciplined
9. Conformist
10. Respectful
11. Loyal
12. Honest
13. Polite
14. Sensitive
15. Having to fulfil the requirements of various kinds of duty (as explained later, these are *Giri, Ninjo*, etc.)
16. Less interested in the letter of a contract or written agreement than its emotional connotation and context
17. Very anxious to avoid uncertainty and stark confrontations in almost all situations (social, business, governmental)
18. Having tendency to dislike and look down on Koreans
19. Having a realistic willingness to learn from them

Chart 3
THE JAPANESE HAVE (IN COMPARISON WITH ENGLISHMEN):

A more realistic willingness to learn from others

A more good-humoured cheerfulness

A more realistic appreciation of the need to cooperate in society

A keener desire for self-improvement

A keener sense of personal honour, less complacently self-righteous

Less sense of social responsibility to remove abuses in their own society

Ability to show greater affectionate warmth and quicker emotional responses in intimate relations

Adapted from R. P. Dore, 'The Japanese Personality', Guy Wint, ed., *Asia Handbook* (Middlesex, England: Penguin Books, 1969), p. 568.

Chart 4

THE JAPANESE PERSONALITY (IN COMPARISON WITH ENGLISHMEN):

JAPANESE ARE	BUT THEY ARE ALSO
More ambitious	Less willing to stand up for individual rights
More imitative	Less men of principle
More introverted	Less selfish
More sentimental	Less afraid of hard work
More childishly naïve	Less busybody, with a more tolerant willingness to live and let live
More slavishly diligent	
More submissive to superiors	
More dishonest and indirect in speech	Less self-confident and more neurotically preoccupied with retaining the good opinion of others
More sensitive to, and less willing to offend, the feelings of others	
More willing to forego the pleasures of self-assertion in the interests of social harmony	
More shy about imposing their views and feelings on strangers	Adapted from R. P. Dore, 'The Japanese Personality', Guy Wint, ed., *Asia Handbook* (Middlesex, England: Penguin Books, 1969), p. 568.

Chart 5

SYNOPTIC VIEW OF JAPANESE CULTURE

1. Politically (in both public and private organization) pluralist
2. Authoritarian
3. Communal
4. Nationally egoistic and assimilative
5. Hierarchical
6. Pre-World War II a romantic attitude towards war. Now?
7. Aesthetic attitudes and values pervasive and important (particularly in upper classes)
8. Competent perfective technology
9. Assertive attitude towards environment
10. Approving attitude towards private property
11. Purposive attitude towards history (a working out of the national destiny)
12. Ideal types are faithful Samurai warrior (and/or faithful servitor); responsible paternalistic Confucian master; and conforming, dutiful Japanese citizen

Chart 6

SPECIAL ISSUES OF JAPANESE CULTURE, SOCIETY, POLITICS, AND NATIONAL CHARACTER

1. Great capacity for purposive communal action
2. Hierarchy, prestige, shame, guilt, and pride
3. Sense of being on display and of being judged
4. Social and group unity and harmony
5. The politics and techniques of 'group-centred' decision-making, Japanese style – the institution of *Ringi*
6. Influencing of Japanese decisions – whether governmental or private
7. 'Duty' – e.g., *Giri, Ninjo, On,* etc.
8. 'Damaged' or 'inadequate' people and things are (usually) regarded as expendable
9. Traditional emphasis on 'spiritual' *v.* materialistic resources and issues
10. Japanese patriotism – *Kokutai* – mystic sense of being special and distinct
11. *Tenkō* transformation
12. *Kanji* barrier
13. Importance of cliques (*Batsu*)
14. 'Japan Inc.' (or Japan : a conglomerate of conglomerates)
15. The Todai club
16. Japanese 'racism'
17. Japanese politics
18. Contracts and litigation – treaties and understandings
19. Japanese exclusiveness
20. Japanese press

Group-Oriented

'For Japanese of all ages, in virtually any situation, have a powerful urge toward group formation : when they wish to do something startling (intellectual, artistic, social, or political), they are likely to go about it by forming, joining, or activating a group. The extraordinary array of student circles, of cultural, professional, political, and neighborhood groups – the "horizontal" groups so prominent at all levels of society – makes Japan one of the most group-conscious nations in the world.'

Robert J. Lifton, 'Youth and History : Individual Change in Postwar Japan', *The Challenge of Youth,* Erik H. Erikson, ed. (New York : Basic Books, 1965 [copyright 1961]), p. 273.

Hierarchy

'Under the feudal system individual man could not have his own value. Instead, he could have his *raison d'etre* only in the hierarchical system from feudal lord down to servants ... His value as a human being increased as his position got closer to the lord and decreased as it got closer to the servants. It was therefore conceived that the highest virtue of the human being consists in serving the superior, the feudal lord, instead of regarding one's individual self as independent from others while living faithful to one's self.'

Charles A. Moore, ed., *The Japanese Mind: Essentials of Japanese Philosophy and Culture* (Honolulu: East-West Center Press, 1967), p. 235.

Emotion

... In the case of the Japanese, emotive expressions are governed by rules of propriety when not actually suppressed. The misconception that the Japanese are devoid of emotion has resulted from the fact that they do not easily show emotion in public. Outwardly composed and calm, a man nevertheless carries within himself the makings of emotional outbursts in which only the time and place are the governing conditions. The concealment of anxiety and grief is as natural as the control of one's temper and not unlike the Englishman's phlegm. But behind such rigid control lies a stronger emotion than behind the habitual outbursts of passion of a more volatile people. Repressed emotions must and do find safety valves for indirect externalization in humor, sports, fine arts, and literature.

'Beneath the rather solid surface of stoicism is found the sentimental, emotional make-up of the Japanese which shows up so clearly once the barrier is penetrated. When the lid of self-control and discipline is lifted the impulsive nature comes to the fore. It is this emotional trait that sustains the various practices and institutions, their social and political and economic activities, and makes them vulnerable to emotional appeals, didacticism, indoctrination, symbols, and myths ...

'Politics has for some time now provided the Japanese with a legitimate arena as an outlet for the emotions not only of the representatives but of the public as well. As an alternative to violence, it is serving a useful function as a safety valve. If political actions are to carry the force of conviction and determination, one can hardly deny an amplitude of emotion to the body politic. The release of emotion is often necessary to clear the atmosphere in politics but it can lead to violent clashes particularly when reason takes the back seat and moderation is forgotten in the heat of argument, as frequently happens on the floor of the Diet.'

Chitoshi Yanaga, *Japanese People and Politics* (New York: John Wiley & Sons, Inc., 1956), pp. 56–7.

Shame

'The Japanese are taught to feel shame before society and to fear it. The result is a self-consciousness which borders on an inferiority complex. This could be part of the origin of the national sense of inferiority the Japanese sometimes exhibit toward the outside world. But it does not seem to have produced among individuals much overt aggressiveness, largely because individual aggressiveness is strongly condemned by society . . .

'To avoid shame and win approval the Japanese must preserve "face" and self respect . . . a sense of shame and the need for self respect provide the Japanese with much the same individual driving force that we derive from conscience and a sense of guilt. Self respect can be as hard a taskmaster for them as conscience was for the Puritans.'

Edwin O. Reischauer, *United States and Japan* (New York: The Viking Press, 1968), pp. 143–4.

Ridicule

'Ridicule is one of the most potent social weapons in community life. To be laughed at is far more painful to an individual who feels the pangs of shame than the mere payment of a monetary fine which does not attract any widespread attention and may not even be noticed by the community.'

Chitoshi Yanaga, *Japanese People and Politics* (New York: John Wiley & Sons, Inc., 1956), pp. 86–7.

Bushido

'. . . Bushido has for its foundation the laying down of one's own life for the sake of one's lord . . . loyalty . . . [is] the centrally significant good.

'Loyalty discounts death, for it is from the start a readiness to die for the cause.'

Josiah Royce

Charles A. Moore, ed., *The Japanese Mind: Essentials of Japanese Philosophy and Culture* (Honolulu: East-West Center Press, 1967), p. 234.

Guilt

'The Japanese seem to suffer from guilt which is not associated with any complex of supernatural sanctions, but is instead derived from the system of loyalties which cements the structure of their traditional society. Guilt in Japanese is hidden from Western observation because we do not understand Japanese familial relationships, and because conscious emphasis on external sanctions helps to disguise the underlying feelings of guilt which, severely repressed, are not obvious to the Japanese themselves. The keystone toward understanding Japanese guilt is held to be the nature of interpersonal relationships within the Japanese family, particularly the relations of the children with the mother. The Japanese mother, without conscious intent, has perfected techniques of inducing guilt in her children by such means as quiet suffering. She takes the burden of responsibility for their behavior and, as also with bad conduct on the part of her husband, will often manifest self-reproach if her children conduct themselves badly or in any way fail to meet social expectations. When a person does wrong he thereby hurts his mother, and he also hurts other familial members; as a result, he suffers unhappiness and feelings of guilt.'

Edward Norbeck and George de Vos, 'Japan', in Francis L. K. Hsu, ed., *Psychological Anthropology: Approaches to Culture and Personality* (Homewood, Ill.: The Dorsey Press, Inc., 1961), p. 27.

Pride

'The universal characterization of the Japanese which is widely accepted is that they are a very proud and sensitive people. Yet, in reality, they are not much more sensitive or proud than any other people in the world. The Japanese, it is true, are highly sensitive to adverse opinion or criticism, expressed or implied, and easily take offense. They are equally sensitive to praise and appreciation. Their sensitivity underlies their strong desire to be accepted and be well thought of by others. On the international scene these attitudes are even more poignantly reflected. Any slight, slur, or discriminatory act has been strongly resented as an affront to national honor. This has been due largely to the inferior diplomatic status to which she was relegated and the uphill struggle she had to carry on before she could achieve a status of equality in the family of nations. In dealing with the nations of the West, Japan had to conduct herself with the eyes of the whole world upon her.'

Chitoshi Yanaga, *Japanese People and Politics* (New York: John Wiley & Sons, Inc., 1956), p. 58.

Self-Discipline

'. . . Japan's shame ethic depends on the one hand on a strong sense of obedience to authority, but at the same time the maintenance of self-respect also calls for the exercise of will power. More important than external conformity to avoid ridicule and shame is the inner force of will power to bolster self-respect. Self-discipline parallels obedience as a fundamental force shaping Japanese character. The self-respecting Japanese can find no more satisfaction in hidden shame than the God-fearing Westerner in concealed sin. The "sincere," self-respecting man must have will power, and to achieve will power he must employ self-discipline.

'The aesthetic Japanese glories in the Spartan virtues. Poet, artist, nature lover though he be, at the same time he believes in subjecting himself to an ascetic regime in the name of self-discipline. Cold baths in winter, strict dietary limitations, and other such dismal austerities are the stuff of which will power is made . . . The Japanese perform physically damaging austerities to strengthen their will power . . . [to perfect their personality] and thus to get the most out of life. All special skills, the Japanese believe, start with self-discipline. Expertness in calligraphy or fencing, painting or judo, depends on the ability to place an iron control over the emotions. The emphasis in archery is more on the self-composure of the archer than on his ability to hit the target. Complete self-discipline will raise the individual above the troubling doubts of shame or the fear of failure. Miracles can be accomplished by the man who knows self-

discipline and has true will power.'

Edwid O. Reischauer, *United States and Japan* (New York: The Viking Press, 1968), pp. 172–3.

Sense of Being on Display and of Being Judged

'[The Japanese child is taught a whole series of restraints. He is told, "If you do this] people will laugh at you." The child is taught not to eschew sin but to avoid *faux pas,* embarrassing or costly errors which would cause others to laugh at him or his family to be ashamed. Although he is taught to acquire certain general virtues, the emphasis is on winning specific approval and praise . . . The family uses the harsh judgments of society to teach the child conformity and obedience.

'This emphasis on the judgment of society makes the individual Japanese a very self-conscious person. "What will they think of me ?" is always his first thought, not "What do I think of them ?" Even the most humble Japanese feels himself to be on a stage before his fellow countrymen and the whole world.'

Edwin O. Reischauer, *United States and Japan* (New York: The Viking Press, 1968), pp. 143.

Kamikaze Pilot

'I believe that my honor has never been greater (since I have been selected for the Kamikaze force) . . . but love for freedom is an essential characteristic of human beings and no one can take it away from them. I believe, as Benedetto Croce said, that although freedom seems to be oppressed at one time, it is always struggling underneath and will finally win . . . The Germany of Nazism has already lost the

war. The countries of authoritarianisms are now crumbling . . . My ambition to make my beloved Japan become a great empire like Great Britain is already in vain . . . Japanese who could walk anywhere in the world, freely – that was the ideal I dreamt.

'(The Kamikaze pilot) can never be understood by reasoning and might be called a "suicider." But probably this can only be understood in a

spiritual country like Japan.
We pilots as instruments, have
no right to say anything; but
sincerely I would plead to the
Japanese people to make Japan
a truly great nation some day
... The above is what I believe
without falsity and please
excuse my disorderly statement.

Tomorrow there will be one less
liberal in the world. He may
look lonely seen in the past, but
he may at least himself have
full satisfaction in his heart.
Goodbye.'

Kyokji Vehara, age 22, Okinawa 1945

Giri

'*Giri* obligations often are
mutual and reciprocal,
especially within a collectivity
.... [it] works well in a society
of lifelong neighbors and
associates. It is measured not
from a single incident or
transaction but from its coloring
of an association that is
expected to extend
indefinitely through time ...
Since ... mutual support often

extends to a network of
persons, *giri* relations may link
not just two but a whole row
of participants ...
    '*Giri* inevitably loses its effect
in an environment of impersonal
transactions among strangers
and incidental acquaintances.'

John W. Hall and Richard Beardsley,
Twelve Doors to Japan (New York:
McGraw-Hill Book Company, 1965),
pp. 95–6.

Towards a Secular Life

'Despite the feverish religious
activity on the part of some
sectors of the population, there
has been no national revival of
religion. The circumstances are
to the contrary. The nation as a
whole moves further and
further from religion and meets
the problems of life in secular
ways. Public opinion polls
show that approximately
two-thirds of the population
disclaims religious faith. A
common response of Japanese

citizens to questions regarding
religious affiliation is to say
that the "family" religion is one
or another of the numerous sects
of Buddhism. Further
questioning reveals that the
speaker himself has no religious
faith. To most people religion
is not a subject of interest.
    'Generally regarded as quite
apart from the realm of religion
are various supernaturalistic
beliefs concerning good and
bad luck. Although customarily

called superstitutions, these retain considerable life, and many citizens find nothing anomalous in referring to "true superstitions."

'In the realm of secular life many of the old ideals and attitudes exist among people of all social strata. One should be faithful to his commitments, however much these might have changed. Thrift, industry, persistent struggles to success against heavy odds, and self-improvement in human skills and capabilities continue to be regarded as virtues. In combination they represent one of the most highly cherished Japanese values, the premium placed upon achievement. This Japanese value has sometimes been likened to the so-called "Protestant ethic" of the United States and Northern Europe, and there are indeed close resemblances. Perhaps the most conspicuous differences are that the role of Japanese religions in reinforcing or engendering the ethic seems comparatively small and that, rather than cherishing work for its own sake, the Japanese people appear to value industry chiefly for the specific economic, social, and associated psychological rewards that it may bring. These words are not to say that the Japanese value lacks moral import. The lazy person in Japan is more than merely lazy; he is regarded as untrustworthy and morally unsound . . .

'Whatever the origin of this ideal, the modern Japanese "naturally" values industriousness and "naturally" wishes to succeed. He desires also the visible symbols of success in the form of material possessions. Self-denial of ordinary necessities of life in order to purchase at outrageous prices such objects as alligator handbags, imported suiting materials, Swiss watches, jewels, and Scotch whisky is by no means exceptional. These are things that may be displayed – the Scotch whisky in a glass case in the living room – and they reflect prestige upon the family or the individual. Rather than being the antithesis of thrift, they are most often in Japan another aspect of it, occasional rewards of thrift that bring great satisfaction. It is not difficult to think that the Japanese emphasis on hierarchy, whether by achievement or prescription, and its accompaniment of tangible symbols of status continue today to reenforce thrift and achievement as virtues.'

Edward Norbeck, *Changing Japan, Case Studies in Cultural Anthropology* (New York: Holt, Rinehart & Winston, 1965), pp. 19–21.

Kokutai

'*Kokutai* is usually translated as "national polity" or "national essence," but it also conveys the sense of "body" or "substance," and its nature is impossible to define precisely. Included in *Kokutai* are the concepts of "national structure," particularly the emperor system; "national basis," the myth of the divine origin of Japan and of its imperial dynasty; and "national character," those special Japanese moral virtues, stemming from both native and Confucian influences, that are considered indispensable for individual behavior and social cohesion (embodied in *Bushido*, or the way of the warrior). Although *Kokutai* is a relatively modern concept — manipulated for political purposes during the Meiji era and again in association with pre-World War II militarism — it had profound roots in Japanese cultural experience and embraced something in the cultural identify of all Japanese.

'Most young people (with the exception of "Rightists") no longer take *Kokutai* seriously; they dismiss it as the propaganda of militarists, and even find it laughable. Nevertheless, the dishonoring of *Kokutai* has created in many Japanese youth a sense of their own past as dishonored, or even of Japaneseness itself as dishonored. The sudden collapse of *Kokutai* revealed its tenuousness as an ideological system. But it also created an ideological void and thus encouraged the polarizing tendencies that still haunt Japanese thought — the urge to recover *Kokutai* and make things just as they were, and the opposite urge to break away entirely from every remnant of *Kokutai* and make all things new.'

Robert J. Lifton, 'Youth and History: Individual Change in Postwar Japan', *The Challenge of Youth*, Erik H. Erikson, ed. (New York: Basic Books, 1965 [copyright 1961]), p. 273.

Kanji Barrier

'Japanese [are] devoid of "self-consciousness" as [evidenced by] the lack of clear distinction between the parts of speech in Japanese as contrasted with the European languages. [In the latter, all sentences are composed of individual words, each] independent of one another . . . In Japanese, on the contrary, there are . . . some [characters] that can be clearly distinguished as forming independent "parts of speech" but there are also not a few that cannot be strictly separated from other words . . . A Japanese sentence is a composite whole, and not an aggregate of individual words or phrases. This corresponds with the fact that in actual life a Japanese has no clear consciousness of his individual self, but recognizes his own existence only in the composite life of the world . . .

'. . . [The Japanese language] is a perfect symbol of the . . . people in its peculiarity of lacking a definite sense of the individual self . . . This "perfectly corresponds with the lack of the individual, the blank of the self, that is to be seen in the clothing, food and shelter of the Japanese in their daily life." '

Inatomi Eijiro

Charles A. Moore, ed., *The Japanese Mind: Essentials of Japanese Philosophy and Culture* (Honolulu: East-West Center Press, 1967), pp. 234–5.

'*Japan, Inc.*' (*or Japan: A Conglomerate of Conglomorates*)

'As implied by the phrase "Japan, Inc.," there is a basic assumption that the objectives of government and business are the same: the maintenance of Japan's economic health and the promotion of the nation's interests . . . "Japan, Inc." is a special kind of corporation: a conglomerate, in U S terms. A conglomerate can channel cash flows from low-growth to high-growth areas and apply the debt capacity of safe, mature businesses to capitalize rapidly growing but unstable ventures. It can move into a dynamic new industry and bring to it financial power that no existing competitor can match. It can increase capacity quickly. The result is that the the conglomerate is in a position to dominate a new industry by setting prices so low that existing competitors cannot finance adequate growth. Its costs are so low, compared with the competition's, that it can sell at the going price and earn large profits. In all these senses "Japan, Inc." is indeed a conglomerate, a *Zaibatsu* of *Zaibatsu*. The bank of Japan is the financial center, and with the bank's help each rapidly growing industry can incur more debt than it could on its own; the borrowing power of the entire portfolio – Japan itself – is available to each industry. Hence the economy as a whole funds new enterprises, holds prices down, competes successfully in the world market and earns large profits.'

James C. Abegglen, 'The Economic Growth of Japan', *Scientific American*, Vol. 22, No. 3, March 1970.

Japanese Racism

'. . . Japanese have a set of prejudices that parallels those of other parts of the world.'

There is a fairly clear ranking in their degree of disdain for foreigners.

At bottom of social ladder are the *Eta*, or *Burakumin* (some one million), believed to be descended from tanners, butchers and others whose work was considered unclean. Living in ghettoes, the *Eta* are generally shunned by other Japanese.

A second group at bottom are the Koreans — most work in low-income jobs and have occasionally reacted with marches, rioting and looting. Some 60 per cent of the over half million Koreans live in ghettoes.

A third group looked down upon are the Okinawans.

Still another group suffering discrimination are the mixed-blood children, especially those of American soldiers and Japanese women.

Adapted from Richard Halloran, 'Racist Japan Aloof from Strife in US', *The Washington Post*, 21 April, 1968.

Politics in Japanese and Western Societies Compared

	Anglo-American countries	Japan
Political sovereignty	Rests with the people and works from the bottom up	Rests with the rulers and trickles from the top down
Citizens	Can be an active participant in the processes of government	Politically passive, usually consenting to to the rule of the establishment
Attitudes towards government	Westerner inherently distrusts, or is sceptical of, government authority; strives to restrain the exercise of political power	Japanese basically trusts governmental authority and accepts the application of its power

	Anglo-American countries	Japan
Political decisions	Made by the majority for the greatest good of the greatest number, without infringing on the basic rights of the minority or the individual	Made by consensus or compromise for the greatest good of the nation-family
Basic ideals and attitudes	1. Western society strives for human fulfillment of the individual	1. Japanese society strives for subordination of the individual to attain harmony within the group
	2. Men are believed to be created equal, even if they are not always treated so	2. Men are inherently unequal and each has his station in a hierarchy
	3. The Western democrat ideally is tolerant and accepts diversity in society	3. The Japanese is intolerant and strives for conformity
	4. The Westerner believes that as a free man he has certain inalienable rights	4. The Japanese believes that as a member of the national family he has certain duties and obligations
Role of the state	The role of the state in a Western democracy is to protect and enhance individual rights	The role of the Japanese state is to preserve a benevolent social order
Rule of law	Western democracies are founded on the rule of law, to which all men are equally subject	Japanese politics are based on the rule of men, who are supposed to govern for the common good but who do so with different standards for superiors and inferiors

Adapted from Richard Halloran, *Japan: Images and Realities* (New York: Alfred A. Knopf, 1969), pp. 100–102.

Politics

'In looking at Japanese politics, it is essential not to confuse political theory with practical politics. Among the oldest of Japanese traditions is duality in government: the separation of the imperial institution, the source of idealism, and legitimacy, from the actual rulers of the country, who are eminently political and pragmatic . . .

'The *Habatsu*, or faction, is the operative unit of Japanese politics . . . [It] has a chief, the modern equivalent of a *Daimyo*, and followers, who are his "*Samurai.*" A *Habatsu* is formed by a politician in the Diet who has the leadership abilities, political skill, access to money in the business community, and the ambition to become prime minister . . . Ideology enters the equation only insofar as the members of a *Habatsu* hold generally similar beliefs. More important are the personal relations that develop over the years.'

Richard Halloran, *Japan: Images and Realities* (New York: Alfred A. Knopf, Inc., 1969), pp. 112–13.

Ethics

'The sharp differences in basic attitudes between the various age groups in Japan are very obvious, and they illustrate another more important point, which itself is not so immediately apparent. Japan today lacks any central core of ethics or any system of guiding ideals. The Japanese religions of Buddhism and Shintoism offer the modern Japanese little solid religious basis for their ethics or ideals; the feudal and Confucian ethics of the past have decayed; and the state-centered system of prewar Japan has been repudiated. Actually what ethics the Japanese have is a composite of old attitudes that have survived piecemeal from the past and elements of the Christian-based ethics of the Occident, with the latter perhaps somewhat in the preponderance, despite the infinitesimal number of professing Christians . . .

'Whatever the origin of modern Japanese ethical concepts, however, there can be no denying that they lack any solid religious basis and vary widely among different social and age groups. And with them goes no generally accepted set of guiding ideals or principles. The Japanese are still self-consciously aware of their national distinctiveness, but the ideal of blind obedience to the state no longer serves as a major unifying principle, and instead they are somewhat apologetic and uncertain in their patriotism. For the most part they are united in their devotion to the concepts of peace and international order, but they are not at all agreed as to how these are to be realized. Most of them approve of democracy, but the principles on which democracy is based do not serve as great unifying beliefs, as they do in such countries as the United States and the United Kingdom. In other words, neither religion, nor ethical principles, nor political and social ideals serve as the great unifying forces they do in many other lands. The keystone appears to be missing in the intellectual or spiritual arch, and this lack in turn gives a certain instability to the whole structure of modern Japan.'

Edwin O. Reischauer, *United States and Japan* (New York: The Viking Press, 1968), pp. 310–11.

National Attitude Towards Happiness

'What seems radically new is the national attitude toward happiness. The pursuit of happiness, a concept that implies maintenance of moral standards and thus does not precisely coincide with pleasure, has become a worthwhile goal of life. Once viewed as an immoral doctrine that threatened the achievement of proper goals of fulfilling obligations, the quest of happiness is an ideal that has gained wide currency throughout the nation.'

Edward Norbeck, *Changing Japan, Case Studies in Cultural Anthropology* (New York: Holt, Rinehart & Winston, 1965), p. 21.

Changes

'While the Japanese remain conscious of class distinctions and hierarchy in a way that is quite unknown to Americans, there has been a decided relaxing of the rigidity of these distinctions. Much of the obsequiousness, even the deference, shown before the war by the lower classes to their supposed superiors has disappeared, and the upper classes too have lost a great deal of their unconscious air of superiority . . . Paralleling the breakdown in class distinctions has been a general weakening of all social controls. A great breath of freedom has blown through the tightly knit, cramped society of Japan. Most Japanese, especially younger ones, think and act with a freedom that was not at all common in prewar days. The control of the family over young people has visibly relaxed. Young men and women nowadays are rarely forced into marriages against their will, and often enough they are permitted to select their own mates . . .

'The changes are most noticeable among two groups, women and young people. The former act with a self-confidence that, if it existed before the war, was carefully concealed. The Japanese woman has become much more of an individual, but without losing any of the charm that characterized her before the war.

'Young people have changed even more markedly. In fact, one could safely say that in most cases the younger a Japanese is, the more he departs from prewar norms. The old have changed very little, but with each younger age bracket the change becomes more noticeable. Japanese under thirty, whose upbringing and education have been largely postwar, are least like their prewar counterparts. Children are more spontaneous and uninhibited, but these qualities are accompanied by a certain degree of brashness and even rudeness that was virtually unknown before the war.

'With the new freedom has gone a great deal of social and emotional confusion. The old iron-bound codes of conduct are now often disregarded, but no new standards have risen to take their place. The postwar Japanese is without doubt more lawless than his police-ridden predecessor. Juvenile delinquency, while in no way as serious as in the United States, has become a real problem for the first time in Japanese history. The Japanese have lost much of their former punctiliousness and with it a certain amount of their politeness. With the relaxing of tensions, there may also have come a certain slackening of will power and even a sloppiness of performance that would not have been tolerated before . . .'

Edwin O. Reischauer, *United States and Japan* (New York: The Viking Press, 1968), pp. 306–8.

Decline in Moral Standards

'A putative general decline in moral standards is a matter of national concern, at least to the extent that it is frequently the subject of public expressions of alarm. Everywhere civic leaders plead for improved standards of morality, and they often refer to sexual morality. Almost any urban citizen of mature years will state that the family system has collapsed, that old values have disappeared, and that confusion reigns. But he generally makes these statements with composure, and it is evident that he has found a way to live with peace of mind.'

Edward Norbeck, *Changing Japan, Case Studies in Cultural Anthropology* (New York: Holt, Rinehart & Winston, 1965), p. 18.

Japanese Post-World War II Economic Miracle

Chart 1 contrasts the performance of Japanese economy with the economies of the other large powers that seem to be among the most important in the world. It should be noted that if we divide the larger and more important powers into three groups — two superpowers, five major, and three intermediate — that the Japanese started out in 1945 as the smallest of the large and end up by 1970 as the largest of these five large powers. This is an enormous feat and raises the issue of how long it will be before they are better classified as the smallest of the superpowers rather than as the largest of the large powers.

We describe in *Chart 2* a number of reasons deriving from the Japanese national character as to why the Japanese did so well.

Chart 3 gives some of the international reasons that were helpful in the Japanese recovery and growth, while *Chart 4* considers some characteristics of the Japanese that were first judged to be serious weaknesses but that in fact turned out, on the whole, to be strengths rather than weaknesses.

Chart 5 gives Japan's recent economic performance, and *Chart 6* points out that the world investor has finally recognized that performance and is putting large-scale investments into Japan.

Chart 7 indicates how well Japan has done in specific areas where it has achieved first, second, or third place. In many of the places where Japan now is second or third, it seems quite likely that they will be in first place within a decade.

Chart 8 highlights one of Japan's most serious economic problems — the rising inflation. Curiously enough, despite rising consumer prices, wholesale prices have remained relatively stable.

Chart 9 demonstrates the serious Japanese research and development effort, at least as compared to the four large European powers.

Chart 1

POSTWAR ECONOMIC GROWTH OF THE
SUPERPOWERS AND 'LARGE' POWERS, 1950–69

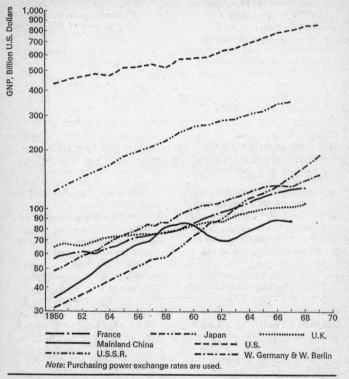

—·—·— France	—— ——— Japan	················· U.K.
—————— Mainland China	— — — — U.S.	
—··—··— U.S.S.R.	—·—·—·— W. Germany & W. Berlin	

Note: Purchasing power exchange rates are used.

Chart 2

JAPANESE 'NATIONAL CHARACTER' TRAITS WHICH
CONTRIBUTED TO POST-1947 GROWTH

1. A great deal of available energy and dedication and the general Japanese capacity for purposive, communal action
2. Stringent population limitation
3. Appropriate and available organizational skills, judgement, and motivation – both governmental and private
4. Relatively high technological and educational levels
5. High savings and investment rate

6. Japanese version of free enterprise
7. Skilful government direction and intervention – (and a reasonably cooperative and sensible US)
8. All kinds of pressures to attain 'higher market shares' and to go into advanced technology and industries of the future
9. Ruthless about non-support of – or even active 'sabotage' against – 'obsolete' or 'not for Japanese' businesses
10. Willingness to switch to 'economic growth' as major tactic in 'catching up with the West'
11. Desirable work force readily available
12. To some degree many of the points in Chart 4 on page 250

Chart 3

INTERNATIONAL POLITICAL AND ECONOMIC CONDITIONS WHICH CONTRIBUTED TO POST-1947 JAPANESE GROWTH

1. Less than 1 per cent of the GNP allotted to defence
2. Stimulus of Korean and later Vietnam wars
3. Influx of American capital
4. US a prosperous and avid customer
5. Technology available at bargain rates – first from the Americans and later from the Europeans
6. General atmosphere of free trade
7. Large discovery in Australia and elsewhere of new mineral deposits
8. Developments in ocean transport

Chart 4

SOME SPECIFIC JAPANESE 'WEAKNESSES'

1. Low ratio of resources to people
2. Low labour mobility, promotion by seniority, compulsory retirement at 55
3. Diffused responsibility
4. Non-competitive practices
5. High debt-equity ratio
6. Postwar legacy of ill will

Chart 5

RECENT ECONOMIC PERFORMANCE

	1966	1967	1968	1969	1970
Real Economic Growth rate (%)	11·4	12·9	14·3	14·2	12·0
Balance of Payments (Billion dollars)	0·06	0·54	1·63	1·85	1·90

Estimated by Japanese Economic Research Centre, November 1969

Chart 6

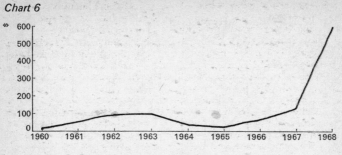

Foreign Gross Portfolio Investments in Japan

Chart 7

JAPAN'S WORLD RANKING, 1969 (SELECTED INDUSTRIAL PRODUCTS)

	1st	*2nd*
Shipbuilding	*Japan*	W. Germany
Radio sets	*Japan*	USA
Cameras	*Japan*	USA
Transistorized TVs	*Japan*	USA
Television sets	USA	*Japan*
Computers	USA	*Japan*
Commercial motor vehicles	*Japan*	USA
Motorcycles	*Japan*	France
Rayon & acetate filament	USA	*Japan*
Cotton yarn	USA	*Japan*
Aluminium	USA	*Japan*
Copper	USA	*Japan*
Crude steel	USA	*Japan*
Caustic soda	USA	*Japan*
Cement	USSR	*Japan*
Plastic resin	USA	*Japan*

Chart 8
INFLATIONARY TREND

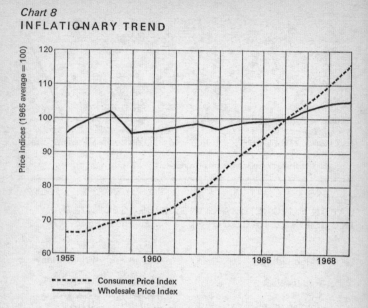

------- Consumer Price Index
——— Wholesale Price Index

The President Dictionary 1969, Diamond Time Co., Ltd., Tokyo

Chart 9
RESEARCH AND DEVELOPMENT COMPARISONS
REFLECT AN IMPRESSIVELY HIGH EMPHASIS BY
JAPANESE, PARTICULARLY ON PRIVATE
RESEARCH

Source: OECD

Selected Countries	R & D Expenditure as % of GNP	R & D Personnel per 10,000 Population	Government R & D as % of Total
Japan	1·5	18·7	28
West Germany	1·4	10·5	41
France	1·6	8·5	64
United Kingdom	2·3	15·9	54
Italy	0·6	3·0	33
United States	3·4	69·6	64

'*Japanese Economy in Western Press*' (*As Quoted by Johannes Hirschmeier in* Oriental Economist, *November 1969*)

Chart 1
THE BATTLE FOR MARKETS

' "Smaller than France with an agricultural area of only 32 per cent, shaken by 54 active volcanoes and 7,000 earthquakes a year, having received a trauma through the only atomic bombs ever being dropped on humanity, humiliated by total defeat in the last war, Japan now challenges the world again to a battle for markets and for power." '
(From *Spiegel*)

' "What kind of nation is this where people do not sleep in beds but travel on the fastest trains of the world, do not sit on chairs but construct the most giant ships, build super-cities but give no names to their streets, boast of the largest newspaper circulation of the world and yet know so well how to pass over the most essential things in silence." '

' "The average time-difference of train arrivals off-schedule is only 18 seconds." ' (From *Die Welt*)

' ". . . Automatic opening and closing of doors, stopping at the exactly marked spot, telephone connections, and all this with Japanese proverbial courtesy." ' (From *Die Welt*)

' . . . Japan by no means owes her success on the world markets to cheap labor, because, while the construction of a 50,000 ton tanker under similar conditions takes 24 months in Spain, 16 in the USA and 12 in Germany, the Japanese shipbuilders need only 7–8 months. Clearly, this is a case of technical superiority and not cheap labor.

'One of the reasons for the new stability is, says the *Economist*, the rapid decline of Japan's imports as per cent of GNP, from 13 per cent in 1956 to only 9·9 per cent in 1966, while that of great Britain is as high as 15·6 per cent.

'By planning Western papers imply that unique close cooperation between government officials, banks and large firms, whereby "the dynamo is out there," in the private sector and not, like in the socialist economies, in the government. The excellent results of Japanese planning are then attributed chiefly to the mutual trust as well as the basic sameness of goals, *v.* fast growth and modernization. The London *Economist* concludes that Japan has the most sophisticated and most closely controlled economic system in today's world.

'According to *Spiegel*, 77 per cent of Japanese machinery are less than 6 years old, giving Japan a tremendous advantage in competition not only in terms of prices but also quality.'

' ". . . The fact that Japan has to import many of the raw materials for the heavy industries (oil, coal, iron ore) is, on the whole, probably an advantage, writes the Frankfurter *Allgemeine.* Why this? Because transport by giant freight ships is probably cheaper than train transport inland would be, given the fact that those factories are located directly at the ports permitting unloading immediately into the factories, and steel mills.

' ". . . Japanese often fail to conform whenever they can gain an advantage by flouting accepted practices, while at other times they demand fair practices from Western competitors." '

' "To sell a $15,000 boiler these guys will send two engineers along just to make the sale while we might send a brochure"; and "they will cut their price 10 to 15 per cent when a 2 or 3 per cent cut would have done the trick." ' (From *Fortune* magazine)

' "There is hardly a nation which fights so relentlessly for her markets as do the Japanese. Where Western businessmen go alone to open up new export markets, the Japanese entrepreneurs will send out teams of experts who make accurate analyses of the markets, who study the mentality of the foreign nation and even the personal characteristics of the future partners in order to take them by surprise in the dealings." ' (From *Spiegel*)

' "Japanese representatives at international business conferences are always clamouring, with loud voices, for free trade concessions while they themselves never make any concessions worth mentioning." ' (From *Die Zeit*)

Chart 2

WHAT MAKES THE JAPANESE ECONOMY TICK?

'Among the many aspects which are brought up, five stand out as most important, as seen by foreign observers: saving habits, the blend of traditional small and modern large scale production, the attitude toward work backed up by group loyalty, a new nationalism and, finally, an optimistic faith in the future.'

Chart 3

HARD WORK WITHIN THE GROUP

'The overall verdict is that Japanese work hard, put in long hours and are disciplined and loyal. Says *Fortune*: "The great edge the Japanese have over us is simply their willingness to work." Japanese "do not work by the clock but by the job" is another such view. A Japanese worker does not rush out of the factory, and an employee from his office, when the time is out. They often finish the job begun, sit around for a while and review some of the problems, clean up together and give thus the feeling that they are personally committed to their work. They do not separate their work time from their leisure so sharply as the Western worker tends to do.'

Chart 4
SAVING ONE THIRD OF GNP

'Japanese consumers, it is noted, saved between 1960 and 1966 the "incredibly high ratio" of 18 per cent of disposable income whereby the comparable figure for the US is 5·5 per cent.

'. . . The Japanese security system is too underdeveloped: families have to save for any kind of "rainy day" like typhoon disaster, long sickness. Further, higher education has to be borne largely by the families, and, it should be added, weddings are also expensive in Japan and need saving ahead of time.

'Several German papers point to the exceedingly high debt/equity ratios of most large enterprises, averaging about 80 per cent. Writes the *Handelsblatt*: "Western bankers would not be able to sleep because of worry. Yet in Japan people are trustful: banks cooperate closely whenever a large enterprise needs backing, while, on the other hand, the small enterprises are dropped."

'. . . Thus, with people willing to save and banks willing to lend incredibly high ratios, and at the same time guiding enterprises into high growth investments, the Japanese growth is carried by a record investment rate of about one third of the GNP. Clearly, investments and hence economic modernization can thus be carried out much faster than in the West. In this process the consuming public actually lends the funds to the business community "free of charge." Considering the fact that banks pay no higher interest than the inflation rate, which means, at a real interest rate of zero per cent — or even less. While making use of bank loans, firms can, under this cover, gradually build up their reserves without diminishing the speed of expansion.'

Chart 5
FAITH IN THE FUTURE

'Some Western papers make much of the prognosis of the Hudson Institute which predicts that, if present trends continue, the 21st century may well be the "Japanese century." Most agree that the constellation of factors is extremely good for Japan and few see any serious signs that would effectively stop Japan's rapid advance toward top leadership position in the world economy.

Die Zeit writes that a British visitor was highly astonished about the overall discipline and dedication of the Toyota workers, finding no cigarette butts lying around, no pin-up girls' photos standing at the working places; and when he then heard that there had been no strike at Toyota for the last 10 years "the British observer understood why that company could, with only one fourth of the working force, produce more cars than the British Motor Corporation." '

The Future of the Japanese Economic Miracle

The following is a recapitulation of the material in Chapter 4, 'Japan, Inc.: The Future of the Economic Miracle'.

Chart 1 examines some of the possibilities. As indicated there, our surprise-free projection estimates more than $10,000 per capita.

Chart 2 gives a list of reasons many people advance in support of the argument that Japan's economy will 'top out' in the near future.

Chart 3 provides a general answer to that list.

Chart 4 provides in turn a list of reasons that the Japanese should continue to do well. In some cases almost any item on Chart 4 should be worth a major fraction of a point in growth rates versus most of the European countries.

The 12 charts on the pages following illustrate respectively the points of *Chart 4*.

Chart 1
JAPAN, GNP PER CAPITA, 1879–2000

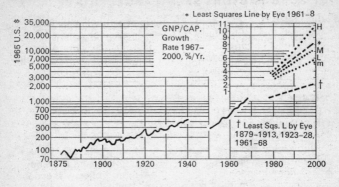

Note: To convert to 1967 dollars at a purchasing power exchange rate, multiply by 1.325.

Chart 2
FACTORS OFTEN SAID TO FAVOUR 'TOPPING OUT' OR EVEN DOWN-TURN IN JAPANESE GROWTH

Cream has been skimmed off European and US technology

Size of Japanese work force no longer increasing rapidly

Lagging infrastructure

Greater defence expenditure

Hedonistic tendencies of younger generation

Young resent system in general and in particular 'escalator system'

Likely difficulties with foreign trade

Economy may become overheated by excessive equipment investments, which might eventually lead to oversupply when the expansion of exports levels off

Rising barriers to American and other foreign investments will introduce managerial techniques that will revolutionize firms still adhering to vertical organizations

Japan is becoming a service economy — soon will be post-industrial

Serious political strains within the existing system

Serious American recession

Chart 3

BUT SUCH FACTORS SEEM LARGELY TO BE:

1. Overstated
2. Assumed to have too great effectiveness and/or
3. Assumed to affect growth rates too rapidly – if they do so at all it will take time
4. Can often be negated – or at least limited – by proper policies and/or likely events

Chart 4

THIRTEEN 'ADDITIONAL' REASONS FOR THE LIKELY CONTINUED GROWTH OF JAPANESE ECONOMY*

1. High saving and investment rates (about twice U S)
2. Superior education and training (i.e., American scale and European quality through high school)
3. 'Adequate capitalization'
4. 'Risk capital' readily available
5. Technological capabilities competitive to West
6. Economically and patriotically advancement-oriented, achievement-oriented, work-oriented, deferred gratification, loyal, enthusiastic employees – probably increasingly so
7. High morale and commitment to economic growth and to surpassing the West – by government, by management, by labour, and by general public
8. Willingness to make necessary adjustments and/or sacrifices – relatively mobile capital and labour
9. Excellent management of the economy – by government, by business, and, to some degree, by labour – this results in a controlled and, to some degree, collectivist economy ('Japan, Inc.') but still competitive and market-oriented (but not market-dominated) capitalism
10. Adequate access – on good and perhaps improving terms – to sufficient world resources and markets
11. Almost all future technological and economic and most cultural and political developments seem favourable to continuation of the above
12. Relatively few and/or weak pressures to divert major resources to 'low economic productivity' uses
13. Current high momentum of growth facilitates further growth

* And, by and large, of the continued lagging of the British economy. The word 'additional' is in quotation marks because not all of the above are in addition to the already discussed issues (many of which would hold for the future as well as the past).

HIGH SAVING AND INVESTMENT RATES

Highest in the world (next to Kuwait)

Saving rate is $1\frac{1}{2}$ to 3 times as much as that of Europe and America

Since average worker's income now goes up about 10 per cent a year or more, the high saving rate does not press on him

Mid-year and end of year bonuses make savings easy

System of savings needed to establish long-term security, given relatively inadequate welfare services

SUPERIOR EDUCATION AND TRAINING

Intelligent education system

Probably highest literacy rate in the world

Mass education at university level (720 college level institutions established since war) ; number of graduates exceeded only by US and USSR

Best use of educational TV

Highest ability in mathematics and science

Ability to read (but not speak) foreign languages

Advantage of almost completely homogeneous population

'ADEQUATE CAPITALIZATION'

Debt-equity ratio of Japanese firms is often 4–5 or even 10–1

Yet it makes little or no difference to the productivity of a machine whether money used is debt or equity capital

Japanese firm gets its capital cheaper than American firm — making it much easier for Japanese firm to expand

'RISK CAPITAL' READILY AVAILABLE

Japanese context is different from US

If large firm is in trouble, it would almost certainly be bailed out by the government, the banks extending loans, etc.

Government and society stand behind firms

Most important of all is high motivation for growth, competitive position, and market shares

TECHNOLOGICAL CAPABILITIES COMPETITIVE WITH WEST

There is now a reverse flow of 'payments for technology'

About 10 per cent of royalties Japanese pay to other countries now comes back to them as royalties for their own technology

In terms of research and development, Japanese in some ways spend more than Europeans particularly in terms of available manpower

ECONOMICALLY AND PATRIOTICALLY ACHIEVEMENT-ORIENTED

High morale work-oriented attitude of Japanese families; for example, weekends and vacations sacrificed for common good

Japanese feel that working hard for the firm helps the country's success

HIGH MORALE AND COMMITMENT TO ECONOMIC GROWTH AND TO SURPASSING THE WEST

Japanese are elated with their current success and watch growth rates with sports-like devotion

Any government which sacrificed rapid growth rates for almost any other objective would find itself in trouble

Old commitment with 'catching up to the West' now changing to 'surpassing the West, (probably soon to be before year 2000 and in total GNP not GNP per capita

Anyone seeking premature distribution of profits and comfortable outlets would be seen as dropout from most exciting project of the nation

MATSUSHITA WORKER'S SONG

For the building of a new Japan,
Let's put our strength and mind together,
Doing our best to promote production,
Sending our goods to the people of the world,

Endlessly and continuously,
Like water gushing from a fountain.
Grow, industry, grow, grow, grow!
Harmony and sincerity!
Matsushita Electric!

WILLINGNESS TO MAKE NECESSARY ADJUSTMENTS AND/OR SACRIFICES

General willingness to sacrifice almost any defective part of the economy — or even culture — that would prevent achieving their growth goal; thus retirement will soon be at sixty, wives are working, escalator system is being modified, investments in sale and joint ventures in South-east Asia to acquire substitute for low-price labour is growing, etc.

EXCELLENT MANAGEMENT OF THE ECONOMY RESULTS IN A CONTROLLED AND, TO SOME DEGREE, COLLECTIVIST BUT STILL COMPETITIVE AND MARKET-ORIENTED CAPITALISM

The drive for growth has not allowed emotion to interfere with efficiency

Growth rate is fuelled not so much by sacrifices as by internal consumption by a people who each year (now) live about 10 per cent or more better than they lived the previous year

ADEQUATE ACCESS TO MOST WORLD RESOURCES AND MARKETS

It is not really true the Japanese export to live; they export in order to buy imports

Imports total is becoming a lesser and lesser proportion of the economy

A good deal of the Japanese investment overseas is designed to create better import or better export situations (for example, steel mills are located on coast of Japan where they can get raw materials more cheaply than a US steel mill in Pittsburgh)

Japanese have made a virtue of their necessities and are now drawing their raw materials in the most economic fashion

Given new forms of transportation and efficient techniques, costs of raw materials for Japan will go down

A good deal of exports will start going to pay for capital investment in foreign countries, for tourism, for luxury imports, and for both 'political' and 'nonpolitical' foreign aid

RELATIVELY FEW AND/OR WEAK PRESSURES TO DIVERT MAJOR RESOURCES TO 'LOW ECONOMIC PRODUCTIVITY' USES

If it takes greater investments to maintain growth rates, the Japanese will be willing to make them

By deferring expenses for defence, infrastructure, welfare,

environmental planning, etc. until country grew very big so that it could afford them, the Japanese will find that a rather small per cent of their budget will still equal an unbelievably large amount by earlier standards

Japan's Foreign Trade

JAPAN'S EXPORTS AND EXPORT MARKETS

	(Average) 1934– 36	1950	1960	1968
Total exports ($ millions)	932	828	4,055	12,972
Share to low-income areas (%)	72·9	60·9	53·2	46·9
Asia	63·7	46·3	37·0	34·0
Africa	5·8	8·9	8·7	7·2
Latin America	3·4	5·7	7·5	5·7
Share to high-income areas (%)	27·1	39·0	46·8	53·0
United States	15·9	21·7	26·7	31·5
Canada	0·3	1·8	2·9	2·7
Europe	8·1	12·0	12·2	14·6
(EEC countries)	(3·3)	(4·9)	(4·3)	(5·3)
(United Kingdom)	(3·9)	(3·1)	(3·0)	(2·8)
(USSR)	(0·7)	(0·0)	(1·5)	(1·4)
Australia and Oceania	2·8	3·6	4·9	4·2

Note: Minor inconsistencies result from rounding.
Warren Hunsberger, 'The Japanese Economy: A Continuing Miracle?' *Interplay*, December 1969, January 1970, p. 18

EXTERNAL TRADE Unit: $100 million
Remarks: *Anticipated figure
          **Estimated figure

	1966	1967	1968	1699*	1907**
Trade Balance	22·75	11·60	25·29	39·0	47·0
Invisible Trade Balance	−8·86	−11·72	−13·06	−15·0	−17·0
Transfer Balance	−1·35	−1·78	−1·75	−2·0	−2·0
Capital Balance	−8·72	−3·06	−0·30	−0·2	−10·0
Discrepancy	−0·45	−0·75	−0·84	0	0
Overall Balance	3·37	−5·71	11·02	20·0	18·0

Industrial Japan, January, 1970, p. 57

JAPAN'S FOREIGN TRADE
(Unit: US $ Million)

		First 7 Months 1969	1968	1967	1966
Total	Exports	8,652	12,972	10,442	9,776
	Imports	8,293	12,987	11,663	9,523
Asia	Exports	2,970	4,415	3,555	3,288
	Imports	2,543	4,004	3,582	3,165
Europe	Exports	1,222	1,896	1,664	1,575
	Imports	1,150	1,878	1,766	1,216
North America	Exports	3,226	4,831	3,618	3,503
	Imports	2,831	4,539	4,172	3,444
Latin America	Exports	257	343	280	279
	Imports	411	610	529	446
Africa	Exports	646	940	850	729
	Imports	553	839	661	420
Oceania	Exports	327	542	472	389
	Imports	804	1,115	951	832

Source: Finance Ministry

TRADE ESTIMATES 1969–70
(US $ Million)

	1969	1970
Exports	$16,200	$19,296
Imports	14,500	17,110
Trade Surplus	$1,700	$2,186

Source: Far Eastern Economic Review Yearbook 1970

BREAKDOWN OF TRADE BY 1968
(IN PERCENTAGES)
Custom's Clearance Basis

	Exports	Imports
Asia	30·9	17·5
Europe	14·3	14·3
North America	34·2	31·5
Latin America	5·7	7·6
Africa	6·5	6·0
Near and Middle East	4·3	14·0
Oceania	3·6	8·5
Others	0·5	1·6

Source: Japan Economic Yearbook 1969, p. 68

JAPAN'S NEED FOR RAW MATERIALS

1. Seventy per cent of all Japanese imports are industrial raw materials
2. Nearly 43 per cent of all direct Japanese overseas investments (1951–67) were for securing raw materials
3. Within a generation Japanese natural resources 'may be totally exhausted.' Common estimate is
   a. Copper — reserves for 17 years
   b. Gold, lead, zinc, mercury — about the same
   c. Iron — reserves for 9·8 years
4. 'Our position as a buyer is quite precarious. We are buying these things almost on a spot basis.' (Naohira Amaya, Director of Planning, The Ministry of Trade and Industry — Miti)

JAPAN'S GROWING HUNGER FOR RAW MATERIALS

Imports:	Fiscal 1967	Fiscal 1975 (Est.) (Thousands of Tons)
Copper	483	742
Lead	86	128
Zinc	182	387
Nickel	53	110
		(Millions of Tons)
Iron Ore	55	200
Coking Coal	24	100
		(Millions of Cubic Metres)
Petroleum	121	261
Lumber and Pulp	33	60

(Mitsui & Co., Japan Iron & Steel Foundation, *Business Week*, 24 January 1970).

Japanese Overseas Investments

JAPANESE INVESTMENTS (1951–1967) : OVERVIEW

1. Asia – \$267 million – 20 per cent of total overseas investments
2. South-east Asia – \$218 million – 18 per cent of total overseas investments
3. Reasons for investments
   a. Securing raw materials
   b. Utilization of local labour
4. Until recently Japanese investments were relatively small because of
   a. Lack of government support
   b. Equipment purchases had higher priority
   c. Japanese companies reluctant to take risks or spend valuable capital when not absolutely necessary

GROWTH OF JAPANESE OVERSEAS INVESTMENT
(Unit : U S \$1,000)

Type Year	Portfolio Investment No.	 Value	Loans No.	 Value	Direct Overseas Investment No.	 Value	Total No.	 Value
1951–5	106	14,930	12	6,125	0	0	118	21,055
1956	54	11,868	17	6,400	2	1,114	73	19,382
1957	37	18,349	16	14,630	4	427	57	33,406
1958	39	25,089	24	28,579	4	10,956	67	64,624
1959	69	22,375	29	20,156	2	9,090	100	51,621
1960	104	34,083	28	21,130	5	37,208	137	92,421
1961	86	46,588	34	38,753	1	77,806	121	163,147
1962	112	39,542	35	31,300	4	24,769	151	95,611
1963	155	64,134	35	23,276	4	37,286	194	124,696
1964	136	68,912	40	38,988	2	11,946	178	119,846
1965	153	75,578	40	69,236	5	11,991	198	156,805
1966	191	74,493	43	121,316	4	30,590	238	226,399
1967	191	118,897	54	85,051	3	20,081	276	224,029
1951–67	1,461	614,838	407	504,940	40	273,264	1,908	1,393,042

Source : Japanese White Paper on Economic Cooperation
Note: 1. Loans exclude those for exports on a deferred payment basis to local corporations but includes emigration agency loans.
2. Direct overseas investments include acquisition of real estate.
3. Because of the difference in the date of compilation, figures do not coincide with those in Table 3.
4. The statistics cover Japanese fiscal years, which end on 31 March.

Source : Yoshizane Iwasa, 'Japan Ventures into Southeast Asia' *Columbia Journal of World Business*, November–December 1969, p. 51.

JAPANESE OVERSEAS INVESTMENT BY AREA AND INDUSTRY, 1951 TO 1967
(Unit: US $1,000)

Area: Type of Industry	North America	Central & South America	East & South Asia	Middle & Near East	Europe	Africa	Oceania	Total
Agriculture & Forestry	650	762	18,464	—	430	208	2,519	23,033
Fishery	2,190	4,536	1,355	143	81	836	441	9,562
Mining	40,827	31,789	93,243	237,927	366	434	23,482	428,068
Construction	3,535	29,170	1,800	—	—	—	—	34,505
Food	1,080	7,786	24,281	—	4,582	1,388	757	39,874
Textiles	3,000	36,746	32,634	—	616	9,965	837	83,798
Chemicals	12,039	3,088	7,494	224	918	19	178	23,960
Ceramics	20	2,549	7,948	30	—	—	—	10,547
Metal	389	64,985	19,801	—	—	1,324	2,097	88,596
Machinery	2,098	92,403	13,894	1,000	31,754	—	49	141,198
Electrical Machinery	15	7,952	10,681	—	278	610	1,011	20,547
Other	106,234	898	16,636	50	486	1,904	1,291	127,499
Total	172,077	282,664	248,211	239,374	39,511	16,688	32,662	1,031,187
Commerce, etc.	224,994	88,596	20,182	831	16,015	574	3,824	355,016
Total	397,071	371,260	268,393	240,205	55,526	17,262	36,486	1,386,203
Percentage	29	27	19	17	4	1	3	100

Source: Yoshizane Iwasa, 'Japan Ventures into Southeast Asia,' Columbia Journal of World Business, November–December, 1969, p. 52.

JAPANESE OVERSEAS INVESTMENT BY AREA AND
TYPE, 1951 TO 1967
(Unit: US $1,000)

Area	Portfolio Investment	Loans	Direct Overseas Investment	Total
Asia	122,750	143,297	923	266,970
Central and South America	205,954	162,637	3,397	371,988
Middle East	2,280	0	237,926	240,206
Africa	12,844	4,656	167	17,667
North America	232,654	137,938	30,755	401,347
Europe	25,222	30,643	96	55,961
Oceania	13,134	25,769	0	38,903
Total	614,838	504,940	273,264	1,393,042

Source : Yoshizane Iwasa, 'Japan Ventures into Southeast Asia,' *Columbia Journal of World Business,* November–December, 1969, p. 51.

Japanese Foreign Aid

TOTAL GOVERNMENT AND PRIVATE AID 1964–75

1964	360·7 million	0·45% of GNP
1965	600·8 million	0·68% of GNP
1966	669·0 million	0·66% of GNP
1967	855·3 million	0·72% of GNP
1968	1,049·3 million	0·74% of GNP
1969	1,200·0 million	0·60% of GNP (est.)
1970	1,400·0 million (est.)	
1975	3–4 billion (projected)	1% of GNP

BREAKDOWN OF AID (1964–68)

Government	39·4%
Private	60·6%
Private Investments	12·2%
Private Exports and Credits	48·4%

JAPAN IN COMPARISON WITH OTHER MAJOR DONORS – 1968

	Total Flow	Official Aid	Private ($ billion)
United States	5·676 (0·65% of GNP)	3·605 (0·41%)	2·071
Japan	1·049 (0·74)	0·507 (0·36)	0·542
West Germany	1·635 (1·24)	0·595 (0·45)	1·040
France	1·483 (1·24)	0·855 (0·72)	0·628
United Kingdom	0·845 (0·83)	0·428 (0·42)	0·417

MORE SPECIFIC BREAKDOWN OF AID DISTRIBUTION (1964–8)

	Government	Government– Private
Asia	85·6%	57·0%
South-east Asia	40·0	25·0
Indonesia	20·4	8·2
Philippines	12·7	9·8
Burma	4·0	2·1
Thailand	1·4	3·5
Others (in S E Asia)	1·5	1·4
South Korea	12·6	12·3
Republic of China	4·6	4·9
Ceylon	1·0	0·7
Pakistan	9·9	3·5
India	17·4	9·9

PERCENTAGE OF TOTAL AID TO SOUTH-EAST ASIA FROM MAJOR DONOR COUNTRIES – 1967

	(Including Aid to South Vietnam)	(Excluding Aid to South Vietnam)
Totals (US $ million)	994·0	538·0
United States	63·2%	35·3%
Japan	19·1	33·5
West Germany	6·8	12·3
France	4·2	7·3
United Kingdom	2·2	3·9
Netherlands	1·8	3·5
Australia	1·6	2·4

SOME CHARACTERISTICS OF JAPANESE FOREIGN AID

1. Japanese fourth in total aid allocations in 1968 among the developed nations
2. Comparative grace periods for direct government loans
   a. Average for direct Japanese government loans in 1967 – 4·7 years
   b. Average of OECD members – 5·3 years
   c. Recommended period by OECD – 7 years
3. Average interest rate registered on Japanese loans – 4·8 per cent per annum (Average for OECD countries – 3·8 per cent per annum)
4. Average redemption period for loans described by some as 'relatively short' at 16·6 years in 1967

ATTITUDE TOWARDS FOREIGN AID

' ". . . Everyone tells us we are No. 2 in the free world now . . .

' "But, deep down in our bones we don't really feel this as yet. Look at the houses and apartments we live in – tiny and overcrowded. Look at the way we go to work every morning – packed into commuter trains like sardines. Look at our sewers, or rather our lack of sewers; look at our hospitals, poorly equipped and with not enough beds; at our roads, at our handkerchief-sized parks, at our traffic accidents, at our problems of pollution and public hazards.

' "We have so much to do at home . . . Yet every underdeveloped country is going to be demanding that we do more to help them reach the economic take-off stage – and of course, for our own sakes we have to do it.

' "If our Gross National Product keeps increasing at the present rate, our foreign aid in the mid-seventies will come to $4 billion. That's a respectable sum – it's more than the US foreign aid appropriations for this year." '

A senior Japanese government official quoted in 'Japan Is Entering the 1970s with Self-Confidence Restored and Economy Thriving', *The New York Times*, 5 January, 1969, p. 12. © 1969, The New York Times Company. Reprinted by permission.

MAJOR CRITICISM OF JAPANESE FOREIGN AID

1. High percentage of government *v.* private aid
2. Hard terms on which aid is given
3. ' "Japan doesn't have a foreign aid program, it only has an export-promotion program" '

(A foreign diplomat – quoted in *The New York Times*, 21 April 1969).

A PLAUSIBLE ECONOMIC SCENARIO FOR THE GNP[1] OF NON-COMMUNIST PACIFIC ASIA (NOCPA) — IN 1967 BILLION US DOLLARS

	1970 Estimated	1980	2000	Assumed Growth Rate (%)[2]
Australia	33·5	54·5	144·7	5·0
Burma	2·3	3·0	5·0	2·6[3]
Cambodia	1·3	2·0	4·9	4·5
China (Taiwan)	5·7	14·9	100·1	10·0
Hong Kong	3·4	12·1	155·0	13·6
Indonesia	15·1	22·4	49·0	4·0[4]
Korea (South)	7·9	19·1	110·9	9·2
Malaysia	4·7	8·6	29·3	6·3
New Zealand	5·6	8·4	18·9	4.15
Philippines	9·4	16·6	52·3	5·9
Singapore	1·9	3·9	15·5	7·2
Thailand	7·7	16·4	73·7	7·8
Vietnam (South)	3·4	5·3	13·1	4·6

TOTAL I (Excluding Japan, Australia, New Zealand)	63	124	609	

TOTAL II (Excluding Japan only)	102	187	772	

TOTAL III (All 14 countries)	302	687	3772	

Note: These projections may be understated if the impact of future Japanese investment is taken into account. GNP projections use exchange rates adjusted upward for relative purchasing power including 10 per cent for Australia and New Zealand, and 20 per cent for the remaining nations, except Cambodia, Hong Kong, and South Vietnam which were not adjusted.

1. GNP forecast is based upon a linear extrapolation of assumed growth rates.
2. Assumed growth rates are based upon recent (up to ten years) economic experience, which is most relevant to the respective nation's long term prospects.
3. This note assumes that the recently experienced economic performance is most likely to be representative of Burma's long term economic prospects, despite better economic performance in the early 1950s.
4. The experience of the post-Sukarno government is likely to be more representative of Indonesia's long term economic prospects than its earlier performance under the Sukarno régime.

Sources: *UN Monthly Bulletin of Statistics; UN 1967 Yearbook of National Account Statistics; US Aid GNP Growth Rates and Trend Data, and Estimates of GNP for Non-Communist Countries.*

MAJOR JAPANESE OBJECTIVES IN REGION

1. Securing raw materials
2. Access to cheap (and usually efficient) labour force
3. Securing reliable outlets for exports
4. Regional security and economic/political development

(The above are probably in order of priority)

CURRENT JAPANESE BUSINESS TECHNIQUES, PRACTICES, AND POLICIES

1. Restrained investment
2. Occasional instances of dumping
3. Very favourable terms
4. Infiltration of domestic market

a. US normally invests only for export trade
b. Japanese attempt to gain some control over existing firms

BASIC PRINCIPLES FOR A PROPOSED NEW JAPANESE POLICY TOWARDS PACIFIC ASIA

1. Awareness among the Pacific nations of their common destiny
2. Regional cooperation to promote trade and economic development
3. 'Free Trade Area' among the advanced Pacific nations
4. Increased assistance by the advanced nations to the developing nations
5. Japan in 'the role of a bridge to link Asia and the Pacific nations'

Adapted from speech by former foreign minister Takeo Miki in May 1967 to the Japan Committee for Economic Development.

POSSIBLE FUTURE POLICIES/PROGRAMMES

1. Japanese 'Marshall Plan'
2. Militarization followed by intensive regional security
3. Closer regional cooperation
4. Asian Ford Foundation
5. Pacific Asian Common Market (or Greater Pacific Asia Co-Prosperity Sphere)
6. Area of interest, responsibility, protection, hegemony, and/or political control

PROBLEMS FACING JAPANESE POLICYMAKERS

1. Indecision
2. Hostility among some South-east Asians towards Japanese
3. Latent guilt feelings about World War II
4. Domestic pacifists
5. Reluctance to assert political influence
6. Preoccupation with internal economic and other domestic matters

POSSIBLE FUTURE TENSION AREAS

1. Japan–China
2. Japan–USSR
3. Japan–USSR–China
4. North Korean invasion of South Korea
5. Some threat to a major source of raw materials
6. A threat to security of Singapore Straits
7. Expropriation of Japanese property (e.g., oil fields in Indonesia)
8. Commercial restrictions against Japanese (e.g., Australia tries to decrease its dependence on Japan)

Japan in NOCPA – Possible Clashes of Temperament – I

Because the issue of how well the Japanese get along in NOCPA (Non-Communist Pacific-Asia) is so important, we append excerpts from three relatively current news stories on some of the initial issues which Japanese activities in NOCPA have created.

MANY ASIANS EXPRESS HARSH CRITICISM OF JAPANESE BUSINESSMEN

'Manila – When a visiting Japanese businessman slapped a female Filipino secretary in a moment of anger several weeks ago, the incident created a public furor throughout the Philippines.

'Manilla newspapers wrote bitter editorials declaring that the businessman's behaviour demonstrated "the arrogance of Japanese prosperity" and that the Japanese are "the most aggressive people in Asia."

'When he was hauled into court, the businessman was admonished by the judge that his action reflected not only on himself but also on the entire Japanese people.

'The incident was by no means isolated. Throughout Southeast Asia there has been swelling criticism of the ubiquitous Japanese traders.

'Politicians and newspapers in the area accuse the Japanese traders of everything from dishonest dealing and contempt for the local country to spending too much time in nightclubs and paying too much attention to local girls.

'A minister of the Indonesian government charged recently that Japanese economic activity in his country was directed only at assuring a supply of raw materials for Japan and was unconcerned with the development of Indonesia.

'A Malaysian businessman in

Kuala Lumpur said that "the word has gone out to be very careful in dealing with the Japanese traders. They are never satisfied with just a reasonable profit."

'In Singapore, a government official asserted that some representatives of Japanese trading and manufacturing companies were acquiring a bad reputation by trying to bribe local officials. "That may be all right in some other countries, but it is not necessary in Singapore," the official said.

'However, thoughtful officials in every country in the region concede that the criticism of the Japanese businessmen is exaggerated. While there are some selfish, greedy and arrogant Japanese traders, the Japanese do not hold a monopoly on these failings, they concede.

'The harshness of the attacks on the Japanese stems in part from left-over bitterness in countries occupied by Japan in World War II. To an even greater degree, perhaps, the criticism is generated by envy of Japan's economic progress in the postwar years.

' "The ugly Japanese is replacing the ugly American in this part of the world," said a Japanese diplomat in a Southeast Asian capital. "It is a penalty we must pay for success, I suppose." Representatives of the big Japanese trading companies such as Mitsui and Mitsubishi are particularly vulnerable to this criticism

because their firms handle the business of much of Japan's industry and because they are so efficient in penetrating markets in every corner of the region.

'But the traders one encounters in Southeast Asia do not, as a rule, correspond to the image of the "ugly Japanese." For example, Mr Morita, a representative of Mitsui Trading Company in Jakarta, is the very antithesis of the stereotyped aggressive, avaricious Japanese.

'A slim, gray-haired, mild-mannered man in his late fifties, Mr Morita has lived in Indonesia for 27 years, first coming here with Japanese occupation forces during World War II. He thinks of Indonesia as his home.

' "I go back to Japan once a year and I can't stand it. Everything is so noisy – so quick, quick, quick. But it is very easy to live in Indonesia. Everything here is so beautiful, so peaceful."

'He has visited almost every part of Indonesia, selling the products of Mitsui's clients and buying raw materials for Japan. "I haven't seen resentment against Japan. Politically, the government is not pro-Japanese, but economically they don't mind us. All they want is cheap goods and quick shipment."

'But sometimes he feels that there may be "too much Japan" coming to Indonesia. The Indonesians say that the Japanese are looking for too much profit and maybe there is something to it. Mr Morita concedes.

'But Japan really has no choice, he adds. "We are not so rich. We cannot come in with huge investments like the Americans and settle for small profit margins."

Mr Morita has many Indonesian friends and cannot help being sorry that Indonesia is so poor. Perhaps, he thinks, Japan can help ease Indonesian poverty.

'Whether or not the Japanese traders are contributing toward alleviating poverty in Indonesia and other Southeast Asian countries, they certainly are an important contributor to Japan's growing affluence.

'Japanese products are everywhere in Asia, sweeping aside competition from the United States and Europe. In the rice fields of Malaysia, the use of small Kubota Company power tillers is so prevalent that farmers there talk about "Kuboting" their fields instead of tilling them. Asian roads are clogged with Nissan and Toyota cars and Honda and Yamaha motorcycles. If an Asian family is rich enough to afford a television set, it is almost certainly a Matsushita or some other Japanese product.

' "I personally don't like the Japanese," said the Chinese-Malaysian owner of a trading company in Kuala Lumpur. "I would like to buy my equipment from the Americans if I could.

' "But the Japanese know how to do business in this country and the Americans do not. An American comes into the country and expects to sell you his product and leave in 24 hours. The Japanese do things differently. They will take the time to get to know you and to find out what you need. They will sit down with you at dinner and go out with you into the countryside to see what kind of problems you have. They are patient.

' "I think maybe it is just easier for Asians to do business with other Asians." '

The New York Times, 14 December 1969. © 1969, The New York Times Company. Reprinted by permission.

THE NEW INVASION OF GREATER EAST ASIA

'From transistor radios to whole steel mills, the Japanese have been able to sell the rest of the world just about everything except themselves. A "hate-Japan wind," as it is called in Tokyo, has been rising as legions of Japanese tourists and hard-bargaining salesmen swarm into the rest of Asia.

'Once it was 'The ugly American' who proved most conspicuous around here," says a Japanese correspondent in Bangkok. "Now it's 'the ugly Japanese.' And wherever he goes, bribery, the kickback routine dumping practices, golfing and sex crazes go with him."

'The Japanese are making

steel in Malaysia, drilling for oil off Indonesia, building cars in the Philippines and assembling television sets in Taiwan. Half a million Honda, Yamaha and Suzuki motor bikes put-put along South Viet Nam's roads, and little Sony radios are to be seen everywhere. "The people feel that," we are being invaded," says Thailand's economic affairs minister Bunchana Atthakor, "This time economically."

'The other Asians are uneasy at the speed, the size and the cost of the invasion. They tend to play down or overlook Japan's growing aid to the area. Tokyo is paying out $1·5 billion in World War II reparations, has given $220 million to the Asian Development Bank, and has lent $100 million to the world bank. Japan's foreign aid, most of which goes to other Asian countries, totals $1·4 billion this year, second only to the U S's $1·8 billion. The figure that most concerns Asians, however, is Tokyo's huge trade balance. Last year Japan sold cars, trucks and machinery worth $4·6 billion to East Asia, but spent only half as much for the purchase of timber, maize and other raw materials.

'Sometimes such reactions are born of sour experience; often, however, they simply reflect envy of Japan's drive and organization. Mitsui, a top Japanese trading company, "is better at information gathering than the CIA," swears one Singapore government official. "They send in 20 men to look

at an investment. They read everything and they take down everything — even the jokes cracked at meetings." Japanese firms are famous for absorbing absurd losses just to get a piece of a market — which is why Toyota has 25% of the Philippine auto business.

'As representatives of an alien culture, foreign businessmen and tourists are easily misunderstood and often resented — the more so if they come from an affluent, highly successful country. The Japanese are no exception, and in their case the resentment is compounded by bitter wartime memories. In Asian capitals, where groups of Japanese tourists are a common sight, marching behind a flag-carrying tour leader, their style and manner are often considered objectionable. They are famed as over-generous tippers and bad (but amiable) drinkers. They are also reputed to be single-minded in their pursuit of sex. Several Tokyo magazines carry frank whoring guides to Southeast Asia, complete with price lists, and all the evidence indicates that they are very well thumbed.

'Above all else, the Japanese have acquired a reputation for being clannish and arrogant. Even more than the Americans, who are famous for bringing the US along with them, the Japanese move in with their own beer, newspapers, chefs, wines, delicacies and restaurants. "They form an empire of themselves," said

Thailand's Bunchana. "They play golf together, eat together, go to their own Japanese schools."

'Many Japanese have an almost masochistic talent for self-criticism. In *Japan Unmasked*, former Japanese diplomat Ichiro Kawasaki ascribes the arrogance of the Japanese to what he calls their preoccupation with social rank. Writes Kawasaki, who was sacked from the diplomatic corps last year because his book created such an uproar: "The Japanese harbor an inferiority complex toward Europeans and Americans, while they tend to treat Asians with a superiority complex. This is why the average Japanese, while feeling at home in the company of Asiatics, often betrays arrogance and disdain."

'Foreign Minister Kiichi Aichi attributes Japan's troubles abroad to the "social maladroitness" of an island people unused to dealing with others. The Japanese realize that much of the criticism is overdrawn, but it stings nonetheless, and they are pondering ways to improve their image. Indonesian Foreign Minister Adam Malik suggests a "Japanese Marshall Plan" for Asia. The idea may be worth exploring as a way to help Japan's neighbors through a crucial phase in their development. It is not necessarily the answer to improving Japan's image, however, as any ugly American will agree.'

Time magazine, 2 March 1970, reprinted by permission from *Time*, The Weekly Newsmagazine; Copyright Time Inc., 1970.

'YELLOW YANKEES' SOUTH-EAST ASIANS FEAR JAPANESE TRADE PUSH

'Tokyo — Japanese businessmen, busily seeking to expand markets in Southeast Asia, are finding a growing fear in the area of an "economic invasion" by Japan.

'Japanese traders are active throughout the region.

'The force behind Japan's export activity, according to Japanese traders themselves, is the keen competition among Japanese firms exporting to Southeast Asia.

'This competition, it is said, has resulted in some Japanese traders getting involved in the internal politics of Southeast Asia.

'In Indonesia, for example, a Japanese trader is said to have told the Suharto government that "as we are affiliated with the new government, we want the orders to be given to us and not to firms which had a say with the Sukarno regime."

'Criticism of Japan is loudest in Indonesia. Japanese traders are called "Yellow Yankees." Indonesians have not yet forgotten Japanese militarism of 25 years ago.

'Indonesian intellectuals are the most vociferous. They say that Japan is trying to establish the "Greater East Asia

Co-Prosperity Sphere" with economic power and is working as a "substitute" for the United States in Asia.

'In Thailand, too, Japan is fast becoming a target of criticism. Japan is talking about "international peace." This is only to win a position in the international political arena, while benefiting greatly from disputes in Asia, Thais say.

'Japan, they add, is trying to make incursions into Asia now that the Vietnam War seems on the way to a settlement.'

JAPANESE TRADE WITH ASIAN—PACIFIC AREA: OVERVIEW

1. Exports (first 7 months of 1969)
   a. US – 37·3% of total exports – $3,226 million
   b. Asia – 34·3% of total exports – $2,970 million
2. Exports: FY 1968
   a. US – 31·4% of total exports – $4,311 million – 35·5% increase
   b. Asia – 28·2% of total exports – $3,865 million – 29·4% increase
3. 1968 favourable balance of trade with Asia – $1,822 million
4. Over-all 1968 Japanese international trade surplus – $427 million

JAPANESE BALANCE OF TRADE

UNFAVOURABLE		FAVOURABLE	
Australia	5:2	Hong Kong	1:9
USSR	2:1	South Korea	1:6
Indonesia	7:4	Singapore	1:4
Malaysia	3:1	Taiwan	1:3
Thailand	2:5		

Japan–Australia Trade

CHARACTERISTICS OF TRADE BETWEEN JAPAN AND AUSTRALIA

1. Australia is Japan's second largest supplier, after the US
   a. Supplies 20 per cent of Japan's entire iron ore needs
   b. Major commodity – wool
   c. Also biggest supplier of coking coal, supplying 40 per cent of Japanese annual requirements
2. Japan is Australia's largest customer
   a. Purchases 60 per cent of Australia's total mineral exports

b. Examples (FY 1967–8)
   88 per cent of Australian
     iron ore exports
   97 per cent of coking coal
     exports
   50 per cent (approx.) of
     crude copper exports
   25 per cent of lead
     exports

c. Other major commodities
  traded:
  38 per cent of raw wool
    exports
  22 per cent of sugar
    exports

JAPAN–AUSTRALIAN TRADE 1958–68
($ in Millions)

1. Japan's Exports to Australia

	1958	1963	1965	1966	1967	1968
Foodstuffs	4	5	9	9	9	11
Fuels	1	3	8	6	5	5
Light Industrial Prod.	47	86	115	116	137	143
Of which Textiles	38	62	75	77	93	92
Heavy & Chemical						
Industrial Goods	11	64	180	167	207	256
Chemical Goods	3	13	21	25	32	39
Metals	3	19	65	37	47	60
Iron & Steel	2	15	53	26	34	46
Machinery	4	33	94	105	127	158
TOTALS	63	158	312	298	359	416

2. Japan's Imports from Australia

Foodstuff	34	94	89	109	139	141
Meats	—	5	15	28	24	25
Wheat	10	25	27	25	35	50
Sugar	13	49	25	30	30	27
Raw Materials	187	349	347	419	477	554
Wool	162	298	285	321	298	299
Iron Ores	—	1	3	25	98	164
Non-ferrous Metal						
Ores	5	18	30	38	48	56
Mineral Fuels	6	46	92	107	121	160
Coal	6	41	89	106	117	155
Mfd. Products	—	25	23	43	54	65
TOTALS	227	514	551	678	798	920

Source: *Oriental Economist*, July, 1969.

JAPANESE–AUSTRALIAN TRADE (FISCAL 1966–8):
PERCENTAGES
(Unit: a $1,000)

	1966–7		*1967–8*		*1968–9*	
	Value	*% of Total*	*Value*	*% of Total*	*Value*	*% of Total*
Imports	296,044	9·7	343,310	10·5	414,296	11·95
Exports	586,437	19·4	642,068	21·1	823,171	24·44
Total Trade	882,481	14·56	985,378	15·6	1,237,467	18·11

Commonwealth Bureau of Census and Statistics, Canberra, Australia.

MINERAL EXPORTS

'By far the most important new development of the last three years has been Japanese interest in the immense new mineral wealth discovered in Australia. The huge iron ore deposits in western Australia are being developed largely for export to Japan under long-term contracts already totaling over $3,000 million and with considerable participation of Japanese capital in joint ventures with American, British, and Australian interests. Japan is also actively interested in securing increased supplies of Australia's established mineral exports, such as coal, copper, lead, and zinc, and of new ones now in prospect, especially alumina, manganese, and perhaps uranium. Some Japanese capital is being invested in Australian manufacturing industries, partly in response to Australian prodding, as in the case of the motor car industry where higher tariffs on imports of completely built-up cars were imposed last year in order to induce Japanese manufacturers to move into local production. Another field in which joint Australian-Japanese ventures are being discussed is the economic development of New Guinea. Total Japanese investment in Australia is still modest, perhaps $60 million. But it is certain to grow.'

India, Japan, Australia. Partners in Asia ?, Canberra, Australian National University Press, 1968, pp. 148–9.

'The major iron ore deposits at Hammersley . . . were tapped only after the signing of an agreement with Japan to supply 65·5 million tons of iron ore over a 16-year period.'

(World Business,
January 1969)

PROBLEMS IN AUSTRALIAN–JAPANESE TRADE

'Japanese–Australian trade relations are not without their problems. The main theme of Japanese complaints, voiced at varying levels of sophistication, is the continuing imbalance of trade, Japanese purchases still running at almost twice the level of Japanese sales. The Japanese find it difficult to contain their impatience with Australian protectionist policies which, as recently in the case of motor cars and chemicals, hit out with higher tariffs at particularly successful Japanese exports and which have so far blocked Japanese entry into banking in Australia. The Australians counter with grumbles about Japanese protectionism, especially quota restrictions on imports of meat and dairy products. But these bickerings are all in the cause of still more trade and closer economic relations between the two countries.'

India, Japan, Australia. Partners in Asia ?, Canberra, 1968, p. 149.

National Policies and Goals

The first three charts are really applicable to the recent postwar years. They indicate respectively that there was a basic consensus on what the major objectives were and that this major concensus has achieved its goals.

Charts 2 and 3 list the kinds of goals that are often discussed in the Japanese press, particularly by intellectuals and the more literate members of the Japanese community.

The next three charts take a much more realistic view of what may be going on in Japan, even though there is relatively little discussion of this in the public press.

Chart 5 is our guess of what the major goals are actually likely to be, whether or not they are explicitly expressed by the authorities or in general newspaper discussion.

The last four charts concern the issue of possible Japanese rearmament with modern nuclear forces. *Charts 7 and 8* try to indicate that current Japanese pacifism and 'nuclear allergy' are not simple phenomena but are actually quite complex matters with meanings and consequences that are not as certain as most commentators seem to think.

Charts 9 and 10 indicate that the Japanese are already engaged in producing some of the equipment they would need for such rearmament. The text points out that by 1975 the nuclear power industry will have grown to the point where they will have a capacity for some thousands of small bombs per year, and that all the other ingredients of modern new weapons systems will be available at that time.

Chart 1

1945 TO 1965 JAPANESE OBJECTIVES
(CONSENSUS OF MIDDLE LEFT TO
EXTREME RIGHT)

1. Restore economy ⎫ Old
2. Physical security ⎭
3. Continue and increase above ⎫
4. Regain status and strength ⎪
5. Restore internal morale ⎪
6. Discharge 'war guilt' ⎪
7. Some political independence ⎬ Recent
8. Reconciliation with Soviet Union and the West ⎪
9. Reconciliation with Asia ⎪
10. Regain lost territory in Ryukyus and Kuriles ⎭

Chart 2

CURRENTLY DISCUSSED JAPANESE NATIONAL
GOALS

1. Continually increasing material prosperity
2. Lead the world in economic growth rate
3. Catch up with the United States
4. Surpass the United States
5. Enter the top class or lead the world in various areas such as: sports, scientific development, art, etc.
6. High status for Japan in non-economic, noncultural (power or leadership) terms
7. Play a central role in Asian development
8. Play a central role in the World Peace Movement
9. Other special foreign policy goals

Chart 3

OTHER SPECIAL FOREIGN POLICY GOALS

1. De-escalation of Asian tension
2. Rapprochement with the Soviet Union
3. Mediate between Moscow and Washington, possibly even creating new Axis
4. Peace Corps and technical programmes
5. Take the lead in bringing Communist China into the world community and cushion the Sino-American confrontation
6. In general act as a mediating and friendly influence trying to be friends with all and enemies with none

Chart 4

'This age group does not know World War II and has not directly experienced the devastation and poverty of the postwar period. It has a belligerently democratic mentality, nurtured by the postwar constitution, the new educational system, and rationalism (even though of an American type). Thus the movement to be organized around such a generation cannot be developed successfully by the practices learned from the older methods; it calls for a new ideology and method. We have failed to work out the necessary policies to cope with the political indifference now spreading among youth.'

Chief of the Youth Department
Japan Socialist Party

Chart 5

JAPAN MAY HAVE AN INCREASING NEED (OR DESIRE) FOR:

1. International (political) status
2. A partial return to prewar values (third generation effect?)
3. Independence (political and military)*
4. New political ideas (either elimination of current 'boredom' or classical oscillation between xenophobia and xenophilia — chauvinism and internationalism — over-respect and resentment — adoration and contempt)
5. Revisionist theories on World War II and the Japanese historical experience
6. In general, a sense of national purpose and cultural identity

* It should be noted that, in the medium or long run, neutrality and disengagement probably mean nuclear armament.

Chart 6

SOME POSSIBLE CONSEQUENCES OF A DESIRE FOR CULTURAL IDENTITY

1. Growing realization of the need for 'Japanese solutions'
2. Pressures against naïve xeno-philism and internationalism of any kind, toleration (or even encouragement) of xenophobia and chauvinism
3. Some degree of political disengagement — even isolationism
4. Perhaps excessive reactions against foreign influence
5. Possibly some reaction against 'American' or even parliamentary democracy
6. Greater interest in Asia or 'Asia for the Asians' themes
7. Pressure for at least 'temporary' nuclear armament

Chart 7

COMMENTS ON THE SO-CALLED JAPANESE NUCLEAR 'ALLERGY'

1. Allergy was (and is) anti-militarism, anti-Americanism, political partisanship, part of the low posture policy, some nuclear pacifism and international idealism, and, most important of all, a basic and widespread belief in the non-existence of an objective and pressing issue for Japanese security or other national interest.
2. All the above are now eroding.
3. In addition, nuclear rearmament may not be as politically disruptive as many now assume. It may fit in with the desire of the left to be independent of the US as well as with desire of the right for national prestige and power as well as independence.
4. Indeed, eventual nuclear armament now appears likely or inevitable to most Japanese, but usually they argue it will take place after Germany or India has created a precedent.
5. That too could change.

Chart 8

AN IMPORTANT TREND

1963	General acceptance of self-defence forces		nuclear issues
1964	Revival of war songs; revisionist theories of the war	1967	Great animosity aroused by NPT negotiations
1965	Relatively great willingness to discuss national security issues	1968	Joint right-left study groups
1966	Relatively great willingness to discuss	1969	Relatively open discussions
		1970	Desire to realize now Japan's 'coming' great power status

---

Chart 9

CURRENT JAPANESE MISSILE RESEARCH

Item	Japanese MU-IV Missile	Minuteman A & B
Length	56–65 feet	53–60 feet
Diameter	5–6 feet	6 feet
Weight	About 80,000 lbs.	70,000 lbs.
Thrust	220,000 lbs.	270,000 lbs.
Speed	15,000 mph	15,000 mph-plus
Range	4,000–5,000 miles?	6,500 miles

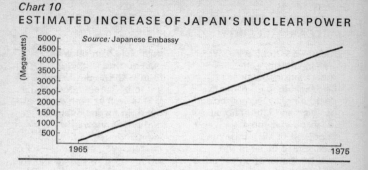

Chart 10
ESTIMATED INCREASE OF JAPAN'S NUCLEAR POWER

Alternative Japanese Futures

The first chart describes what we call The Standard Japan. It would be 'surprise-free' to most Americans, because it seems to be what they expect. Some Americans are even more hopeful, expecting something like *Chart 2*. My own guess is that something closer to *Charts 3, 4,* or *5* is more likely. The reasons for favouring *Charts 3, 4,* or *5* over *Charts 1* and *2* is that the latter take the special conditions of postwar Japan too seriously and expect too much that there will be more of the same. *Charts 3, 4,* and *5* take more account of historical Japan and the kinds of attitudes that the Japanese have shown in the past and that are still very much part of the Japanese tradition. When we say that the first charts take postwar Japan 'too seriously' we refer specifically to the example of the so-called nuclear allergy. They assume that the intense pacifist sentiments of the postwar years are permanent, and they lack understanding of the re-emergence of nationalism and Japanese desires for national prestige.

Chart 1
THE STANDARD JAPAN

1. By the end of fiscal year 1970, Japan will have finished twenty years of high growth rates, and be looking ahead for twenty to thirty years of much of the same. (Her Gross National Product should be about $200 billion — the third largest in the world.)
2. World War II will have been over for twenty-five years and there will have been extensive revisionist

literature on World War II
– little or no guilt feelings
will remain.
3. Many new desires and
reactivation of some old
desires – 'third generation'
and 'youth' effects.
4. Some desire to 'pass' but
strong desire for cultural
identity – great desire for
international status among
the conservative and the
old – to some degree
among others as well.
Qualitatively changed
international and national
context – contributes to
generational conflicts and
general confusion on how
much old concepts and
constraints apply, on what
new concepts and
constraints are applicable.
5. Politics of compromise and
factionalism continue; but
while intensity goes out of
some of the old issues, new
controversies around
shifting national priorities
and goals will arise –
economic growth and
technological advancement
considered as ideal interim
goals.
6. Old left still nationalist,
racist, xenophobic, Marxist,
dogmatic, and subject to
considerable (revisionist)
factional stress and strain
. . . New left is?
7. Vigorous pursuit of some
policies – moderately
rank-oriented.
8. No strong centre party – no
charismatic leader, but
'centrist' parliamentary
government.

9. National emphasis on trade
and economic growth
(achieving planned rate of
perhaps close to 10 per
cent); expanded defensive
military forces with
emphasis on technologically
advanced equipment
(nuclear and missile
options); emphasis on
consumer prosperity.
10 US security treaty extended
– probably without explicit
amendments; US bases in
staged transition to
Japanese control with
strictly qualified US
emergency access.
Moderate but steady
reduction of US influence
justified as Japan's
assuming 'proper
responsibilities' in defence
and foreign affairs.
11. Improved relations with
USSR including peace
treaty and profitable joint
economic projects;
cultivation of close relations
with Australia, Indonesia,
India.
12. Diplomatic recognition of
China; increasing but still
moderate level of trade.
Some attempts to mediate
between China and West.
This role fraught with
potentially grave conflicts
and may contain seeds for
grand debate on Japan's
place in world.
13. Active but non-controversial
role in world diplomacy
primarily as supporter of
UN peacekeeping and aid
programmes – 'good
citizen' and 'honest broker'

roles; primary interest in defending Japanese access to markets and free flow of international trade. Will probably attempt to hew to 'protectionist' trade policies.

14. Great attention to developing Asian regional political cooperation but avoiding anti-Communist identification. This will pose problems of great diplomatic delicacy between Japanese and former victims of Japanese imperialism.

15. Extensive economic penetration of Africa, Middle East, and South America.

Chart 2
(PRO-AMERICAN)

1. Continued conservative parliamentary government; waning socialist and leftist party strength.

   Moderately expanded military forces including non-nuclear cooperation with United States; conventional troop commitments to UN peacekeeping activities.

2. US security treaty continued or strengthened. Active cooperation with US in political and economic programmes in rivalry with China.

3. Moderately improved, 'correct' relations with USSR.

   Sizable aid programme, primarily in South-east Asia.

   Active role among Afro-Asian anti-Communist states including tolerance of some controversy in support of goals held in common with US

4 Pressure for a partnership role — perhaps including nuclear armament and perhaps even an offer to relieve US of need to maintain forces in North-east Asia — or even the rest of Asia.

5. A Pacific collective security pact including US, Japan, Australia, Canada, New Zealand and Philippines. Could also include Indonesia, Malaysia, Thailand, South Vietnam, or South Korea.

   The above could also include a collective or multilateral nuclear force.

6. Some increased degree of renunciation of military capability — perhaps under umbrella of US–Soviet agreement (following an Indian guarantee?).

Chart 3
(REVISIONIST)

1. 'Progressive' coalition government of elements from Socialist Party, left wing of Conservatives, independent left, and ex-Communist factions.

Expanded social welfare and economic growth policies with extension of government role in industry, labour, national planning. Moderate growth rate actually achieved (6 per cent).

Enlarged military forces; no nuclear weapons but option maintained.

Foreign policy of assuming 'responsibility' in a world governed by national self-interest. Within Japan greatly revised assessments of the legitimacy and 'inevitability'

of prewar policy.

2. US security treaty terminated on conciliatory terms; yet decisive Japanese dissociation from US.

3. Expanded political and trade relations with Russia and Europe. Ambitious programme to enlarge Japanese economic intrerests in Asia — with implicit political significance. Frank programme of competition with China but devoid of ideological content.

Chart 4
(CONSERVATIVE NATIONALIST)

1. Centre-rightist coalition government; some restriction on Communist and Socialist activity; constitution rewritten.

National emphasis on trade in international environment of restrictive regional groups; moderate rate of economic growth; deliberate fostering of economic, political and military programmes promoting Japanese national prestige; less emphasis on consumer prosperity.

Substantially expanded military forces, nominally defensive but with nuclear submarine programme, missile development, and nuclear weapons option — possibly an ABM programme.

Possible introduction of military draft.

2. US security treaty greatly revised or terminated. Much unofficial criticism of US occupation policies, cold war role, but official good relations maintained.

3. Many joint economic projects with USSR.

Extensive trade and joint development projects with China; guarded political rapprochement with both sides expecting eventual domination of the other.

Vigorous role as opponent of all 'foreign' political interventions in Asia and promoter of Afro-Asian trade groupings; formal demands for return of Kuriles.

Chart 5
(LEFTIST NATIONALIST)

1. Neo-Socialist government with some Komeito and

Communist parliamentary support (intra-Communist

party splits on nationalist-internationalist lines).

National emphasis on expanded welfare programmes (but otherwise relatively limited consumption), planned economic growth (autarchic tendencies; actual 3–5 per cent growth rate with some sectors nearer stagnation); serious balance of payments programme; reduced conventional forces; eventually wholly defensive nuclear deterrent posture.
2. U S security treaty renounced. National campaign to end foreign (American) influences on Japanese politics, economy, culture.

3. Peace treaty signed with Russia, partial restoration of lost territories; recognition of China; active programmes greatly to expand Soviet and Chinese trade.
International role of Afro-Asian neutralist leadership, implicit rivalry with China; programme to mobilize Afro-Asian nations as leftist economic and political bloc rivalling established great powers. Selective aid programme to 'progressive' Afro-Asian governments designed to develop exclusive market and trade zone, contributing to international environment of increasing trade restriction.

Chart 6
OTHER JAPANS

Komeito Japan: Neutralist, reformist, intolerant, collectivist (welfare-oriented); much domestic controversy – naïve, unstable régime; probably without consistent foreign policy of major consequence although a factor for instability in the world system.
Neo-Ideological: Relatively collectivist society with dramatic, sophisticated, implicitly anti-Western ideology – possibly with universalist or Pan-Asian claims; probably a response to major internal or international crisis.
Reactionary–Nativist: Militarist

and probably isolationist; much domestic instability; possibly racist (anti-white); possibly deteriorating economically in environment of world trade restriction or depression.
Communist: Nationalist, politically efficient and (politically) aggressive, hyper-competitive and a contender for world Communist leadership – militarily ambitious, dangerous, again probably plausible chiefly as reaction to internal or world crisis (probably economic, possibly political).

Chapter Notes

Prefatory Note

[1] A summary of these issues can be found in 'The Emergent US Post-Industrial Society' by Herman Kahn, prepared for the US House of Representatives Committee on Science and Aeronautics, Panel on Science and Technology, 27–28 January, 1970.

Foreword

[1] For an early review of part of this study, see Eleventh Annual Meeting of Panel on Science and Technology, sponsored by the Committee on Science and Astronautics, US House of Representatives, Washington, DC, 27–28 January, 1970.

Chapter 1

[1] 'Nuclear Proliferation and Rules of Retaliation', *Yale Law Journal*, Volume 76, Number 1, November, 1966 and 'Criteria for Long-Range Nuclear Control Policies' by Herman Kahn and Carl Dibble, *California Law Review*, Volume 55, No. 2, May, 1967.

Chapter 2

[1] Alexis de Tocqueville, *Democracy in America* (New York: Vintage Books, 1958).

[2] Ruth Benedict, *The Chrysanthemum and the Sword* (Cleveland: Meridian Books, The World Publishing Company, 1967 [copyright 1946]).

[3] Benedict, op. cit., pp. 1–3.

[4] Chitoshi Yanaga, *Big Business in Japanese Politics* (New Haven: Yale University Press, 1968), pp. 1–2.

This book is, of course, rather specialized compared to *The Chrysanthemum and the Sword*, but it is also likely to be useful to many readers who may wish to pursue further their interest in 'The Japanese Challenge' or 'The Emerging Superstate'.

[5] Michiko Inukai, 'Agreeing to Differ', *Japan Quarterly*, Vol. XIII, No. 2, April/June, 1966, pp. 182–3.

John Whitney Hall and Richard K. Beardsley, ed., *Twelve Doors to Japan* (New York: McGraw-Hill Book Company, 1965 [copyright 1961]), p. 387.

[7] Robert Jay Lifton, 'Youth and History: Change in Postwar Japan', *The Challenge of Youth*, ed. Erik H. Erikson (New York: Basic Books ,Inc., 1965 [copyright 1961]), p. 269.

[8] This paraphrase is in R. P. Dore, 'The Japanese Personality', Guy Wint, ed., *Asia Handbook* (Middlesex, England: Penguin Books, 1969), p. 565.

[9] Edward Norbeck, *Changing Japan*. Copyright © 1965. (New York: Holt, Rinehart & Winston, 1965), p. 18.

[10] Inukai, op. cit., p. 182.

[11] *Asahi Journal*, New Year's Issue, 1966.

[12] Lifton, op. cit., pp. 272–74.

[13] Bruno Bettelheim, 'The Problem of Generations', *Youth: Change and Challenge*, ed. E. Erikson (New York: Basic Books, Inc., 1963), p. 73.

[14] Robert Huntington, 'Comparison of Western and Japanese Cultures,' *Monumenta Nipponica*, Tokyo, Vol. XXIII, No. 3–4, p. 477.

[15] Richard Halloran, *Japan: Images and Realities* (New York: Alfred A. Knopf, 1969), pp. 92–3.

[16] Chitoshi Yanaga, *Japanese People and Politics*. (New York: John Wiley & Sons, 1956), pp. 58–9.

[17] ibid., pp. 59–60.

[18] Hall and Beardsley, op. cit., p. 95.

[19] ibid., pp. 94–5.

[20] Benedict, op. cit., p. 116.

[21] ibid., pp. 35–6.

[22] ibid., pp. 36–7.

[23] Lifton, op. cit., pp. 269–70.

[24] ibid., pp. 285–6.

[25] Hall and Beardsley, op. cit., p. 409.

[26] Inatomi Eijiro, *The Japanese Mind: Essentials of Japanese Philosophy and Culture*, ed. Charles A. Moore (Honolulu: East-West Center Press, 1967), pp. 234–5.

[27] Benedict, op. cit., pp. 180–81.
[28] Yanaga, op. cit., pp. 27–8.
[29] ibid., p. 29.
[30] ibid., p. 22.
[31] ibid., p. 24.
[32] ibid., p. 31.
[33] For further discussion see Halloran, op. cit., Chapter 5.
[34] ibid., p. 154.
[35] B. James George, 'Law in Modern Japan', in Hall and Beardsley, op. cit., p. 517.
[36] Halloran, op. cit., pp. 174–5.

Chapter 3

[1] Correspondents of *The Economist*, *Consider Japan* (London: Gerald Duckworth & Co., Ltd., 1963).
[2] Halloran, op. cit., p. 134.

Chapter 4

[1] See Peter Drucker, *The Age of Discontinuity: Guidelines to Our Changing Society* (New York: Harper & Row, 1969).
[2] Jules H. Masserman, *Psychiatry: East and West*, (New York: Grune & Stratton, Inc., 1968), pp. 52–3.
[3] ibid., pp. 51–2.

Chapter 5

[1] See *Nihon Shimbun* (*Japan Economic Journal*), 14 April 1970.

Chapter 6

[1] See Kahn and Dibble, op. cit.
[2] *Far Eastern Economic Review*, 18 December, 1969, p. 601.
[3] *The Washington Post*, 'Japan Arms Makers Push Buildup', 7 November 1969.
[4] *The Times* (London), 5 January 1970.

[5] *Le Monde*, 10 November, 1969.

[6] 'Christ Und Welt', *Atlas* (Stuttgart), December, 1969, p. 29.

[7] *Far Eastern Economic Review*, 23 October, 1969, p. 232.

[8] Yoshizane Isawa, 'Japan Ventures Into Southeast Asia', *Columbia Journal of World Business*, Nov./Dec. 1969, p. 52.

[9] 'Japan-Australian Partnership', *The Oriental Economist*, July, 1969, p. 17.

Bibliography

Books

Allen, G. C., *A Short Economic History of Modern Japan 1867–1937*, with a Supplementary Chapter on Economic Recovery and Expansion 1945–1960, London, George Allen & Unwin Ltd, 1946.

Ballon, Robert, *Doing Business in Japan*, Englewood Cliffs, New Jersey, Prentice-Hall, Inc., 1967.

Beasley, W. G., *The Modern History of Japan*, London, George Weidenfeld & Nicolson Ltd, 1963.

Belli, Melvin M., and Danny R. Jones, *Belli Looks at Life and Law in Japan*, New York, The Bobbs-Merrill Company, Inc., 1960.

Benedict, Ruth, *The Chrysanthemum and the Sword*, London, Routledge & Kegan Paul Ltd, 1967.

Clyde, Paul Hibbert, *The Far East, a History of the Impact of the West on Eastern Asia*, Englewood Cliffs, New Jersey, Prentice-Hall, Inc., 1966.

Economist (correspondents of), *Consider Japan*, London, Gerald Duckworth & Co., Ltd, 1963.

Craig, William, *The Fall of Japan*, London, George Weidenfeld & Nicolson Ltd, 1968.

Dempster, Prue, *Japan Advances, a Geographical Study*, London, Metheun & Co. Ltd, 1967.

de Tocqueville, Alexis, *Democracy in America*, London, Frederick Muller Ltd, 1956.

Erikson, Erik H., editor, *The Challenge of Youth*, chapter by Robert J. Lifton, 'Youth and History: Individual Change in Postwar Japan', New York, Basic Books, Inc. (copyright 1961), 1965.

Erikson, Erik H., editor, *Youth: Change & Challenge*, chapter by Bruno Bettelheim, 'The Problem of Generations', New York, Basic Books, Inc., 1964.

Feis, Herbert, *Japan Subdued, the Atomic Bomb and the End of the War in the Pacific*, London, Oxford University Press, 1961.

Hall, John W., and Richard K. Beardsley, *Twelve Doors to Japan*, New York, McGraw-Hill Book Company, 1966.

Halloran, Richard, *Japan: Images and Realities*, New York, Alfred A. Knopf, Inc., 1969.

Haring, Douglas G., *Japan's Prospect*, London, Oxford University Press, 1946.

Hasegawa, Nyozekan, *The Japanese Character, a Cultural Profile*, London, Ward Lock & Co. Ltd, 1966.

Hsu, Francis, editor, *Psychological Anthropology: Approaches to Culture and Personality*, chapter by Edward Norbeck and George de Vos, 'Japan', Homewood, Illinois, Dorsey Press, 1961.

Huh, Kyung-Mo, *Japan's Trade in Asia, Developments Since 1926 – Propsects for 1970*, New York, Frederick A. Praeger, Inc., 1967.

Kajima, Morinosuke, *A Brief Diplomatic History of Modern Japan*, Englewood Cliffs, New Jersey, Prentice-Hall, Inc., 1966.

Kajima, Morinosuke, *Modern Japan's Foreign Policy*, Englewood Cliffs, New Jersey, Prentice-Hall International, Inc., 1970.

Kawasaki, Ichiro, *Japan Unmasked*. Englewood Cliffs, New Jersey, Prentice-Hall, Inc., 1969.

Kennan, George F., *American Diplomacy 1900–1950*, London, Martin Secker & Warburg Ltd, 1952.

Lockwood, William W., *The State and Economic Enterprise in Japan*, Princeton, New Jersey, Princeton University Press, 1966.

Maki, John M., *Government and Politics in Japan – The Road to Democracy*, London, Thames & Hudson Ltd, 1962.

Maraini, Fosco, *Meeting with Japan*, London, Hutchinson & Co. Ltd, 1959.

Maruyama, Masao, *Thought and Behaviour in Modern Japanese Politics*, London, Oxford University Press, 1963.

Masserman, Jules H., *Psychiatry: East and West*, London, William Heinemann Medical Books Ltd, 1968.

Moore, Charles A., editor, *The Japanese Mind: Essentials of Japanese Philosophy and Culture*, Honolulu; East-West Center Press, 1967.

Murata, Kiyoaki, *Japan's New Buddhism*, New York, Walker/Weatherhill, 1969.

Nakamura, Hajime, *Ways of Thinking of Eastern Peoples*, London, Luzac & Co. Ltd, 1960.

Norbeck, Edward, *Changing Japan, Case Study in Cultural Anthropology*, New York, Holt, Rinehart & Winston, Inc., 1966.

Packard, George R., III, *Protest in Tokyo, The Security Treaty Crisis of 1960*, London, Oxford University Press, 1966.

Passin, Herbert, editor, *The United States and Japan*, Englewood Cliffs, New Jersey, Prentice-Hall, Inc., 1966.

Reischauer, Edwin O., *The United States and Japan*, London, Oxford University Press, 1950.

Reischauer, Edwin O., *Japan Past and Present*, London, Gerald Duckworth & Co. Ltd, 1964.

Riesman, David, *Conversations in Japan*, Harmondsworth, Penguin Books Ltd, 1967.

Sansom, G. B., *The Western World and Japan*, London, Cresset Press Ltd, 1950.

Schnaps, Maurice, and Alvin D. Coox, editors, *The Japanese Image*, Philadelphia, Orient/West Inc., 1965.

Seidensticker, Edward, *Japan*, New York, Time-Life Books (copyright 1961), 1965.

Stone, P. B., *Japan Surges Ahead, The Story of an Economic Miracle*, London, George Weidenfeld & Nicolson Ltd, 1969.

Storry, Richard, *A History of Modern Japan*, Harmondsworth, Penguin Books Ltd, 1960.

Takahashi, Kamekichi, *The Rise and Development of Japan's Modern Economy*, Tokyo, The Jiji Press, Ltd, 1969.

Thayer, Nathaniel B., *How the Conservatives Rule Japan*, Princeton, New Jersey, Princeton University Press, 1969.

Thomsen, Harry, *The New Religions of Japan*, Englewood Cliffs, New Jersey, Prentice-Hall, Inc., 1963.

Vogel, Ezra F., *Japan's New Middle Class*, Los Angeles, University of California Press, 1967.

Ward, Robert E., *Japan's Political System*, Englewood Cliffs, New Jersey, Prentice-Hall, Inc., 1967.

Wint, Guy, editor, *Asia Handbook*, chapter by R. P. Dore, 'The Japanese Personality', Harmondsworth, Penguin Books Ltd (copyright 1966), 1969.

Yamamura, Kozo, *Economic Policy in Postwar Japan*, Los Angeles, University of California Press, 1968.

Yanaga, Chitoshi, *Big Business in Japanese Politics*, New Haven, Yale University Press, 1969.

Yanaga, Chitoshi, *Japanese People and Politics*, London, Chapman & Hall Ltd, 1957.

Magazines, Pamphlets, Newspapers

Abegglen, James, C., 'The Economic Growth of Japan', *Scientific American*, March, 1970.

'Christ Und Welt', Stuttgart, *Atlas*, December, 1969.

Economic Planning Agency, Japanese Government, *Economic Survey of Japan* (*1967–1968*), London, HMSO, 1968.

Far Eastern Economic Review, 23 October, 1969.

Far Eastern Economic Review, 18 December, 1969.

Far Eastern Economic Review Yearbook 1970.

Hunsberger, Warren, 'The Japanese Economy: A Continuing Miracle?', *Interplay*, December, 1969/January, 1970.

Huntington, Robert, 'Comparison of Western and Japanese Cultures', *Monumenta Nipponica*, Tokyo, Vol. XXIII, No. 3–4.

India, Japan, Australia. Partners in Asia?, Canberra, 1968.

Industrial Japan, January, 1970.

Information Bulletin 1967, Public Information Bureau, Ministry of Foreign Affairs, Japan.

Inukai, Michiko, 'Agreeing to Differ', *Japan Quarterly*, Tokyo, April/June, 1966.

Iwasa, Yoshizane, 'Japan Ventures Into Southeast Asia', *Columbia Journal of World Business*, New York, November–December, 1969.

'Japan-Australian Partnership', *Oriental Economist*, Tokyo, July, 1969.

Japan Economic Yearbook 1969.

'Japanese Economy in Western Press', *Oriental Economist*, Tokyo, November, 1969.

'Japan – Salesman to the World', *Newsweek*, 9 March, 1970.

Keidanren (Federation of Economic Organizations), *Economic Picture of Japan, 1968.*

'Mitsui & Co., Japan Iron & Steel Foundation', *Business Week*, 24 January, 1970.

Nakamura, Hajime, *Ways of Thinking of Eastern People*, London, Luzac & Co. Ltd, 1960.

'The New Invasion of Greater East Asia', *Time*, 2 March, 1970.

The President Directory 1969, Tokyo, Diamond-Time Co, Ltd.

Statistical Handbook of Japan, Bureau of Statistics, Office of the Prime Minister.

World Business, January, 1969.

Index

*uniqueness (exclusiveness)
  race and Japanese techniques
    and, 83–4
United Nations
  role of as perceived by Komeito,
    188
United States of America *see* US
  universities
  internal conflict in Japan and, 8
  resentment against 'system' in,
    96
  student rebels on, 112–14
  See also Tokyo University
urban problems
  In Osaka and Tokyo, 152
  role of CNDP in, 152
*US
  abdication in Asia and Japanese
    rearmament, 204
  advantages of co-prosperity
    sphere with Japan in Asia,
    201
  aid and defence burden of
    Japan, 16
  attitudes towards advancement-
    orientation, compared with
    Japan's, 125
  attitudes towards business, com-
    pared with Japan's, 101
  attitudes towards contracts,
    compared with Japan's, 79–81
  attitudes towards Japan's role in
    Asia, 16–17
  attitudes towards Japan's role in
    world trade, 37
  bases of, in Japan as provocation
    for China, 196–7
  business attitudes towards risk
    in, 122–3
  creativity in technology by, 27
  cultural changes in, 112
  debt-equity ratio of, compared
    with Japan's, 121
  decision making in, compared
    with Japan, 50
  desire for emulation, 43

desire for greater participation
  in Asia by, 199
dilution of relations with, by
  Japan, 210
economic impact on foreign
  trade, compared with Japan's,
  115
educational system as model for
  Japan's, 35
erosion of productivity motivation in, 108
failure of aid to India from, 206
form of Tenko Transformation
  in, 64
GNP and GNP per capita,
  surpassing of by Japan, 149
Hudson Institute study of, xiii
in superpower hegemony with
  Japan and USSR, 179
increases in GNP and pro-
  ductivity of, if run by Japan,
  107–8
innovation and implementation
  in decision making in, 51
intended reduction of military
  presence in Asia of, 182
introduction of computers by
  business in, 95
Japan as bridge to USSR for,
  167
Japan–USSR cooperation and,
  203–5
Japan's attitudes towards
  'Americanization' by, 103
Japan's need for protection by,
  while developing nuclear programme, 193–4
Latin American constitutions
  and, 43
loosening of Japan's political
  ties to, 146
manufacturing subsidiaries in
  PA, 199–200
military power of, and Japan's
  economic power united in
  PA, 200–201

More about Penguins
and Pelicans

Penguinews, which appears every month, contains details of all the new books issued by Penguins as they are published. From time to time it is supplemented by *Penguins in Print*, which is a complete list of all available books published by Penguins. (There are well over four thousand of these.)

A specimen copy of *Penguinews* will be sent to you free on request. For a year's issues (including the complete lists) please send 30p if you live in the United Kingdom, or 60p if you live elsewhere. Just write to Dept EP, Penguin Books Ltd, Harmondsworth, Middlesex, enclosing a cheque or postal order, and your name will be added to the mailing list.

Note: *Penguinews* and *Penguins in Print* are not available in the U.S.A. or Canada

Japanese Imperialism Today

'CO-PROSPERITY IN GREATER EAST ASIA'

Jon Halliday and Gavan McCormack

One Japanese design for 'co-prosperity with its Asian neighbours' ended in disaster in the 1940s. Since then, with solid backing from its old enemy, the United States, Japan has achieved a remarkable recovery.

Jon Halliday and Gavan McCormack have written a lively and convincing Marxist study of Japan's new economic empire in Asia, detailing the new forms of dependency and control built into its relations with the region. They argue that Japan, having established during the 1960s a powerful grip on South-East Asia's markets, is now tightening its fist on the supply of raw materials: by 1980 it plans to monopolize 30 per cent of the entire world's raw-material exports.

While concentrating on East and South-East Asia, the authors set their analysis firmly in the context of Japan's changing relations with the United States and China, adding appendices on the Soviet Union and Australasia. To complete the picture, they describe the internal restructuring of Japan's society and economy that has accompanied overseas expansion, and in particular they pinpoint the speed and extent of Japan's rearmament.